The Digital Courtroom

The digitalisation of courtrooms brings both opportunities and challenges to the judicial process, shaping our understandings of trials and their participants in a myriad of, at times, unexpected ways, and transforming how we participate in, attend, engage with, and consume trials. While digital tools offer potential benefits, they can also impact core aspects of judicial integrity, such as the conduct of legal proceedings and participants' experiences, as well as introducing additional layers of complexity – sometimes problematic – in how trials are portrayed in popular culture. By exploring these developments, the book highlights the importance of a thoughtful approach to digital integration – one that carefully considers its implications for procedural fairness, public trust, and the perceived legitimacy of the legal system. The author examines the social construction of courts in the digital age, arguing that digitalisation is not merely transforming the tools of justice but also redefining the very essence of the justice experience and reshaping our perceptions of trials and their participants. The work will be a valuable resource for scholars and students in the social sciences, law, and all those interested in digitalisation and society.

Lisa Flower is Associate Professor at the Department of Sociology, Lund University, specialising in a sociological approach to digital technologies in courts, the social construction of trials, and court ethnography. She is currently leading the ERC-funded "VIRTUTRIALS" project on virtual participation in trials.

Routledge Contemporary Issues in Criminal Justice and Procedure

Series Editor Ed Johnston is an Associate Professor of Criminal Justice and Procedure at the University of Northampton, UK.

Social Rehabilitation and Criminal Justice
Edited by Federica Coppola and Adriano Martufi

Neurolaw in the Courtroom
Comparative Perspectives on Vulnerable Defendants
Edited by Hannah Wishart and Colleen M. Berryessa

Contemporary Challenges in the Jury System
A Comparative Perspective
Nicola Monaghan

Implementation of Rights for Crime Victims in Theory and Practice
Lessons from India
Anupama Sharma

Justifying Punishment
Perspectives from Post-Communist Europe
Edited by Jakub Drápal

International Perspectives of Neuroscience in the Youth Justice Courtroom
Edited by Hannah Wishart and Ray Arthur

Poor Defence Lawyering in Criminal Proceedings
A Comparative View
Edited by Ashlee Beazley, Michele Panzavolta and Andrew Sanders

The Digital Courtroom
Participation, Attendance, Engagement and Consumption
Lisa Flower

See more at www.routledge.com/Routledge-Research-in-Legal-History/book-series/CONTEMPCJP

The Digital Courtroom

Participation, Attendance, Engagement and Consumption

Lisa Flower

Routledge
Taylor & Francis Group
LONDON AND NEW YORK

First published 2025
by Routledge
4 Park Square, Milton Park, Abingdon, Oxon OX14 4RN

and by Routledge
605 Third Avenue, New York, NY 10158

Routledge is an imprint of the Taylor & Francis Group, an informa business

The development of the theoretical framework and contextual foundation for this book was made possible through the support of the Swedish Research Council [2023–01183]. The analytical work in chapter six was made possible through the support of the Wahlgrenska Foundation.

British Library Cataloguing-in-Publication Data
A catalogue record for this book is available from the British Library

ISBN: 978-1-032-38362-0 (hbk)
ISBN: 978-1-032-38364-4 (pbk)
ISBN: 978-1-003-34464-3 (ebk)

DOI: 10.4324/9781003344643

Typeset in Galliard
by Apex CoVantage, LLC

For Dad

Contents

Figures

Tables

Acknowledgements

I would like to thank the Crime, Control, and Culture research environment at the Department of Sociology, Lund University. In particular, I am grateful to David Wästerfors, David Sausdal, Malin Åkerström, and Max Persson, for their valuable feedback on earlier chapters of this book, along with Magnus Ring and Sara Eldén for their comments.

A special thanks to Lorna, Lucy, Liz, Rach, Rach, Anna, and Esta – not for their involvement in this book, but for their profound and inspiring lack of spa voices.

Likewise, my mum and sister had no direct involvement in this book, but they still deserve a big thank you for keeping me focused on life's greatest question: can you milk it?

And finally, my deepest gratitude to Martin: thank you for your endless patience and support. Despite your promises to make cake having become even more seldom, you remain my rock. And to Daisy and Harriet: you are, and always will be, the best kids I could ever wish for!

1 Introduction to the digital courtroom

This book examines how the digitalisation of courtrooms brings both opportunities and challenges to the judicial process, shaping our understandings of trials and their participants in a myriad of, at times, unexpected ways, and transforming how we participate in, attend, engage with, and consume trials. While digital tools offer potential benefits, they can also impact core aspects of judicial integrity, such as the conduct of legal proceedings and participants' experiences, as well as introducing additional layers of complexity – sometimes problematic – in how trials are portrayed in popular culture. By exploring these developments, I highlight the importance of a thoughtful approach to digital integration – one that carefully considers its implications for procedural fairness, public trust, and the perceived legitimacy of the legal system. *The Digital Courtroom* explores the social construction of courts in the digital age and argues that digitalisation is not merely transforming the tools of justice but is redefining the very essence of the justice experience and transforming our perceptions of trials and their participants.

The traditional courtroom setting is increasingly being replaced or supplemented by digital platforms, allowing judges, prosecutors, lawyers, defendants, plaintiffs, and witnesses to participate via video conferencing platform tools such as Zoom or Microsoft Teams from locations outside the physical courtroom. In some cases, entire proceedings are conducted remotely, with all participants joining through video link. This shift extends even further in places like Colombia and China, where virtual trials have utilised online environments in which each actor is represented by a digital avatar. Such developments indicate a broader trend towards the normalisation of fully virtual legal proceedings, raising profound questions about the future of justice, public access, and the social meaning of the courtroom as a space of accountability.

This transformation of the courtroom extends far beyond its walls. Today, trials are not confined to physical spaces – they are livestreamed on court websites and platforms such as CourtTV and YouTube, allowing anyone to attend in real time. Detailed, blow-by-blow descriptions of courtroom events can be followed through live blogs, giving audiences a sense of "being there." True crime podcasts, documentaries, and streaming services have become popular mediums through which legal events are consumed, shaping public

DOI: 10.4324/9781003344643-1

perceptions of justice and those involved. The courts, judges, lawyers, and prosecutors now actively engage with the public on social media platforms such as X, Facebook, and Instagram, sharing updates, information, educational content, and insights into their work.

The digitalisation expands public access and redefines the experience of justice, stretching the trial's reach far beyond the courtroom walls to a greater extent than ever before. This shift reshapes how legal professionals, lay participants, and the broader society understand and interact with legal processes. As courts become more transparent and digitally integrated, new practices and expectations emerge, raising important questions about how to maintain the legitimacy of judicial institutions in a digital age.

This shift is also changing our collective understandings and experiences of the legal sphere, shaped by an endless stream of stories and accounts of court events that are readily accessible given their digitalised format. Interactions with courts have become both more detailed, nuanced, and complex and at the same time more mundane. We can now open our laptops or turn on our TVs and be transported to a trial happening thousands of miles away from the comfort of our own homes or listen to the latest true crime podcast on our daily commute.

In this book, I argue that the perception, accomplishment, and experience of justice – of the courts, legal professionals, lay participants, and the processes going on within the courts – are increasingly shaped by digitalisation. Our understanding of legal proceedings, the roles of legal professionals, victims, perpetrators, and even crime itself, is being influenced by the multitude of digitally enabled depictions, reports, interactions, and accounts. At the same time, legal professionals are adapting to a new reality, where digital tools and heightened public scrutiny are integral to their daily practices.

This shift has important implications for ensuring the continued legitimacy of courts, a fundamental pillar of democratic societies. It also affects the daily routines of legal actors, who are now expected to develop and negotiate new practices, ways of working, presenting themselves, preparing for trial work, and interacting in the courtroom. For example, while the increased use of digital technologies enabling remote participation has been widely embraced, as I will demonstrate, their implementation and use has outpaced the research needed to fully understand their impact on justice, legal processes, and the actors within.

Open justice continues to play a central role in democratic societies, ensuring that legal proceedings are transparent and accountable. A central argument in this book is that the drive towards increased transparency in Western societies has been heavily enabled by digitalisation, yet there are unexpected consequences of this increased openness which risk, ultimately, damaging justice. For instance, the ubiquity and longevity of the information now available thanks to the digitalisation of court records, audio recordings, and so on mean the consequences can be more comprehensive than ever before. Indeed, I will argue the trial has become a public spectacle once again.

At this early point in the book, it is important to reveal that I am not a techno pessimist, nor am I arguing for a return to closed courts. The plethora of ways in which courts have been opened has contributed to upholding fair and just trials, injustices being uncovered, easier accessibility and reduced costs, and far more. However, critical reflection and investigation of the range of digital tools that have been introduced into courts is vital. The introduction and widespread use of many digital technologies has progressed more rapidly than the research needed to fully comprehend how they interplay with justice, legal processes, and the individuals involved. As a result, we lack a comprehensive understanding of, amongst other things, how these tools are reshaping courtroom dynamics and influencing the behaviour of legal actors.

Understanding the interplay between courts and wider society is important as courts sit at the heart of democratic societies. They resolve disputes and quarrels, determine guilt or innocence, and settle questions of freedom, security, and more. They include parties ranging from family members, businesses, states, and individuals. Courts play a vital role in fostering peace and security in the lives of citizens, whilst also contributing to stability in the commercial sector. They discourage and penalise unacceptable behaviour, ensuring accountability, and provide a necessary balance in governmental affairs and operations. The everyday functioning of independent courts serves to reinforce shared morals and values, thereby strengthening social cohesion in society.

Courts thus play a crucial role in maintaining the stability of societies, influencing our lives in various ways. For some individual, a legal proceeding can be a life-changing event, while for others may it simply be another task on their to-do list. Participating in a trial may be a rare, once-in-a-lifetime event, or it may just be another workday. Some may attend to support a friend or loved one or may have visited a trial as part of an educational fieldtrip. Conversely, there are those who have never had reason to set foot inside a courthouse. Their exposure to trials may only come from reading about trials in newspapers, watching the news on TV, or listening to a podcast.

The point I wish to make is that remaining oblivious to the courts and the goings on within has becoming increasingly difficult, largely due to the impact of digitalisation. By applying a sociological lens to the digital courtroom, I will unpack the ways in which contemporary digital tools are shaping how we participate, attend, engage with, and consume the courts and therefore show how digitalisation is shaping practices, understandings, and experiences. Courts not only reflect the societal dynamics, but also actively engage with and shape society. They are thus a microcosm of society and a driving force in its construction.

The book explores four central themes within the overarching topic of digitalisation and open justice: participation, attendance, engagement, and consumption. Participation addresses the ways in which digitalisation has enabled new forms of participating in trials, in particular via video links. The next theme of attendance looks at how digitalisation has enabled the public gallery to be divorced from spatial restraints with attendance possible from locations other than the courtroom. Engagement focuses on how the courts use social media to engage with society, how trials are depicted in social media, and how social media can be used and abused by legal actors and others taking part in, or following, a trial. Finally, consumption takes a deep dive into the multitude of ways in which the courts are consumed as a form of entertainment, distraction, or even education. I will return to a more developed structure of the book at the end of this chapter. My goal with this book is also to orientate the reader to the wider context of digitalisation, video links, social media, news media, and true crime and how these interplay with open justice.

In the quest for contemporary openness, normative ideas regarding open justice often prevail. Such enhancements can therefore lead to a "transparency paradox" (Moran 2016) whereby opening up the courts has unexpected and even contradictory effects. For instance, the role of the news media and social media in this process can have damning implications on witnesses and procedural correctness as I will show in the following chapters (see also Flower 2023b).

In this book, I argue that the rush towards transparency is boosted by technological developments that enable increased openness and thus risks being paired with a lack of appropriate reflection regarding what comprises an appropriate amount or level of access to legal documents and proceedings (Schofield 2006, 267; Moore, Clayton, and Murphy 2019; Resnik 2013; Flower 2023b). Hence, rather than leading to a concomitant enhancement of the courts' legitimacy (Tyler 2003; Moran 2016), increased transparency may lead to a decline in confidence and trust, or even new forms of self-censorship and anxiety (see Hansen, Christensen, and Flyverbom 2015, for an overview).

Within this, the news media and social media play a central role in opening up trials to a wider public than those physically attending in the courthouse. This is particularly pertinent given current temporal patterns, whereby many people no longer have time to attend legal proceedings, and spatial patterns in society, whereby architectural changes have reduced the size of public galleries thereby also diminishing the possibility of attending (Hans and Dee 1991; Mulcahy 2010; Rodrick 2014; Bosland and Townend 2018). And, whilst opening up trials in this way does not guarantee the transformation of "passive seeing into active scrutiny" (Moore 2018, 428), it nevertheless contributes to information reaching out to wider society (Peters 2013).

In this book, I explore the tension between the rhetoric and practice of open justice stemming from the implementation of a range of digital tools and platforms into courts such as video links, live blogs, livestreams, and social media, together with the widespread digitalisation of legal materials such as preliminary investigation files, judgements, and audio recordings. Here the work of legal scholars Townend and Welsh (2023, 120) and their finding of a "disjuncture between the ideal and the reality" regarding the principle of open justice in the digital age is of particular inspiration. They argue that inadequate resources and management contribute to the practices of open justice failing to achieve the goal of transparency (Townend and Welsh 2023).

I aim to build on their work, by taking a sociological perspective to show how digitalised transparency is shaping such practices, as well as experiences and understandings.

For those looking for a deep dive into *all* things digital, I'm afraid disappointment awaits, although I hope to keep your attention, nonetheless. The digitalisation of courts encompasses so many different aspects it would be nigh on impossible to include them all in one short book. Moreover, rapid advances in technology, combined with an increased degree of open-mindedness towards digital solutions in many courts – spheres traditionally considered technologically conservative – has led to multitudinous developments. Indeed, many courts include digitalisation in their strategic plans, reflecting the central role digitalisation now plays.[1]

The aim of this book is thus to provide an overview of the – admittedly – ever-evolving state of the art regarding the courts which, in turn, will serve as a basis for a sociological framework which can help us to recognise how these changes in participation, attendance, engagement, and consumption impact our understandings of the courts along with the people and goings on within. Within this, open justice – that trials and hearings are made public trials – is foundational.

Digitalisation

Digitalisation is the practice of converting analogue texts, pictures, or sounds into a digital format which can then be processed by a computer (Härtel and Härtel 2020; Scott and Marshall 2009). Digitalisation breaks down time-space barriers and produces globalised information distribution, flow, and storage (Schaefer et al. 2018). The digital age (or information age) is thus characterised by the speed and ease of information transference using digital technology. This postindustrialist stage of economic development has been labelled informationalism by sociologists and represents a third industrial revolution,

1 According to Susskind (2019), these developments can be split into two subdivisions: automation and transformation. The first of these entails grafting new technology to old practices: doing old things in new ways. In contrast, transformation involves the displacement of old practices: doing new things in new ways. For instance, taking part in a trial via video link is a new take on an old practice. Here participants still participate synchronously – at the same time – just via video link. Further examples of automation which I will not be delving into in this book include digital court files, electronic case management, and electronic evidence bundles. Within this category also falls radically transforming trials by introducing asynchronous hearings whereby there is no physical courtroom and no temporal hearing, rather arguments, evidence, and decisions can be sent without parties being physically or virtually present simultaneously (Susskind 2019, 60). Another transformation of the courts is the introduction of algorithms and artificial intelligence – AI. For instance algorithms are used to determine recommended criminal sentences (e.g. in Wisconsin) (Beriain 2018) and risk assessment (McKay 2020), although warning flags have been raised regarding the absence of oversight regarding responsible, ethical, and accountable design and implementation (Wales 2019; Kroll 2015).

following the first which saw the invention of the printing press, steam engine, and machinery and the second which harnessed electricity and realised the creation of internal combustion and telecommunications (Castells 1996; Warschauer 2004). The digital age is thus an age in which information is central and in which the internet plays a central role enabling networking and communication. Although computer-mediated communication has been used since the mid-1960s, it was the creation of the World Wide Web in 1989 that revolutionised how we communicate with the introduction of a range of information and communications technologies (ICT).

Over the following decades, email rapidly developed, followed by the capability of communicating audio-visual elements as well as networking on a global scale (Warschauer 2004). By 2020, 60 percent of the world's population were internet users (Bank 2022). However, the digital divide separating those with the means and capability of accessing the internet remains vast and digital inequality continues (Cullen 2001; van Dijk and Hacker 2003; DiMaggio and Hargittai 2001). For instance, in 2020, 92 percent of North Americans were internet users in contrast with 30 percent of those in Sub-Saharan Africa (Data 2023). Furthermore, beyond cost and capabilities, the design of digital technologies may function as disabling barriers which also leads to digital exclusion (Warschauer 2004; Egard and Hansson 2021), including access to justice. The entanglement of justice and internet is reflected in the finding that "more people in the world now have access to the internet than access to justice" (Susskind 2019, 27): approximately 5.1 billion people (two thirds of the world's population) lack appropriate access to justice, in contrast to around 5 billion people who have access to internet (Project 2019; Data 2023). Hence although there is still a long way to go before digitalisation encompasses the social and legal lives of the majority of people, the ways in which many work, learn, feel, socialise, relax, consume, and interact have already changed remarkably.

Open justice

The roots of today's open justice can be traced back to the mid-1700s and Cesare Beccaria, an Italian philosopher, jurist, and economist, who criticised the lack of insight into legal systems with trials shrouded in secrecy and with punishments that were inhumane, arbitrary, and disproportionate to the crime. For Beccaria, punishment must be public, prompt, and necessary, as minimal in severity as possible under given circumstances, proportional to the crime, and prescribed by the laws (Beccaria 2016).

Beccaria's writings were later developed in the early 1800s by the British philosopher and jurist Jeremy Bentham, who pushed for the reformation of legal systems. Bentham argued that making legal proceedings and legal documents public would fulfil three key functions: (1) education: allowing observers into the courtroom – including those who watch proceedings and then distribute summaries of events – will help to educate the public about legal proceedings; (2) truth: participants of a trial are more likely to tell the truth if they risk being found out in a lie due to the openness of proceedings; and (3) discipline: opening up the courts to observers would ensure that legal actors behaved appropriately (Bentham 1843).

The work of Beccaria and Bentham led to widespread changes in the law and legal processes such as codified laws and public legal hearings. This became a universally accepted and widely implemented legal rule that required courts to conduct proceedings publicly (see e.g. Hess and Koprivica 2019) and which stands to this day. Open justice remains a central tenet in contemporary democratic legal proceedings, indeed the right to a fair and *public hearing* is considered a basic human right (European Convention on Human Rights and Fundamental Freedoms 1950, 5). This means that in many modern states, trials are open to the public, judgements are announced, and certain legal documents can be requested and accessed.

Contemporary open justice

Contemporary open justice utilises digitalisation in order to answer more recent calls for the increased scrutiny of legal processes and proceedings (Bogoch and Peleg 2014; Rodrick 2014; Jaconelli 2002). This is in line with wider societal trends towards what Moore (2018) calls "institutional transparency" where demands for the accessibility of information within the public sector are also mounting.

Open justice has, unsurprisingly, undergone subtle changes since its beginnings. For instance, the disciplinary function as envisioned by Bentham, traditionally centred on moral control but, as I will show in Chapter 3, has since expanded to encompass a broader surveillance purpose. Surveillance is the "focused, systematic and routine attention to personal details for purposes of influence, management, protection or direction" (Lyon 2007, 14) and constitutes a set of practices with two purposes: control and safety/care. Whilst the control aspect aligns with open justice's original disciplinary function aimed at ensuring morally correct conduct by legal actors, today's open justice also focuses on ensuing the safety of the legal system, that is, that trials are conducted in a legally correct manner and that the rights of all those involved are upheld. By widening the gaze in this way, contemporary open justice can instead be understood in terms of fulfilling a surveillance function rather than the original, more confined, disciplinary function. I argue that open justice has thus shifted in line with the "surveillance society" (Lyon 2001).

Correspondingly, this also means that "surveillance practices" (Lyon 2018) – the things we do in relation to surveillance, along with shared understandings and expectations regarding surveillance – "surveillance imaginaries" (Lyon 2018) – are being constructed by legal actors and the wider society in response to digitalisation. These practices and imaginaries capture how we evaluate and engage with surveillance. Again, this shift towards a surveillance society aligns with a wider societal shift towards increased "institutional transparency" (Moore 2018).

The synopticisation of the courts

Along with codified laws and open proceedings, Bentham believed that punishment should act as a deterrent, inspiring him to design a prison that was architecturally planned to ensure maximum observation of inmates by staff, which he named the "panopticon."[2] The panopticon was an annular design where all cells could be monitored from one watchtower positioned at the centre of the circle of cells. Each cell had two windows – one facing outwards, and one facing inwards towards the tower. This enabled those standing in the watchtower to observe each inmate as the sun backlit the inmate's actions. These prisons were also planned to be built near the centre of towns in order to serve as a reminder of the consequence of crime, and thus serve as a deterrent.

Whilst the panopticon as a prison design never fully came to fruition, Bentham's ideas were picked up by Michel Foucault over 100 years later. Foucault (1975/1991, 200) highlights Bentham's panopticon design as enabling the inmate to be seen, but without seeing. A central effect is therefore inducing in the inmate "a state of conscious and permanent visibility that assures the automatic functioning of power" (Foucault 1975/1991, 201). The inmate begins to self-monitor their own behaviour as they can never be sure if they are being watched by a guard in the watchtower. In this way, the "permanent, exhaustive, omnipresent surveillance" of the panopticon could make inmates' actions visible whilst itself remaining invisible (Foucault 1975/1991, 214). Extrapolating these ideas to society, Foucault (1975/1881, 214) writes that the panopticon is "like a faceless gaze that transformed the whole social body into a field of perceptions: thousands of eyes posted everywhere, attentions ever on the alert."[3] It is the interplay between the synopticon and panopticon that I am interested in. In the original understanding of the panopticon, the few watch the many, leading to self-monitoring which, in turn, led to widespread monitoring of each other on a societal level, according to Foucault (1975/1991). For Foucault (1975/1991, 205), the panopticon was "polyvalent in its applications" and that, "without disappearing as such or losing any of its properties, was destined to spread through the social body; its vocation was to become a generalized function" (Foucault 1975/1991, 207). This generalised function was turbo-boosted by social media and other digital means, enabling surveillance to be freed from physical or temporal restraints.

Foucault's writings on the panopticon are central to understanding modern forms of social control and surveillance and were later developed by Mathiesen

2 Bentham's brother was actually the inspiration for this as his brother had a factory with a similar design aimed at monitoring the workers.

3 I attempt to move away from Foucault's normative and dystopian "visibility is a trap" (Foucault 1975/1991, 200). I also endeavour to present a contextualised understanding of surveillance as to how it can be understood in a courtroom context. Thus, once again in agreement with Haggerty (2006), I suggest that a one-size-fits-all approach regarding surveillance should be resisted.

(1997) who presents the "synopticon" and includes the role of the mass media, which he claims Foucault overlooks. In the synopticon, the "see/being seen dyad" (Foucault 1975/1991, 201) is reversed; hence, rather than the few watching the many as in the panopticon, in the synopticon, the many watch the few (Mathiesen 1997). These two processes work in parallel to each other.

The concept of synopticon is valuable for analysing how digitalisation is enabling the many – the public – to observe the few, such as those involved in a trial – to an unprecedented degree. As this book will demonstrate, live blogging from courts through live blogs and livestreams, as well as podcasts and documentaries, can serve as tools of open justice, breaking free from the traditional from a spatial and temporal dynamics of seeing and being seen.

Digitalisation thus enables the de-spatialisation of surveillance as this relationship is no longer tied to physical presence. This will be further explored in Chapter 3 where I will discuss how digitalisation is driving the ongoing – though the term may be a bit awkward – "synopticonisation" of trials.

The social construction of courts and the interactions within

So why does the digitalisation of the courtroom matter? As already noted, the courts play a central role in democratic societies, but it also matters because our social reality – the shared beliefs, values, norms, attitudes, and meanings that we collectively construct and accept as part of our everyday lives – is shaped by the interactions we engage in. This social reality also encompasses the courts and the actors within. This means that how we understand this institution and the roles within, as well as crime more generally, are shaped by what we read, what we watch, and what we listen to. It means that how we perceive a trial, what we think of when we think of a lawyer or a judge or a prosecutor, and also the extent to which we trust the legal institution are all shaped by the images, depictions, and stories we interact with. This also means that, for instance, filmed images of trials, live blogs, and podcasts should not be understood as a window into reality – of "pure vision" (Thompson 2005, 36) – rather, these depictions constitute a prism – representations or versions of reality shaped by editorial, budgetary, political, and individual factors (Moran 2016, 238). Courts and the actors within are thus socially constructed by choosing out and framing events in certain ways, producing and circulating cultural meanings (Hall 1974; Hjarvard 2013; Strömbäck 2008).

Another way in which digitalisation matters is that it has changed, and is continuing to change, the everyday work life of legal professionals. This has led to the construction of new practices as well as new ways of interacting and new ways of performing one's role. In sociological terms, it has disrupted the "traffic rules of social interaction" (Goffman 1967, 12) which guide what we do and how we do it in any given situation. The social rules for interacting which Goffman (1983) called "interaction orders" are used as invisible roadmaps for how to navigate face-to-face interactions. In these situations, interactants attempt to manage the impression they make on the other and interpret the impressions others are attempting to make on them. The strategies that are used by actors to convey this social information about themselves to others is known as "facework" (Goffman 1963). For instance, in Swedish criminal trials, defence lawyers use eye contact to intimidate the prosecutor, to produce remorse in clients, and to check with the judge that they are not questioning a plaintiff too harshly (Flower 2019).

For Goffman, for sustained, intimate, and coordinated actions to be possible – that is, for interactions to run smoothly – co-presence is necessary, and this co-presence also demands co-location; that is, that two or more people are physically located close to each other. Co-presence ensures a mutual flow of information and feedback between interactants (Goffman 1963) and it emerges when each person is "close enough to be perceived in whatever they are doing, including their experiencing of others, and close enough to be perceived in this sensing of being perceived" (Goffman 1963, 17). In short, people can read each other and act accordingly, enabling interactions to flow smoothly. Central to these interactions is that there is a shared understanding of what is going on, or a shared definition of the situation (Goffman 1959, 1963). This means that interactants know what kind of interaction is taking place, that there is a shared agreement as to the roles and rules to be followed and know how to act accordingly. Digitalisation challenges all of this by moving interactions either wholly or partially online, removing co-location, and making the definition of the situation less clear.

However, placing a contemporary spin on this, some scholars argue that a new form of co-presence – mediated co-presence – is possible in video link interactions because of the opportunity for synchronous mutual monitoring and the shared timeframe (Rettie 2009; Zhao and Elesh 2008; Campos-Castillo and Hitlin 2013). Co-presence is therefore decoupled from co-location. This means that, just as it is possible to be *in* the same location as others without being *with* them, for instance two people may sit next to each other on the bus without engaging in conversation, it is also possible for us to be *with* others even when we are not *in* the same location, for instance two people can be reciprocally oriented, mutually accessible, and available to each other in a video conference call without physical co-presence (Zhao and Elesh 2008).

Consequently, although interactants are not physically co-present, their mutual focus and shared temporality means that they are able to accomplish Goffman's (1983, 3) "sustained, intimate, coordination of action" as is central to social situations. Indeed other scholars take for granted that communicating via webcams entails a form of digital facework (Jenkins 2010, 262) and that a digital interaction order grounded in temporal co-presence, not physical co-presence, can be found (Jenkins 2010, 263).[4]

4 The digital interaction order has previously been used to analyse virtual spaces such as social networking sites, chatrooms, and virtual worlds (Walsh and Clark 2019; Walsh and Baker 2017; Humphreys 2005; Pinch 2010) and has also begun to be applied to understand situations in

Digital justice rituals

A ritual is a collection of organised practices and ceremonies that symbolically reinforce the beliefs, values, and norms within a community or society. These rituals play a crucial role in community building and fostering a sense of togetherness (Durkheim 1912/1995). According to Durkheim, the law, morality, and religion serve as forms of social control. Legal proceedings such as trials are thus extensions, enactments, re-enactments, and enforcements of the moral ideas deemed significant to society and are aimed at restoring a sense of social order when societal values are deviated from. Accordingly, gathering around the "justice ritual" (Rossner 2013) of a trial can serve to bind a society together. This means not just participating in a trial, but also listening to podcasts on the latest high-profile trial, tuning in to a livestream of a particularly gruesome murder trial, or discussing an ongoing trial in social media can all be ways of reinforcing moral values. Trials are therefore sacred objects around which society gathers and that within the trial there are symbols which have been infused with meaning.

Digitalisation also means that the well-established ritual of a trial is transitioned to a digital setting where participation takes place via video link by either one or more participant. Whilst some of these symbols of justice can easily be moved into this digital interaction, such as the scales of justice or a court's coat of arms, other fuzzier symbols which engage with other senses than purely visual, such as the soundscape of the courtroom or the courtroom atmosphere, may be harder to evoke yet are also important. Virtual justice rituals – those taking place partially or wholly online – thus need to be adjusted when they no longer take place in traditional, customary, and well-established settings in order for them to retain their symbolic power.

Central to virtual justice rituals is understanding the importance of physical settings and, within this, the absence of this physical setting. Physical social interactions take place in settings that are associated with specific kinds of activity. For instance, a home is divided into different rooms: kitchen, living room, bathroom, bedroom, and so on. Each of these areas or rooms has specific social functionalities and specific social activities associated with it. Likewise, a courthouse is divided into different areas: courtroom, waiting room, restrooms, chambers, and so on, each with specific social functionalities and social activities. To this, I add that there are also emotional expectations as to what one should feel and how this should be displayed in each area. For instance, certain behaviours and emotions are permitted in the waiting room such as displays of happiness with loud, raucous laughter and clapping each other on the backs which are often considered inappropriate in the courtroom. In the waiting room, the defence lawyer and prosecutor can have a

which interactants are "partly 'there' as well as 'here'"(Jenkins 2010, 271) referring to interactions where digital technologies, such as iPods and mobile phones, interrupt face-to-face interactions.

more relaxed and informal chat with each other about shared interests, interacting more as friends than legal actors. Again, this would not be appropriate in the courtroom. I explore taking part in an extraordinary event, such as a trial, from an ordinary setting, such as one's home, by introducing the concept of "emotional landscapes" in order to unpack the clash of emotional expectations and rules that can arise.

This book explores the opportunities and challenges posed by video links which interrupt the traditional flow of interaction in a trial, an interactional flow that is vital for justice rituals to run smoothly and which is thus vital for the reinforcement of solidarity and shared morality and, hence, trust in the legal system (Tyler 2006).

Emotions and newsworthiness

In this book I am also interested in exploring the role of digital tools in reporting from trials where the news media sphere risks clashing with the legal sphere. Whilst both spheres can be understood as grounded in the search for finding facts, the way in which these facts are presented differs. The legal sphere values the neutral presentation and evaluation of facts, and whilst the news media sphere (perhaps not all aspects, but many) is also driven by this, there is also a drive to construct news stories from these facts. Within this, the way in which emotions are perceived also differs, with the courts often seen as rational and emotionless entities, in contrast with the news media where reports and stories are filled with drama and sensationalism. Although current research shows that the courts are indeed emotional spheres wherein judges, prosecutors, and defence lawyers actively work with their emotions to make them appropriate to the courtroom context, and their roles within (Flower 2019; Bergman Blix and Wettergren 2018; Bandes 1999; Maroney 2011; Törnqvist 2021), there remains a schism between these two spheres.

Previous studies of news stories show that one of the key factors in deciding what becomes the news, and the extent to which it is covered, is a story's newsworthiness. Newsworthiness is a set of criteria which are used as guides to choosing and constructing the news (Jewkes 2015; Chibnall 1977; Galtung and Ruge 1965). Chibnall's (1977, 23) eight criteria for newsworthiness are immediacy, dramatisation, personalisation, simplification, titillation, conventionalism, structured access, and novelty. As part of the affective turn in journalism, emotion has been suggested as a ninth professional imperative (Pantti 2010; Allern 2002). The use of emotional depictions and characterisations and their use as tool to draw in readers have previously been confined to tabloid journalism, but their strategic use has more recently gained mainstream acceptance.[5] This widespread acceptance should not be surprising because, as

5 Certain types of news – for instance tabloid news – are often denounced as sensationalist due to the perceived focus on the bodily and emotional, rather than appeals to our reason

Pantti (2010, 170) argues, "news matters as a central site for emotion production, as an important source of political and moral emotions as well as a site of emotion management." This book will therefore also discuss the clash of the media and legal sphere and how digitalisation has shaped how courts are reported on. There is thus a clash between the "newsworthiness" of a trial that rests on specific criteria, which conflict with the factually and traditionally unemotional legal logic of a trial (Peleg and Bogoch 2012; Bogoch and Peleg 2014).[6]

Overview of each chapter

In this book I engage with a range of empirical materials including ethnographic fieldnotes written during trials, transcripts from interviews I have conducted with judges, lawyers, prosecutors, and journalists, and live blog transcripts gathered from new websites, as well as social media posts and podcasts.

Data was collected between 2019–2022 as part of two research projects. The first was a scoping comparative study between Denmark and Sweden exploring the use of live blogs as a form of court reporting, the second was focused on the Swedish context. The empirical material drawn on in this book consists of 44 interviews with judges, prosecutors, defence lawyers, and journalists in Sweden (30 interviews) and Denmark (14 interviews) who had experience of working on trials that were live blogged. All interview respondents have been given pseudonyms. All live blogs from Swedish news organisations' websites published between 2012 and 2020 and still available were collected, constituting 95 in total (randomly numbered between 1 and 95), and 20 purposely chosen live blogs from Danish websites. A wide range of experience levels are included, from newly qualified legal actors to those with long legal careers, with data collected until empirical saturation was reached (Fugard and Potts 2015). The aim of these studies was to explore how legal professionals relate

(Örnebring and Jönsson 2004). Such stories tend to entail an over-simplification of complex stories (Wahl-Jorgensen 2020, 176), within which emotions may be depicted or staged for particular purposes, so-called mediated emotion (Wahl-Jorgensen 2020). Mediated emotions thus drive the construction of certain ways of understanding and, in the case of court reporting, may contribute to the construction of the courtroom as a highly emotional sphere (see also Pantti 2010).

6 However, trials and, in particular, criminal trials, by their very nature, focus on personal experiences, events, and tragedies, thus fulfilling Chibnall's (1977) criteria of personalisation. Direct reporting – by its very nature – fulfils the imperative of immediacy. Whilst it could be argued that the imperative of structured access is also attained as journalists have access to the legal professionals involved in the trial who have an expert position, indeed direct reports regularly include an interview conducted with primarily a defence lawyer, but also prosecutor (although many choose not to comment on a trial until the end of proceedings, much like judges); this imperative is perhaps not as relevant with regards to this form of reporting.

to live blogging, how journalists accomplish it, and how legal professionals are emotionalised in such reports. I have conducted different analyses on the data collected, including a frame analysis on how trials and the legal professionals within are framed in live blogs (see Chapters 3 and 6), a quantitative content analysis focusing on the gendered nature of live blogs (see Chapter 6), a thematic content analysis exploring which types of crime are covered in live blogs and how they are made newsworthy (see Chapter 6), and a narrative analysis of the interview material (see Chapters 3 and 6). For a more developed overview of the methodologies used see, for instance, Flower and Ahlefeldt (2021) and Flower (2023a, 2023c).

Chapter 2 examines the use of video links in courts as a form of participating in trials. Although initially introduced as a way of ensuring safety for vulnerable victims and enabling participation in trials in rural areas, video links as a tool for legal professionals and lay participants to participate in a trial has seen a recent boom, with the implementation and use of this form undergoing a rapid expansion during and since the COVID-19 pandemic. In Chapter 2 I begin with a short overview of the history of video links before providing a summary of the opportunities and problems associated with this digital form of participation. I then analyse the virtual justice rituals by focusing on the sensorial aspects, in particular the soundscape of a trial, and the emotional landscape of a trial before tying these aspects together to analyse how a certain atmosphere emerges and the role this plays in trials, which interrupts the established interaction order and risks going lost in a virtual setting. Next, I explore the ways in which video links disrupts courtroom interactions, focusing on eyework, bodywork, and props. The penultimate section discusses digital co-presence as a possible solution to some of the challenges virtual justice rituals face before closing the chapter with final reflections. Throughout the chapter the theme of de-spatialising trials is discussed. The central argument made in this chapter is that there is a risk that video links have been rushed into courts without appropriate reflection and without the law keeping up to speed.

Chapter 3 focuses further on the interplay between digitalisation and open justice, in particular by analysing digital means of attending trials without the need to physically visit the courthouse, and the associated implications. The function of the media in enabling these forms of attendance is also examined. The chapter begins with a brief history of attending trials, open justice, and the role of the news media. I then focus on two forms of attending trials via livestreams and live blogs, with a specific focus on analysing interviews with Swedish and Danish legal professionals regarding how these insiders relate to live blogging and open justice. The central argument made in this chapter is that strategies for enabling open justice must be balanced against the level of transparency they facilitate to ensure that their implementation does not jeopardise fair and just trials.

In Chapter 4, I switch focus to open justice and social media by zooming in on the use and abuse of social media by courts and the actors within. There are therefore two streams to be explored: first, how the courts use social media as a tool of open justice to engage the wider society with the legal sphere, and second, how social media is used for beneficial means by legal professionals to educate about the legal system but also how social media can be used inappropriately by legal professionals and others participating in trials. The chapter begins with a short overview of social media and its evolution in the judicial sphere, drawing on the International Criminal Court as an example. I then explore the duality of social media engagement, highlighting the advantages and disadvantages. Next, I move to judicial use of social media and discuss the balance between judicial neutrality and freedom of speech before touching briefly on the phenomenon of Google mistrials. The next section examines the changing perception of the judicial system stemming from social media engagement before ending the chapter with a closing discussion. The key argument made in this chapter is that social media can be a useful tool for ensuring open justice, however the integrity and rights of all parties must be upheld. The use of social media to engage with wider society can therefore spill over into the misuse of social media with more damaging consequences.

The convergence of the digitalisation of courtroom documents and proceedings and the explosion in interest in crime is explored in Chapter 5 to examine the true crime trial and to investigate the clash between open justice and personal integrity. I begin by presenting a short background on true crime before introducing the true crime trial and the role played by the digitalisation of court proceedings. I then show how juridical documentaries and podcasts shape our understandings and expectations before closing the chapter with a specific focus on the Swedish context and the rise of podcasts using audio recordings from trials, along with the boom in online forums which circulate legal documents now available digitally. In this chapter I argue that in the drive towards increased transparency, the digitalisation of the courts has contributed to the trial becoming a form of public spectacle and ask, how much access is too much?

Chapter 6 continues the focus on Sweden, to delve deeper into several of the themes presented in the book. Video links are discussed before diving into a detailed analysis of live blogs, which highlights the types of trials reported on and how trials and the actors within are depicted, including a Bechdel test which demonstrates female legal professionals are under-represented in this form of reporting. Beyond drawing on extensive empirical material in the form of live blogs, I also analyse interviews with judges, lawyers, prosecutors, and journalists to discuss whether live blogs can be understood as a form of education or entertainment. I then show how the functions of open justice have shifted in the digital age, from disciplinary goals to a purpose of surveillance, and show that live blogs constitute a distinct threat to the execution of fair trials with regards to the truth function of open justice. The central argument in this chapter is that digitalisation tools for ensuring open justice and increased access have been rushed into courts without appropriate reflection. The final chapter sums up the key findings in the book and suggests future areas of research.

To summarise the main points made in this book:

- Digitalisation has enabled courts to be more open than ever before empowering public insight, boosting the courts' engagement with the wider community, and improving the media's capacity to monitor trials; however, this has had several unwanted consequences which have a negative impact on justice and the experience of justice.
- The law has not kept up with digital technologies leading to confusion as to their appropriate usage and intrusions of personal integrity.
- The digitalisation of legal information has contributed to the trial becoming a public spectacle.
- Trials have become de-spatialised with physical presence no longer necessary, yet without fully understanding the implications of this decoupling.
- Some technology has been rushed into the courts without appropriate reflection and empirical investigation.
- We need to ask, how much access is enough and how much access is too much?

Once again, I want to reiterate that I am not anti-open justice or a technophobe! Rather, I want this book to be seen as a call for more critical attention to be paid to the ways in which digitalisation has enabled more insight into our legal proceedings than ever before.

References

Allern, Sigurd. 2002. "Journalistic and Commercial News Values." *Nordicom Review* 23 (1–2):137–152.

Bandes, Susan, ed. 1999. *The Passions of Law*. New York: New York University Press.

Bank, World Data. 2022. "Individuals Using the Internet (% of Population)." Retrieved from https://data.worldbank.org/indicator/IT.NET.USER.ZS, accessed 11th January 2023.

Beccaria, Cesare. 2016. *On Crimes and Punishments*. Transaction Publishers.

Bentham, Jeremy. 1843. *The Works of Jeremy Bentham*. Edited by John Bowring. Vol. II. Edinburgh: William Tait.

Bergman Blix, Stina, and Åsa Wettergren. 2018. *Professional Emotions in Court*. Abingdon: Routledge.

Beriain, Iñigo De Miguel. 2018. "Does the Use of Risk Assessments in Sentences Respect the Right to Due Process? A Critical Analysis of the Wisconsin v. Loomis Ruling." *Law, Probability and Risk* 17 (1):45–53. https://doi.org/10.1093/lpr/mgy001.

Bogoch, Bryna, and Anat Peleg. 2014. "Law in the Age of Media Logic." In *Mediatization of Communication*, edited by Knut Lundby, 443–462. Berlin: De Gruyter.

Bosland, Jason, and Judith Townend. 2018. "Open Justice, Transparency and the Media: Representing the Public Interest in the Physical and Virtual Courtroom." *Communications Law* 23 (4):183–202.

Campos-Castillo, Celeste, and Steven Hitlin. 2013. "Copresence: Revisiting a Building Block for Social Interaction Theories." *Sociological Theory* 31 (2):168–192. https://doi.org/10.1177/0735275113489811.

Castells, Manuel. 1996. *The Information Age: Economy, Society and Culture*. Malden, MA: Blackwell.

Chibnall, Steve. 1977. *Law-and-Order News: An Analysis of Crime Reporting in the British Press.* London: Tavistock.
Collins, Randall. 2004. *Interaction Ritual Chains.* Princeton: Princeton University Press.
Cullen, Rowena. 2001. "Addressing the Digital Divide." *Online Information Review* 25 (5):311–320. https://doi.org/10.1108/14684520110410517.
Data, Our World in. 2023. "Share of the Population Using the Internet, 2020." Retrieved from https://ourworldindata.org/grapher/share-of-individuals-using-the-internet.
DiMaggio, Paul, and Eszter Hargittai. 2001. *From the 'Digital Divide' to 'Digital Inequality': Studying Internet Use as Penetration Increases, Center for Arts and Cultural Policy Series, Working Paper Series 15.* Woodrow Wilson School: Princeton University.
Durkheim, E. 1912/1995. *The Elementary Forms of Religious Life.* New York: The Free Press.
Egard, Hanna, and Kristofer Hansson. 2021. "The Digital Society Comes Sneaking in. An Emerging Field and Its Disabling Barriers." *Disability & Society*:1–15. https://doi.org/10.1080/09687599.2021.1960275.
European Convention on Human Rights and Fundamental Freedoms, ECHR. 1950. "Convention for the Protection of Human Rights and Fundamental Freedoms." Retrieved from https://www.echr.coe.int/documents/d/echr/convention_ENG.
Flower, Lisa. 2019. *Interactional Justice: The Role of Emotions in the Performance of Loyalty.* Abingdon: Routledge.
Flower, Lisa. 2023a. "Constructing Clickable Criminal Trials: Framing Trials and Legal Professionals in Digital News Reports." *Emotions and Society* 5 (1):48–66.
Flower, Lisa. 2023b. "Live Blogs Can't Handle the Truth." *Oñati Socio-Legal Series.* https://doi.org/10.35295/osls.iisl/0000-0000-0000-1402.
Flower, Lisa. 2023c. "Live Blogs Can't Handle the Truth? A Contemporary Cross-Cultural Consideration of Transparency and Procedural Justice." *Oñati Socio-Legal Series* 13 (5):1690–1710.
Flower, Lisa, and Marie-Sophie Ahlefeldt. 2021. "The Criminal Trial as a Live Event: Exploring How and Why Live Blogs Change the Professional Practices of Judges, Defence Lawyers and Prosecutors." *Media, Culture & Society* 43 (8):1480–1496.
Foucault, Michel. 1975/1991. *Discipline and Punish: The Birth of the Prison.* Translated by Alan Sheridan. New York: Random House.
Fugard, Andrew J. B., and Henry W. W. Potts. 2015. "Supporting Thinking on Sample Sizes for Thematic Analyses: A Quantitative Tool." *International Journal of Social Research Methodology* 18:669–684.
Galtung, Johan, and Mari Holmboe Ruge. 1965. "The Structure of Foreign News." *Journal of Peace Research* 2 (1):64–91.
Goffman, Erving. 1959. *The Presentation of Self in Everyday Life.* Harmondsworth: Penguin Books Ltd.
Goffman, Erving. 1963. *Behavior in Public Places: Notes on the Social Organization of Gatherings.* New York: The Free Press.
Goffman, Erving. 1967. *Interaction Ritual: Essays on Face-to-Face Behavior.* New York: Anchor Books.
Goffman, Erving. 1983. "The Interaction Order: American Sociological Association, 1982 Presidential Address." *American Sociological Review* 48 (1):1–17.
Hall, Stuart. 1974. "Deviance, Politics, and the Media." In *Deviance and Social Control*, edited by Paul Rock and Mary McIntosh, 261–286. London: Tavistock.
Hans, Valerie P., and Juliet L. Dee. 1991. "Media Coverage of Law: Its Impact on Juries and the Public." *American Behavioral Scientist* 35 (2):136–149. https://doi.org/10.1177/0002764291035002005.
Hansen, Hans Krause, Lars Thøger Christensen, and Mikkel Flyverbom. 2015. "Introduction: Logics of Transparency in Late Modernity: Paradoxes, Mediation and Governance." *European Journal of Social Theory* 18 (2):117–131. https://doi.org/10.1177/1368431014555254.

Härtel, Jasmin C. R., and Charmine E. J. Härtel. 2020. "What the Digital Age Is and Means for Workers, Services, and Emotions Scholars and Practitioners." In *Emotions and Service in the Digital Age*, edited by Charmine E. J. Härtel, Wilfred J. Zerbe, and Neal M. Ashkanasy, 9–17. Emerald Publishing Limited.

Hess, Burkhard, and Ana Koprivica, eds. 2019. *Open Justice: The Role of Courts in a Democratic Society*. Baden-Baden: Nomos Verlag.

Hjarvard, Stig. 2013. *The Mediatization of Culture and Society*. Abingdon: Routledge.

Humphreys, Lee. 2005. "Cellphones in Public: Social Interactions in a Wireless Era." *New Media & Society* 7 (6):810–833. https://doi.org/10.1177/1461444805058164.

Jaconelli, Joseph. 2002. *Open Justice: A Critique of the Public Trial*. Oxford: Oxford University Press.

Jenkins, Richard. 2010. "The 21st-Century Interaction Order." In *The Contemporary Goffman*, edited by M. H. Jacobsen, 271–288. Abingdon: Routledge.

Jewkes, Yvonne. 2015. *Media and Crime*. 3rd ed. London: Sage Publications Ltd.

Kroll, Joshua Alexander. 2015. *Accountable Algorithms*. Princeton: Princeton University Press.

Lyon, David. 2001. *Surveillance Society: Monitoring Everyday Life*. Buckingham: Open University Press.

Lyon, David. 2007. *Surveillance Studies: An Overview*. Cambridge: Polity Press. Book.

Lyon, David. 2018. *The Culture of Surveillance: Watching as a Way of Life*. Cambridge: Polity Press.

Maroney, Terry A. 2011. "Emotional Regulation and Judicial Behavior." *California Law Review* 99 (6):1485–1555.

Mathiesen, Thomas. 1997. "The Viewer Society." *Theoretical Criminology* 1 (2):215.

McKay, Carolyn. 2020. "Predicting Risk in Criminal Procedure: Actuarial Tools, Algorithms, AI and Judicial Decision-Making." *Current Issues in Criminal Justice* 32 (1):22–39. https://doi.org/10.1080/10345329.2019.1658694.

Moore, Sarah. 2018. "Towards a Sociology of Institutional Transparency: Openness, Deception and the Problem of Public Trust." *Sociology* 52 (2):416–430. https://doi.org/10.1177/0038038516686530.

Moore, Sarah, Alex Clayton, and Hector Murphy. 2019. "Seeing Justice Done: Courtroom Filming and the Deceptions of Transparency." *Crime, Media, Culture*:1741659019883764. https://doi.org/10.1177/1741659019883764.

Moran, Leslie J. 2016. "Visible Justice: YouTube and the UK Supreme Court." *The Annual Review of Interdisciplinary Justice Research* 5:223–263.

Mulcahy, Linda. 2010. *Legal Architecture: Justice, Due Process and the Place of Law*. London: Routledge.

Örnebring, H., and A. M. Jönsson. 2004. "Tabloid Journalism and the Public Sphere: A Historical Perspective on Tabloid Journalism." *Journalism Studies* 5 (3):283–295. https://doi.org/10.1080/1461670042000246052.

Pantti, Mervi. 2010. "The Value of Emotion: An Examination of Television Journalists' Notions on Emotionality." *European Journal of Communication* 25 (2):168–181. https://doi.org/10.1177/0267323110363653.

Peleg, Anat, and Bryna Bogoch. 2012. "Removing Justitia's Blindfold: The Mediatization of Law in Israel." *Media, Culture & Society* 34 (8):961–978.

Peters, Anne. 2013. "Towards Transparency as a Global Norm." In *Transparency in International Law*, edited by A. Bianchi and A. Peters, 534–607. Cambridge: Cambridge University Press.

Pinch, Trevor. 2010. "The Invisible Technologies of Goffman's Sociology: From the Merry-Go-Round to the Internet." *Technology and Culture* 51 (2):409–424.

Project, World Justice. 2019. *Global Insights on Access to Justice*. Washington, DC: World Justice Project.

Resnik, Judith. 2013. "The Democracy in Courts: Jeremy Bentham, 'Publicity', and the Privatization of Process in the Twenty-First Century." *NoFo: An Interdisciplinary Journal or Law and Justice* 10 (1):77–119.
Rettie, Ruth. 2009. "Mobile Phone Communication: Extending Goffman to Mediated Interaction." *Sociology* 43 (3):421–438.
Rodrick, Sharon. 2014. "Achieving the Aims of Open Justice – The Relationship between the Courts, the Media and the Public." *Deakin Law Review* 19 (1):123–162.
Rossner, Meredith. 2013. *Just Emotions: Rituals of Restorative Justice, Clarendon Studies in Criminology*. Oxford: Oxford University Press.
Schaefer, Stephan, Magnus Andersson, Elizabeth Bjarnason, and Kristofer Hansson, eds. 2018. *Working and Organizing in the Digital Age*. Lund: The Pufendorf Institute for Advanced Studies.
Schofield, Philip. 2006. *Utility and Democracy. The Political Thought of Jeremy Bentham*. Oxford: Oxford University Press.
Scott, John, and Gordon Marshall. 2009. "Information Society." In *A Dictionary of Sociology*. Oxford: Oxford University Press.
Strömbäck, Jesper. 2008. "Four Phases of Mediatization: An Analysis of the Mediatization of Politics." *The International Journal of Press/Politics* 13 (3):228–246. https://doi.org/10.1177/1940161208319097.
Susskind, Richard. 2019. *Online Courts and the Future of Justice*. Oxford: Oxford University Press.
Thompson, John B. 2005. "The New Visibility." *Theory, Culture & Society* 22 (6):31–51. https://doi.org/10.1177/0263276405059413.
Törnqvist, Nina. 2021. "Drizzling Sympathy: Ideal Victims and Flows of Sympathy in Swedish Courts." *International Review of Victimology*:02697580211035586. https://doi.org/10.1177/02697580211035586.
Townend, Judith, and Lucy Welsh. 2023. *Observing Justice: Digital Transparency, Openness and Accountability in Criminal Courts*. Policy Press.
Tyler, T. R. 2003. "Procedural Justice, Legitimacy, and the Effective Rule of Law." *Crime and Justice* 30 (1):283–357.
Tyler, T. R. 2006. *Why People Obey the Law*. Princeton, NJ: Princeton University Press.
van Dijk, Jan, and Kenneth Hacker. 2003. "The Digital Divide as a Complex and Dynamic Phenomenon." *The Information Society* 19 (4):315–326. https://doi.org/10.1080/01972240309487.
Wahl-Jorgensen, Karin. 2020. "An Emotional Turn in Journalism Studies?" *Digital Journalism* 8 (2):175–194. https://doi.org/10.1080/21670811.2019.1697626.
Wales, Law Society Commission on the Use of Algorithms in the Justice System and the Law Society of England and. 2019. "Algorithms in the Criminal Justice System." Retrieved from www.lawsociety.org.uk/topics/research/algorithm-use-in-the-criminal-justice-system-report, accessed 12th January 2023.
Walsh, James Michael, and Shannon Jay Clark. 2019. "Co-Present Conversation as 'Socialized Trance': Talk, Involvement Obligations, and Smart-Phone Disruption." *Symbolic Interaction* 42 (1):6–26.
Walsh, Michael James, and Stephanie Alice Baker. 2017. "The Selfie and the Transformation of the Public–Private Distinction." *Information, Communication & Society* 20 (8):1185–1203. https://doi.org/10.1080/1369118X.2016.1220969.
Warschauer, Mark. 2004. *Technology and Social Inclusion: Rethinking the Digital Divide*. MIT Press. e-book.
Zhao, S., and D. Elesh. 2008. "Copresence as 'Being With': Social Contact in Online Public Domains." *Information Communication and Society* 11 (4):565–583. https://doi.org/10.1080/13691180801998995.

2 Participation

In the beginning of 2021, the now infamous "I'm not a cat" Zoom hearing took place at a district court in Texas in which one of the attorneys accidentally enables a cat filter that shows a white kitten face over his own, giving the appearance that it is the cat speaking. This prompts the attorney to clarify for the judge, "I'm here live. I'm not a cat." This exchange became a viral sensation as it struck a chord with many regarding the perils and pitfalls of online meetings which, at that time, were washing over the COVID-19 pandemic-ridden globe.

Similar incidents of amusing, remarkable, and even worrying instances of video link usage soon followed. Defendants have participated in trials from a range of locations, such as a defendant charged with driving whilst suspended (punishable by up to 93 days in prison and a fine of up to 500 dollars) who videolinked into his trial whilst sitting in the driver's seat of his car in clear view of the judge.[1] Others have participated from unusual locations, whilst engaged with unexpected activities. For instance, a plastic surgeon defendant attempted to take part in his Zoom traffic court trial direct from the operating room, whilst operating on a patient (11 KHOU 2021). Despite assuring the court that he was available for trial; a new date was scheduled.[2] In other trials there have been instances of a defendant who joined proceedings whilst kayaking (Mike 2023) or another who was accused of drugs possession, who rolled a joint and smoked it whilst waiting in the virtual waiting room in full view of the prosecutor (A&E 2023).[3] The juxtaposition of taking part in

1 The defendant apologises for joining the trial late as "I'm so sorry I'm late, this looks so terrible" to which the judge responds "yeah it does, you're charged for driving whilst suspended and you're sitting in the driver's seat of your car indicating that you just drove to work" (Watch 2021).

2 As of November 2023, the Medical Board of California said it would investigate, but no arrest has been made yet.

3 Although marijuana use is legal in Michigan, the defendant was on bail and therefore prohibited from taking illegal substances and was also required to take a drug test twice a week. His trial was promptly ended and he was ordered to appear for a drug test the following day (which he failed to show for and which led to his bond being revoked).

DOI: 10.4324/9781003344643-2

an extraordinary event from an ordinary place is also reflected in the comments sections of video link trials that are also livestreamed, such as "Imagine getting sentenced to life while taking a bath in your own house." Even more worryingly, an assault trial with all parties participating via video link[4] came to an abrupt halt after the prosecutor became worried for a plaintiff's safety. The prosecutor suspected the defendant was currently located in the same apartment as the plaintiff. The police were called to the plaintiff's address and found the defendant, who had claimed to be elsewhere, was indeed, there. The defendant was promptly taken into custody for violating his bond.

This brief overview makes it clear that the widespread implementation of video links is changing trials in several ways. Video links have opened new spaces from which one can participate – from the surgical operating room to the driver's seat of a car, to a kayak on open water or, perhaps more commonly, from another courthouse, or specially designed spaces.[5] This, in turn, raises important questions regarding how not being physically present shapes the experience and practices of participating in a trial, and how the space from which one participates shapes the experience of taking part in a trial. It also leads to inquiry as to how the ritual of a trial can be upheld when proceedings can take place from – to put it flippantly – anywhere with internet access. This, in turn, leads to questions regarding how the gravity and solemnity of proceedings as are inherent to a legal trial can be conveyed in online settings when cat-filter accidents, participation from lakes, or defendants using illegal substances in the waiting room are possible. Questions also arise regarding the ways in which the absence of face-to-face interaction and the associated absence of feelings of being-thereness risk impacting on how trials are perceived and experienced. Indeed, the legal trial is a situation that is deeply entrenched with the fundamentality of physical co-presence. What happens to this when the physical courtroom is absent? Finally, video links prompt inquiries regarding the legal security of a trial, as the digitalisation of participation enables plaintiffs' testimony to be influenced in real time, proceedings to be disrupted by hacking into livestreams to disrupt proceedings, or by mistrials being called due to inappropriate usage of video links. For instance, in January 2024, during the trial for rapper Young Thug accused of racketeering and gang conspiracy, the Zoom feed which was livestreaming the trial was hacked with shouts of "Free Thug! Mistrial!" broadcast over the stream (CourtTV 2024).

In this chapter I explore the current state of the art regarding video links covering such topics as prevalence, advantages, problems, and the future,

4 Presided over by Judge Jeffrey Middleton whose court became an internet sensation.

5 Such as Nightingale courts which were makeshift courts implemented during the COVID-19 pandemic in England to enable hearings to continue. However, Nightingale courts soon faced widespread criticism due to the associated underestimation of the scale of the problem which was described as "like taking a bucket to a house fire" (Hyde 2020) and because of the restricted space in these courts, making criminal hearings and supporting victims of crime particularly problematic (Moore 2023).

raising themes such as the senses, atmospheres, eyework, and co-presence. As people's obedience to follow laws and their acceptance of legal decisions, including their willingness to accept "losing" their case, is affected by the degree to which they experience their encounter with the courts as fair (Tyler 2006, 1988; Tyler 2007), participation via video link needs to be fully understood, and we need a clear understanding of the benefits and risks of video links as I will explore more fully.

Video links in courts

I begin with a couple of points on terminology. I use the term "video link" to refer to all forms of audio-visual technology that enable participation in court proceedings from a location other than the courtroom using platforms such as Zoom, WebEx, and Pexip, which enable participation via different devices such as computers, laptops, mobile phones, and tablets. My focus is on the use of two-way live video links and not on the use of pre-recorded videos of testimony (although many of the findings presented will be of relevance to both).

Several terms are used to describe trials which take place either partially or entirely via video link, such as "remote hearing," "virtual hearing," "virtual proceedings," and "distributed hearing." In this book I use the term "remote participation" to refer to participation via video link and "virtual court" to refer to courts whereby one or more are present via video link. I also briefly discuss "virtual reality trials," which are those taking entirely in virtual reality spheres with the use of avatars.

A very brief overview of the history of video links

The concept of video conferencing – the use of technology to conduct live, two-way video communication between individuals or groups located in different places – is not new. As early as 1924, Alexander Graham Bell stated, "the day would come when the man at the telephone would be able to see the distant person to whom he was speaking" (Schnaars and Wymbs 2004, 199). Video links – which used technology to transmit video signals over distance – were first used in Germany in the 1940s, with the invention of the video tape recorder capable of recording live images coming in 1951. In conjunction with this, videophone communication began to develop in earnest with the "Picturephone" in the 1960s. However, despite AT&T's sustained efforts, video calling booths and, later, desktop videophones failed to root themselves as established communication forms largely due to a depressed economy, low picture quality, low consumer demand, and high prices (Schnaars and Wymbs 2004). It was not until the digitalisation of the video camera in the 1980s and, more importantly, the explosion of the internet in the late 1990s and 2000s that video conferences became more commonplace. Alongside this, in the early 1990s, the first video conferencing platforms were developed along with the first webcam and, in the early 2000s, the rise of smartphones saw the introduction of front-facing cameras aimed at enabling video conferencing (Patrizio 2021). Skype was first released in 2003 and became market-leading until the early 2010s when Zoom swept in with higher quality audio and video, thus taking over leadership of the field (Walsh 2020). Digital video cameras came along in the late 1980s, further opening up the possibilities and opportunities for video links to be used. Although the digital divide remains – disconnecting those who have the means and capabilities of accessing the internet from those who do not (van Dijk 2019), the inventions and widespread implementation of video conferencing platforms and the introduction of CCTV and video surveillance now means that video links are a commonplace, mundane aspect of the day-to-day lives of many.

The early form of video links, known as "videophones," were first used in bail hearings in the US in the early 1970s (Davis et al. 2015; Courts 1995; Bermant and Woods 1994). Although the United States was the first country to implement video links in courts, Australia introduced widespread use of technology in the 1980s in response to increasing awareness of victims' rights and the need to separate vulnerable witnesses from offenders, combined with the vast distances of travel in Australia[6] (Smith, Savage, and Emami 2021; Wallace 2008; Wallace, Roach Anleu, and Mack 2017; Macdonald and Wallace 2004). The US and England and Wales[7] followed suit, introducing video links hearings when the protection of vulnerable witnesses was warranted[8] (Wiggins 2003; Lederer 1998; Frazier et al. 2021; see Ariturk, Crozier, and Garrett 2020 for an overview). Likewise, Sweden has used video links for children taking part in sexual criminal cases since 1995 (Landström, Willén, and Bylander 2012; see Bylander 2006 for an extensive overview). Indeed, in 2018, the government in England and Wales embarked on a £1.2-billion

6 Current legislation in Australia thus authorises video links to be used by witnesses and parties, including criminal defendants, and is up to the primary judge's discretion exercised in accordance with the circumstances of each particular case (Legg and Song 2021). However, most jurisdictions in Australia state that a person should be physically present for their first appearance and initial bail application, and those facing criminal charges should be physically present in court for an inquiry into their fitness to stand trial, at committal and trial (Wallace, Roach Anleu, and Mack 2017).

7 In 1999, England and Wales introduced the Youth Justice and Criminal Evidence Act to ameliorate difficulties associated with giving oral evidence by vulnerable or intimated witnesses, hence video links, previously reserved for child witnesses, were able to be used by a wider range of participants (Ellison and Munro 2013; see also Tomlinson 2019; Terry, Johnson, and Thompson 2010). In 2016, the Ministry of Justice acknowledged, "more and more cases or parts of cases will be carried out virtually or online" (Justice 2016). After the temporary emergency provisions of the Coronavirus Act 2020 were found to be successful, video links are now able to be used by advocates, members of the court, defendants, witnesses, and victims when the judge deems it suitable (Judiciary 2022). Even juries may be permitted to take part virtually, however this is currently deemed to be rare (Godfrey, Richardson, and Walklate 2022; Judiciary 2022).

8 Video links have since been used in federal, appellate, and state courts since the late 1990s/ early 2000s.

court modernisation scheme which includes "fully video hearings" whereby all parties participate via video link (Rossner and McCurdy 2020, 2018).

Then came the COVID-19 pandemic which sparked lockdowns and the implementation of social distancing rules across the globe. Many jurisdictions were already facing enormous backlogs prior to the outbreak; for instance, Brazil had a backlog of 78 million lawsuits (Brehm et al. 2020), India had 44 million cases waiting (Thakur 2021), the average backlog in state and local courts across the US increased by one third during the pandemic (Jurva 2021), and other countries such as England struggled to keep the courts functioning smoothly (Robins 2021; Godfrey, Richardson, and Walklate 2022). The pandemic thus forced many countries to either introduce video links, for instance in Ireland, San Marino, and Andorra, or bring in emergency measure limited to the pandemic such as in Switzerland, or further develop those capabilities already established, such as in Australia, Canada, China, Kenya, Norway, England, and the US (e-Justice 2020; Sanders 2021; see also Worldwide 2023 for comprehensive information). Video links thus became a widely used way of enabling access to justice (Legg and Song 2021; Viglione, Peck, and Frazier 2023; Daftary-Kapur, Henderson, and Zottoli 2021). Video links are now widely used to hear expert witnesses, provide interpreters, and enable judicial officers to cover regional courts, and they are used in jury and non-jury criminal trials across the globe (Macdonald and Wallace 2004; Rowden et al. 2013; Legg and Song 2021).

Post-pandemic, video links have therefore stayed as a central part of legal proceedings in many jurisdictions (Worldwide 2023; Sanders 2021) and, indeed, may even continue to become more prolific (Sourdin and Zeleznikow 2020; Dale and Smith 2021). Video links are therefore becoming the "new normal" (Rossner, Tait, and McCurdy 2021, 96) across the board, however their usage in specific trials is often up to the discretion of the judge to decide whether virtual participation is appropriate (e.g. in Sweden).[9] Herein lies the problem: video links were first introduced for specific participants, in specific instances; however, they quickly engulfed the legal system during the pandemic despite a lack of sufficient knowledge regarding their appropriateness and despite much of the research being outdated.

Why video links?

As already noted, video links can be a useful tool for protecting vulnerable participants in trials. For instance, in early studies, the use of video links by

9 In Sweden, video links were first suggested in 1995 and were initially used by children taking part in sexual criminal cases. Video links were later introduced more broadly to trials as part of a two-year pilot study in 2000 and are currently permitted, for instance, in criminal trials when there are extenuating circumstances such as unreasonable costs, inconvenience for participating on site, or safety concerns (SFS 1942:740 5 kap).

children or intimidated witnesses (e.g. in Australia, Sweden, England, and Wales) indicated that children preferred to give testimony via video link, were less nervous or fearful, and more likely to report the trial as fair (Davies and Noon 1991; Government 1995; Hamlyn, Phelps, and Sattar 2004). Subsequent studies have also found that video links increase the confidence of victims in criminal trials when describing intimate experiences and that this format also raises the quality of testimony (Burton, Evans, and Sanders 2007; Mulcahy 2008).[10]

However, we should already pause here as a deeper dive into some of these findings already reveals concerning aspects to video links. For instance, another study of vulnerable or intimidated witnesses found that although witnesses were more likely to give evidence via video link in comparison to in court, 10 percent reported that they felt this format was not helpful (Hamlyn, Phelps, and Sattar 2004), whilst in other studies, such witnesses reported that they had little choice with regards to whether this format of participation could be rejected in favour of in-court participation (Hall 2007). It seems that video links are not the panacea as originally envisioned.

Hopping back to the benefits: video links can improve the safety of trials by reducing the need for those sitting in custody having to travel to court. This increases the possibility of defendants taking part in their trial via video link from a prison, detention centre, or similar and removes the risk of escape during transportation or during the trial itself;[11] indeed, in the first four months of 2023, three prisoners escaped during transportation in Sweden.[12] This form of participation also reduces the risk for other types of disruption during the trial with instances of defendants attacking judges (Madani 2021) or their own lawyers (Steinbuch 2023), or victim's families attacking the defendant (Mayer 2022). Even in non-criminal cases such as paternity cases (Wright 2023) and divorce hearings (Zahra 2017) courtroom brawls can break out. Indeed, there have been instances where even the prosecutor and judge have come to physical blows.[13]

The reduction of travel needs also reduces the costs and hassle associated with travelling to participate in a trial. Linked to this, the right to a trial without unnecessary delay is the backbone of many jurisdictions, hence video links can contribute to ensuring the swiftness of a trial. This is particularly pertinent in countries with large rural areas requiring vast distances to be covered in order to take part, such as in Canada (Puddister and Small 2020) and Australia (McKay and Macintosh 2023). Moreover, video link technology enables evidence to be taken from overseas thereby meeting a range of legal requirements, such

10 Although a study on barristers prosecuting and defending rape had mixed findings, with those prosecuting not in favour and those defending more supportive (Temkin 2000).

11 For escape attempts in the US captured on Court Cam see A&E (2024).

12 Escaping from prison or prison transport is currently not illegal in Sweden, however aiding such an attempt is illegal.

13 For such a trial see www.cbsnews.com/video/judge-brawls-with-public-defender-in-court/#x.

as the Hague Evidence Convention (Legg and Song 2021). In Sweden, an increase in the number of people placed in detention centres has led to many being placed in locations far away from the court their trial will take place it, which increases travel costs in order for them to attend. Video links are thus often presented as a way of reducing the time, money, and bother of travelling to a courthouse to participate in a trial and reducing the need to postpone due to illness or scheduling conflicts (see e.g. Johnson and Wiggins 2006; Prescott 2017; Sela 2017). Although not often mentioned, video links also contribute to reducing the carbon footprint of a trial, which can considered to be a positive aspect of this technology.

Having read thus far, you may think video links sound terrific! They ensure participants' safety and integrity, they reduce costs, and they are environmentally friendly. What's the problem?

The problems of video links

There are, in fact, a number of problems related to video links which stem from research being outdated, findings that are contradictory, and gaps in the research field. For instance, several studies have been conducted aimed at exploring how participation format changes our perception of other people. Landström and colleagues have explored perceptions of credibility when witnesses participate via video link, finding that witnesses are perceived as less credible when taking part via video link, in contrast to witnesses who are communicating in person (Landström, Ask, and Sommar 2015; Landström, Granhag, and Hartwig 2005; Landström, Ask, and Sommar 2019; Landström, Granhag, and Hartwig 2007). Whilst other studies have supported this finding (Tait and Tay 2019), contrasting results have also been found, indicating that participation format has no impact on evaluations of credibility (Ellison and Munro 2013; Munro 2018; Goodman et al. 1998). For instance, a study on sexual assault complainants found mode of victim testimony – in-court, video link, telephone – had no impact on evaluations of credibility (Taylor and Joudo 2005) whilst yet another study found no difference in perceptions of credibility between in-court and video participation (however, phone testimony was rated less favourably) (Jones et al. 2023).

Perhaps more worryingly, as Jones and colleagues (2023) note, in some cases, the same team of researchers has yielded contradictory results: Orcutt and colleagues (2001) found that mock jurors were less likely to find a defendant guilty if a child witness testified via video link as they found the witness to be less credible, however as part of the same project, Goodman and colleagues (1998) found that mock jurors' verdicts *did not* change when a child witness gave evidence in court compared to via video link.

Moreover, if we begin to dig more deeply into certain aspects that – on the surface – appear beneficial, we may find hidden issues. For instance, to return to vulnerable participants: video links are often presented as suitable for this category, however this may include many different categories, such as neurodiversity, children, and people with physical disabilities. Rather than blanketing all vulnerable participants in one category and presenting video links as a useful solution for them, it is perhaps more apposite to attend to "who should be excluded in the interests of inclusion" (Mulcahy and Tsalapatanis 2022, 456). For instance, for some people with physical disabilities or neurodiversity, an online hearing may be preferred to avoid travel and reduce anxiety (Mulcahy and Tsalapatanis 2022). However, as Mulcahy and Tsalapatanis (2022) highlight – for the "digitally disadvantaged" (Mulcahy and Tsalapatanis 2022), who lack the necessary equipment, bandwidth, skills, or confidence and who are also more likely to be unemployed, disabled, older, less well educated, and more socially isolated (Mulcahy and Tsalapatanis 2022; Helsper and Reisdorf 2016; Group 2023) – digital participation may lead to feelings of nervousness, stress, and anxiety. This means that when reasoning about the suitability of digital participation, nuanced evaluations need to be made, which include consideration of the implications of digital disadvantage.

The research on the risks and benefits of video links is thus divided. A study of Swedish judges, lawyers, and prosecutors indicated they were positive to the use of video links but that they nevertheless preferred face-to-face presentations in court, as "live" performances were perceived as more reasonable and it was easier to read an interrogation persons' emotional expressions in court when in the courtroom (Landström, Willén, and Bylander 2012). Live interrogations also provided a better basis for critical examination and had a higher evidential value. The study also found that statements in Swedish courts can be evaluated differently depending on if the statement is presented live (in district court) or on video as is the case at the Court of Appeal. In extension this could mean that different evaluations are made at different courts, depending on the presentation format. Whilst an initial comparison did not find any difference (SOU 2012, 93; Levén and Wesäll 2011), other studies have found that there is no difference between how, for instance, a defendant is perceived when participating via video link and when participating in the courtroom (Rossner and Tait 2021).

Video links are therefore not as friction-free or beneficial as appears on the surface, and I argue there is a risk that video links have been rushed into the courts without appropriate reflection and investigation into the impact they have on trials and the actors within. In the next sections I focus on three themes which are important to consider as we continue towards ever-increasing digitalisation of trial participation. Each of these themes highlights a fundamental aspect of physical trials which is jeopardised by the switch to trials partially or fully taking place via video link: justice rituals; courtroom atmosphere and emotional spaces; and courtroom interactions.

The sensorial ritual of a trial

A ritual, as already noted in Chapter 1, is a series of acts or actions which are heavily symbolised, steeped in tradition, and well established. Rituals often indicate critical turning points in life, such as a wedding or a funeral, and have a "sacred and timeless quality" (Rossner 2021, 342). Taking part in rituals enables participants to reaffirm their commitment to a shared normative order, anchoring morality and solidarity and thereby strengthening society. Laws function as a way of highlighting collective values which, when violated, demand punishment. A trial can therefore be understood as a justice ritual, resplendent with symbols, roles, and expectations wherein these collective values are gathered around and upheld.

Shifting a trial into the digital realm, even partially, means shifting firmly established and deeply entrenched routines, practices, and symbols into a sphere so vast and eclectic, yet possibly also mundane. This is a challenge. We use video links to regularly take part in work meetings, club meetings, board meetings, an array of meetings. We use video links for catching up with friends and relatives who are far away. We use video links for attending lessons, lectures, and workshops. It is difficult to distinguish between taking part in a trial from participating in one of these other everyday events; to recognise the gravity of participating in a trial when all we must do is turn on our computer and log in. Or, as Mulcahy (2010, 162), writes, "encounters within the courtroom are in danger of becoming sanitised as participation in the trial becomes akin to a fleeting televisual encounter."

Questions regarding virtual justice rituals have begun to be explored with some worrying findings. For instance, in Rowden's (2018) study of Australian courts, many of the respondents, including judicial officers, expert witnesses, and lawyers, described a "sense of loss" when proceedings were held via video link. Whilst difficult to pinpoint, this feeling of something missing, of something different, of a change in some way, is one that I am sure many readers will recognise. Think back to the height of the pandemic when celebrations, funerals, meetings, and teaching all took place online. It just wasn't the same, was it?

I want to focus on one aspect of justice rituals that play a key role in their construction and which is a fascinating yet relatively unexplored area when it comes to courts, namely the senses. This relative lack of research is surprising as "the political, symbolic, and ideological are not only inherent to places and processes of punishment and social control but are encoded in the sensorial outputs and transmissions occurring within those places and processes" (Herrity, Schmidt, and Warr 2021, xxiii). Sensorial experiences conjure up previous encounters and interactions which may be associated with official and formal settings (see Pink 2015, 107–110). The senses thus play an integral role in recognising, interpreting, and communicating justice. By analysing the senses we can assuage, account for, and manage any transitional issues and future problems of virtual participation. Thus, to fully understand and theorise about such institutions, and to prevent injustice being enabled by technological developments in trials, we must also pay attention to the senses experiences and how they shape experiences.

Part of the problem in both studying and also designing courtrooms is the tendency to emphasise certain senses when considering the ritual of a trial, within which certain sensorial aspects are focused on over others. For instance, we tend to focus on the oculocentric, that is, we focus on the visual. We see the blindfolded lady justice, we see the judges sitting in a row at the front of the courtroom, lawyers sitting with their clients, perhaps we see legal actors bowing to the judge upon entering the court. We see nervous witnesses, upset victims, and concerned family members. We see evidence presented on screens, perhaps we even see a murder weapon held up in the courtroom. Many of these visuals have symbolic meaning, denoting the values being conveyed, the roles being performed, and the purpose of the interactions within. And, as many of these things may also be possible to see in an online setting, there is a risk that the transition to the online is assumed to be friction-free, that nothing is lost, and that the ritual of a trial remains unchanged.

Perhaps even more prominently, we tend to think of courtrooms as places where the spoken word is supreme, not least in jurisdictions grounded in the principle of orality – which means all evidence to be considered in the judgement should be presented orally to the court as in common law jurisdictions (in contrast to continental processes in which proceedings are more or less based on the investigative file) (Roberts and Zuckerman 2022; for research on orality in court, see for example, Conley and O'Barr 1990; Atkinson and Drew 1979). This means that when we think about courts and the ritual of a trial, we often think about the rhetoric and argumentation of lawyers; we think about gripping accounts of events told by victims. We focus on what we hear, and as we can still hear things online, there is once again, a risk that the move online is not considered to be problematic.

Moreover, within each of these senses – intrasensorially – we tend to privilege certain aspects over others. For instance, when we think about the "acoustic landscape" (Young 2023) of a trial we think of the aforementioned argumentation and accounts given, rather than the background murmur of the waiting room or the legal clerk's tapping on a keyboard. Likewise, other senses tend to be neglected more completely. We do not think about how the taste of bureaucracy in bad coffee, the feel of boredom in hard waiting room chairs, or the smell of nervous sweat in the corridors all shape the experience of a trial (Flower 2021).

In short, we tend to notice, reflect, and thus place a sensorial premium on certain aspects, perhaps we assume they seamlessly transition to online rituals, or that they are unimportant, rather than engaging with the full sensorium of a trial (see also Hastrup and Hervik 1994). This is problematic as all these sensorial aspects play a vital role in constructing the ritual of a trial and play a key role in how a trial is experienced: all these factors lead to the social construction of a certain something going on which changes when it takes place online. Together they help to position us as taking part in a certain kind of interaction and help us to make sense of it. It is therefore unavoidable that the absence of these factors will change how we interpret and experience the situation we are interacting within.

The soundscape of a trial

I will exemplify this by focusing on the soundscape of the trial. In my extensive ethnographic fieldwork in courts in Sweden, as well as England and France, I have observed that the soundscape of a trial includes the background murmur of small talk in the waiting room, the slightly louder chatting next to the coffee machine, the pling of the loudspeaker system as a case is called into court, the whirr of the vending machine, the echoing of footsteps through the hallways, the laughter between friends and colleagues milling outside courtrooms, the rustling of magazines being flicked through to kill time, the subdued soothing whispers given to a nervous plaintiff, and the slamming of courtroom doors (see Hendy 2014; Parker 2011). These sounds and noises construct an understanding of what is going on: these are backstage interactions happening in an "in-between" place. The theme of what is "going on" is liminality – of transitioning from the outside social world to that of the courtroom, or vice versa. It is a gathering of people and things, of preparations, debriefings, expectations, celebrations, and commiserations, and it contributes to an atmosphere of liminality.

This soundscape shifts once again upon entering the courtroom where the silence of a criminal trial can be the silence of a funeral – an inescapable, engulfing, and ceremonial silence. The hush of the courtroom as a witness talks about the gaping hole left in their lives after the murder of their child is one of completeness. The interruption of this stillness, by scraping one's chair back, by coughing, or by dropping one's keys on the floor, is jarring – a sign of disrespect even, polluting the sacredness of silence (Douglas 2002).

The sound of crying is a particularly germane example for contrasting the difference in soundscapes. Crying is a response often observed in plaintiffs, witnesses, defendants, members of the gallery, and even legal professionals at times,[14] both in and outside the courtroom. An example of this is from an assault trial I observed in a Swedish district court, where the defendant and plaintiff are women in their early twenties and who, prior to the incident, had been good friends. The plaintiff has claimed that the defendant hit her, but during the trial, the defendant claims that it was, in fact, the plaintiff who attacked first. As the trial continues, it becomes apparent that many of the circle of friends that the defendant and plaintiff once belonged to are in the courtroom or are going to be called as witnesses. We join proceedings as a witnesses enters the courtroom.

> One of the witnesses enters the courtroom and the defendant starts to cry upon seeing her. At first tears fall silently but then the crying becomes more and more intense so that her whole body is shaking, yet she is still soundless. Her chin is wobbling, and it seems as though she

14 For more on crying judges, see for instance Delgado and Stefancic (2019).

> is struggling to stay quiet, taking in air through her mouth, chest heaving upwards. She wipes her eyes and nose with her hand. Her crying intensifies. After about three minutes she reaches over and takes a tissue from the box on the table in front of her. This gets the attention of her defence lawyer sitting next to her, who looks at her with slightly raised eyebrows, as though in surprise or in annoyance as the noise of her taking a tissue is quite loud. The defendant wipes her nose (she does not blow it) and wipes her face. She takes one more tissue after another minute or so. She continues to cry until the end of proceedings which continue for another 12 minutes, after which all those in the courtroom are asked to leave for the judges to deliberate. In the waiting room, her crying becomes full-blown, the sobs are now heard, the sniffing is very audible. Her parents and sister comfort her, their arms wrapped around her, calming words spoken.
>
> (Fieldnote)

The defendant begins to shed tears upon seeing the witness – one of her former friends – enter the courtroom, tears which rapidly escalate into a crying that consumes her whole body, yet which nevertheless remains unobtrusive, almost silent, so inconspicuous that her defence lawyer seated next to her does not notice. It is not until the hush is broken – by the noise of a tissue being pulled from a box – that its presence and importance makes itself known. It is a noise that disrupts the social norm of hush. It is not until the end of proceedings, when we exit the courtroom and enter the waiting room, that the defendant's inconspicuous crying becomes conspicuous, audible crying. A different soundscape is permitted in the waiting room, one which allows a different gamut of sounds and noises.

Mapping the acoustemology of the courthouse in this way is helpful as all of these noises and sounds contribute to the construction of the "soundscape of justice" (Parker 2011) and to the generation of "knowledge, meaning, affect, and experience" (Young 2023, 147; see also Russell and Carlton 2018). Mapping the acoustemology of the courthouse brings sounds out of the shadows and gives a voice to the hush. It raises the importance of these subtle sensorial aspects that unreflectingly yet unavoidably contribute to the construction of a justice ritual. When this switches to online, many of these nuances are lost, the implications of which are currently unclear.

The emotional landscape of a trial

Inextricably linked with the sensorial landscape of the trial is the emotional landscape of the trial (see Flower 2021; also Walenta 2020; Anderson and Smith 2001). The emotional landscape maps which emotions are appropriate to be felt and displayed in different areas of the courthouse and in relation to the different actors involved and the interaction at hand. A courthouse can thus be broken down into emotional places, each of which has a set of implicit emotion rules consisting of "feeling rules" and "display rules" (Hochschild 1983). For instance, in the Swedish courtroom, anger should be displayed in subtle ways such as a lawyer furrowing his/her eyebrows, a judge placing a pen on the table in front of them, or a prosecutor noticeably shaking his/her head (Flower 2016b, 2019b; Bergman Blix and Wettergren 2018). In the Swedish waiting room, other rules apply, and anger can be more explicitly conveyed by these legal actors, yet still in line with wider societal norms. Similarly, in the assault trial between two young women already described, the defendant's display of sadness with crying follows the implicit rules of the Swedish criminal courtroom which require that emotional displays are toned down, in contrast to her more audible emotional expression after exiting the courtroom (Flower 2019b). The rules are well established and clear to follow for legal professionals, and easy for them to help those uninitiated into the landscape with the help of cues and reminders (Flower 2019b).

The concept of emotional places can be used to identify and analyse the distinction between the appropriateness of emotions in different settings and shows us there are rules implicit to the emotional places in the courthouse. The waiting room plays a particularly significant role as it functions as a transitional or liminal space between one event and another and therefore between one set of emotion rules and another. The waiting room thus serves not only as a place to wait, but as a place to prepare and to transition. It is a liminal space, enabling participants, both legal actors and lay participations, to prepare and shift to a front stage performance, one which requires a different range of emotional displays, experiences, and expectations (Goffman 1959).

When participation switches to online, enabling one to participate from a mundane space such as one's living room or kitchen, there is no clear transition – no liminal space for moving from one context into the next, beyond the click on a link which risks blurring emotional spaces, no clear switch of one set of rules and expectations to another. Instead, an extraordinary event may take place in an ordinary setting. This may shape experiences in ways that threaten the perceived legitimacy of the trial and one's participation within as it may be unclear to participants which emotional space they find themselves in and hence which emotion rules should be followed. Indeed, scholars have previously suggested that removing participants from courthouses leads to inappropriate behaviour – as argued by Rowden and colleagues (2010), however other scholars suggest that "reimagining symbols that evoke formality and authority" (Rossner 2021) will safeguard such concerns. Still others suggest that the ritual of a trial is only successful if participants are removed form daily life and take part in a special or sacred place (Leader 2018; see also McKay 2021 for an excellent overview). Conflicting findings pervade yet video links are used nonetheless, and moving forwards I suggest that the concept of emotional places can be used to identify and analyse the distinction between the appropriateness of emotions in different settings to understand and solve issues arising from the lack of liminality.

Integral to emotional places are "affective arrangements" (Slaby, Mühlhoff, and Wüschner 2017; Bens 2018) wherein the sociomaterial setting, including the architecture, layout, positioning, furniture, technological equipment, and décor, interplays with the actors within to construct certain ways of feeling (Slaby, Mühlhoff, and Wüschner 2017, 5). For instance, in the Swedish courtroom the prosecution and defence typically sit behind desks on opposing sides of the courtroom, facing each other. The judicial bench is positioned at the front of the courtroom and witnesses sit behind a desk at the centre and back of the courtroom (see Figure 2.1). The layout of the courtroom thus communicates the adversarial nature of the Swedish trial wherein the prosecution presents evidence, the defence attempts to identify weaknesses or flaws in said evidence, and the judge neutrally presides over proceedings, only interrupting to ask for clarifications (the neutrality reflecting the adversarial nature of Swedish proceedings, the judge asking questions reflecting the inquisitorial nature of the Nordic model trial). It also contributes to producing feelings of antagonism as are inherent to such adversarial processes: prosecution versus defence. The décor is muted with beiges, greys, and purples used, and desks are made in beech, a typical wood for Sweden and, indeed, many other modern courtrooms such as the courtroom in the Palace of Justice in Paris, which was designed and built to hold the trial for the terror attack in 2015 (see Figure 2.2).

Figure 2.1 A courtroom in Norrtälje District Court.

Source: Photograph by Tim Meier.

Figure 2.2 The courtroom designed and built to hold the 2015 terror trials in the Palace of Justice, Paris.

Source: Photograph by Lisa Flower.

We see that the seating for the prosecution and defence is the same: black office chairs. In contrast, the seating furniture of the judges are a different colour (grey), with higher backs. Indeed, the judge, who is seated in the middle, appears to have the highest back of all. This conveys the status of each person in the courtroom and, in particular, the elevated power of the judicial bench.[15]

When this layout is instead mediated via screens, it can change perceptions and experiences in important ways. For instance, contrast the following two photos of a physical trial and an online trial from American courts (see Figures 2.3 and 2.4).

In the physical trial (Figure 2.3) it is clear who the judge is based on where he or she is seated: in a separate booth, slightly elevated from the others at the focal point of all in the courtroom. The prosecutor and defence lawyer are also easy to identify due to their positioning behind separate tables, each with space for either plaintiff or defendant seated next to them. The chair for the

15 In other courts, however, the judge's chair is the same as the lay judges'; however, the seating for the judges and lay judges does tend to be different to the prosecution and defence.

Figure 2.3 United States District Court for the Eastern District of Missouri.

Source: Public domain, via Wikimedia Commons.

Figure 2.4 Jurors are sworn in Tuesday 11 August 2020 in the United States' first virtual criminal jury trial in Travis County, Texas.

Source: Screen-grab taken from Courthouse News (www.courthousenews.com/texas-judge-holds-first-virtual-jury-trial-in-criminal-case/).

witness to sit in, next to the judge, is also obvious, and we can clearly discern who belongs to the jury.

In contrast, in the photo from a virtual trial (Figure 2.4), it is not immediately clear who is who. Each box is equally sized, and randomly positioned with jury members (who are blurred) interspersed by legal professionals. The judge is easier to distinguish due to his robes and perhaps even the US flag in the background and the title at the bottom of his box showing "Judge Nicholas. . . ." Although the defendant and prosecutor are also clearly labelled, their names aren't visible. Jurors are also clearly denoted as "Juror #26, Juror #27," and so on.

Now imagine that there are no labels for the participants and no distinct positioning of the boxes. This would make it far harder to interpret the different roles of each participant. Even though trials tend to begin with a presentation of all the parties, so the *who's who* aspect of a trial is perhaps not the most worrisome, it can still lead to confusion for those joining proceedings later on, or those with attention issues, or indeed, anyone feeling overwhelmed with the trial as can be the case for what may be a life-changing event.

Another troublesome aspect is the lack of tie-signs indicating team membership in the virtual courtroom. Tie-signs help participants to interpret and understand the interaction order: what is going on in any social setting, including a trial (Goffman 1959, 1963). The interaction order gives us important social information as to which roles and rules there are within and how these roles should be performed and rules negotiated. The tie-sign of sitting next to each other can also signal team membership, also helping us to navigate what we can expect of each team member. For instance, in physical trials in the US, the defence team – which may consist of the defence lawyer and defendant – are clearly signified by their positioning in the courtroom, seated next to each other behind a desk. This positioning thus symbolises that the defendant and defence lawyer are together, a team, and that the defence lawyer is there to represent the defendant, that they stand united (Flower 2019b).

When this physical positioning is lost, not only are the fine strategies of impression management using touch, such as a defence lawyer placing a calming hand on the shoulder of his or her client to placate them, in line with the impression the defence team may be attempting to convey to the court, but it can also become difficult for the defendant, and indeed others in the courtroom, to recognise the constellation of the different teams. For instance, a defendant may only meet his or her defence lawyer immediately before the trial starts and may become confused as to which "box" is his or her teammate. This can lead to feelings of uncertainty and powerlessness. Also, the positioning of the prosecutor's box next to the judge's box on a screen may communicate that these two together represent the state, with the judge perceived as a member of the prosecution team, rather than an impartial adjudicator, again leading to similar feelings. We see that the courtroom layout online is also affectively arranged, shaping the emotions emerging within.

McKay (2018) also focuses on the role of screens and emphasizes the importance of screen size by focusing on prisoners in Australia who participate in trials via video link from prison. She finds that screens used in courtrooms to show the defendant may be very large, something I have also observed in Swedish trials, with remote participants being displayed on screens covering entire walls. This can lead to the prisoner being perceived in a particular way (McKay 2018). For instance, a slightly built defendant accused of a violent crime may come across as burlier on a large screen which, in turn, may impact how evidence is interpreted with assumptions drawn regarding his or her strength. Likewise, screens with very high resolution can reveal every small facial expression and movement, and in other cases, poor picture quality thus hides any such subtleties. Again, this can lead to differences in how a participant is perceived, pertaining to the quality of the cameras and screens used.

For the prisoner, each person appears far smaller – one little box on a screen or, in some cases, two screens (McKay 2018). It is therefore harder for them to discern facial expressions, to understand who is addressing whom, and to gain a sense of the atmosphere in the room. This is important for defendants, but perhaps more strikingly for the legal professionals working in the courtroom. My research shows that reading the emotional room is an essential way to ensure that the rules of interaction are followed, a skill that becomes, in many ways, redundant in a virtual setting when the judge is no longer able to assess the mood, the prosecutor cannot get a clear understanding of how uncomfortable a defendant is in a certain line of questioning, or a defence lawyer cannot gauge a witnesses' uncertainty. It can thus change how legal professionals are able to perform their roles appropriately. Indeed, many of the respondents in my studies on technology in courts talk about such problems, for instance, the judges I have interviewed talked about difficulty in upholding their authority in courtrooms where video links are used (see also Rowden 2018).

For some of these prisoner defendants in McKay's (2018) study, participating via video links was akin to being physically present in the courtroom during the trial; however, others complained about the restricted view of the courtroom they had. For these prisoners, not being able to see who was sitting there could be experienced as upsetting, for instance missing the opportunity to view one's loved ones, or disconcerting when it was unclear who was sitting in the public gallery, such as strangers, journalists, and enemies. McKay (2018) concludes that the "see/being seen dyad" (Foucault 1975/1991) for prisoner defendants not physically present in the courtroom during their trial is disrupted and that video link can therefore be understood as a "disciplinary technique that generates a new hierarchical observatory of criminality" (McKay 2018, 142–143). By stripping defendants of their sensuality and presenting them instead as abstract images on a screen, video links serve to frame, repress, and objectify defendants, challenging the equality of arms and the presumption of innocence (McKay 2018, 151).

The arrangement of the courtroom is thus designed for actors to become "affectively involved or immersed in specific ways" (Slaby, Mühlhoff, and Wüschner 2017, 5). This is not to say that the actors within lack agency, interacting in an unreflecting manner, rather that there is an entanglement of roles (judge, lawyer, prosecutor, defendant, plaintiff, witness), emotions, and arrangements which mutually shape each other. As McKay (2018, 2021) has insightfully shown, the removal of actors – for instance, prisoners – from this physical setting leads to feelings of disempowerment and segregation. Hence whilst video links enable judicial institutions, prison services, and prisons to be interconnected in the "justice matrix" (McKay 2018), there are concerning disadvantages to the "de-spatialised simultaneity" (McKay 2021, 199) they afford.

The atmosphere of a trial

The sensorium, emotional spaces, and affective arrangement described earlier all contribute to the construction of a certain *tone* or *air* – an intangible sense emerging from interactions between people, things, and the constellations within (Wästerfors 2018; Böhme 1993; Pink and Leder Mackley 2016). Together they create an atmosphere. An atmosphere is not something that is objectively palpable, rather it is a reflexive sensing of *what is going on*, often produced and reproduced collectively, and difficult to reduce to individuals and their bodies (see Anderson 2009). It emerges from a blend of senses, emotions, and arrangements between human and non-human materialities (Anderson 2009). For Brennan (2004, 1) an atmosphere is "how one feels the others' affects" and emerges from the transmission of emotions whereby "the emotions or affects of one person, and the enhancing or depressing energies these affects entail, can enter into another" (Brennan 2004, 3). This is a social process with emotion not only arising in individuals but also between individuals and between individuals and things.

Atmospheres can thus be constructed, and a key aspect of this is the materiality of the setting within which the atmosphere should emerge. For instance, entering a café filled with plush cushions, velvet sofas, and muted lighting emerges you into an atmosphere of cosiness, comfort, and relaxedness. This is a place to hang out and unwind. In contrast, another café may be filled with plastic stools and tables and bright neon lighting. The atmosphere upon entering this café is one of sterility, speed, and urgency. This is not a place to dwell and enjoy, rather it is a place to consume and go. A particular something emerges, in part radiating from the meaning conveyed by the particular materials, for instance cosy, sterile, or comfort. The physical arrangement and choice of material objects can therefore be used to construct very specific atmospheres (Böhme 2017, 147). Another example of this is in pedagogical settings where all chairs are facing the front of the classroom in rows, thereby creating an "institutional-authoritative" (Griffero 2014, 72), much akin to the courtroom. This means that an atmosphere can also shape social interactions by the materials and objects within conveying socially ingrained habits, styles, and skills (Griffero 2014). As already noted, the atmosphere of the waiting area can be one of liminality – one of in-betweens and transitions. In the courtroom itself, the atmosphere can shift from the charged atmosphere of cross-examinations to the evocative atmosphere of plaintiff testimony, to more light-hearted atmospheres at times of minor mishaps.

So, if the emotional landscape should be understood as a map interlinking specific places with what is permitted to be felt and shown and by whom, along with how it may be displayed, within these emotional landscapes, different atmospheres can emerge from the interplay and interaction of actors, affective arrangements, sensorial experiences, and material objects. Just as the atmosphere in a nightclub or bar is partially produced by actors actively using their bodies by dancing and drinking (Tutenges and Bøhling 2019), the construction of courtroom atmospheres is an interactional process which produces a subjective experience in the individuals within (cf. Böhme 2017, 1). This means that the perception of an atmosphere requires reflection on behalf of the individual to get a sense of what is going on, but the individual also brings with them their own expectations of the situation and setting which can shape how they perceive the atmosphere, and hence that an atmosphere may be sensed differently by different individuals. An atmosphere is therefore never concrete or singular, rather it is an individual's "atmospheric-personal reaction" (Griffero 2014, 135) but which may nevertheless be shared by others. This further complicates our understanding of the role of atmospheres to some extent, due to their individuality. Different atmospheres can emerge from within the same sensing, depending on the specific context and previous experiences, all of which shape each person's specific definition of the situation as to what is going on. What is important here is the idea that an atmosphere can, at least in part, be actively constructed through specific choices made in courtroom design which shape how we interact and feel in them.

If we then consider that atmospheres are traditionally understood as "spatial bearers of moods" (Böhme 1993, 119; Griffero 2014), bounded to a certain space, we add another layer to the description of the emergence of atmospheres online. However, what remains unclear in these earlier writings is whether physical presence is necessary for the construction of atmospheres within this spatiality. Although two of the key scholars on atmospheres – Böhme (1993, 2017) and Griffero (2014) – appear to focus on the construction and emergence of boundaries in physical spaces, Griffero (2014, 126) suggests that these boundaries can be understood as continuities that are not immediately perceptible. This, combined with his standpoint that atmospheres are " 'in-between', made possible by the (corporeal but also social and symbolic) co-presence of subject and object" (Griffero 2014, 121), indicate that an atmosphere could still be constructed in an online setting such as in a virtual justice ritual.

To explore the construction of an atmosphere more fully, I am also going to use the following fieldnote excerpt from a murder trial at a district court in Sweden. We join proceedings as the victim's sister is talking about the impact the murder has had on the family. She has asked for the defendant to not be present in the courtroom, so the defendant is sitting in an adjoining courtroom, listening and watching via video link.

> The sister is holding a glass of water and is having difficulty swallowing, as though she might vomit. When she starts to speak, she is so quiet to begin with that the judge must ask her to talk a little louder. She begins to describe how the victim was her very best friend and says that her daughter has "lost her aunt, her role model" and that "it feels so empty, it's indescribable." The defence lawyer looks over at her. He looks like he might be chewing or moving something from his back teeth and gums. The sister says that she is currently on sick leave from her job because of this and that this leave will probably be extended as she still feels so awful. She says that the same is true of her mother who is also deteriorating, feeling worse and worse as the days go by. When the counsel for the plaintiff asks why this is, she replies "it's because of the knowledge that we have to live a whole life without [her]," referring to her murdered sister. There is no reaction from the defence lawyer, but tears begin to fall from the sister's eyes again. Many of those sitting in the public gallery also become upset and wipe their eyes and noses discretely.
>
> (Fieldnote)

From reading this excerpt from my fieldnotes, it is possible to get a sense of the atmosphere in the courtroom. For me, it was difficult to not be moved by the stirring story told by the sister, with many others in the public gallery visibly upset. It is an evocative atmosphere, filled with sadness and loss. It is a gathering and a focusing on absence. While the crime itself takes centre stage during a trial, it is the intertwining stories of individuals affected by the event that possess the ability to construct a certain air. It is the reactions of family members in the courtroom, sobbing, sitting close to one another and holding each other. It is the absence of the defendant in the courtroom. It is the defence lawyer's stone face performance of showing no emotion. It is the lay judges' tilted heads and soft facial features conveying sympathy. It is the judge's neutral facial expression with a hint of empathy. It is the witness sitting alone. It is the slightly bureaucratic décor but with a touch of pondus. It is the sound of sobbing. It is legal clerk tap, tap, tapping on the computer keyboard. It is the slight buzzing from the overhead lights. It is all these things. And it is all these things that become harder to see, sense, and read, to be a part of the emotional room, in the shift to digital participation.

Digital participation thus endangers the opportunity to construct a sense of being part of something, the sense of belonging and a clear understanding of what is going on. Another vital aspect to be considered within this is that how people interact with each other in an online in contrast to a physical setting is different. However, whilst we know a great deal about physical courtroom interactions, we currently know very little as to how they translate into a digital setting. In the next section I explore what we currently know about courtroom interactions and flag the dangers of shifting online.

Courtroom interactions

Sociological research has shown nonverbal cues and gestures to be an important part of everyday interactions, including in legal work, whereby legal professionals and lay participants observe, interpret, and negotiate each other's gestures in the courtroom. This, in turn, shapes understandings and experiences, as well as perceptions of justice. Legal roles are therefore performed by following implicit rules which outline role performances and which include the feeling and display of emotion. Whilst the rules of interaction in face-to-face courts is well established, how roles are accomplished in online settings is less known. So, what do we know so far?

In my research on defence lawyers in the Swedish context over the past decade, I have identified the implicit and invisible game rules of the courtroom and the subtle ways in which these rules are negotiated, interpreted, and followed (Flower 2023, 2020, 2019b, 2019a, 2018, 2016a, 2014a). These rules stem from an overarching regime, the "emotional regime of the courtroom" (Reddy 2001; Flower 2019b), the purpose of which is to maintain an illusion of the courts as a sphere of rationality that is free from the pesky and perilous influence of emotions in order for us to believe that the law is exercised *sine ire et studio* (without anger and passion) (Bandes 1999; Maroney 2016, 2011, 2006; Bergman Blix and Wettergren 2018; Bandes 2009; Bandes and Blumenthal 2012). This means that the display and/or experience of certain emotions are inappropriate, and emotions should be performed by legal professionals in toned down and subtle ways. This emotion work is a vital part of legal work and is nothing that is taught on law programs, rather the rules and strategies for negotiating these rules are acquired via professional socialisation – on the job, in the courtroom (Flower 2014b, 2019b). We therefore know that the ability to perform one's role and associated emotions appropriately in court is paramount. And we know that appropriate performances constitute a key component of legal work as not only to do they ensure that a trial runs smoothly, but they also entail professional pride. So how are these roles accomplished and what problems does this pose for the digitalisation of participation?[16]

As already noted in this chapter, the display rule for anger in the courtroom differs to how anger may be displayed in other settings. The following excerpt is an illustrative example of how anger should be suitably displayed by a defence lawyer in the Swedish courtroom. We join proceedings as an expert

16 Perceptions of legal professionals may also be altered: prosecutors in one study were found to be less aggressive, less believable, less credible, less convincing, and weaker when appearing via video link (Tait et al. 2017).

witness is telling the court how high the temperature inside a vehicle can reach when left in the sun and the danger this presents to any living thing sitting in the vehicle. The testimony of the expert witness is damaging for the defence, who claim that the car was not left in the sun and therefore posed no threat to the creature in the car:

> The defence lawyer looks up sharply and says, very quietly but also very forcibly "what?!?" (*nämen*). The defence lawyer looks at the prosecutor, then the judge and then his client and shakes his head. Later on, when it is the defence lawyer's turn to talk, he sits up straighter in his chair, speaking rapidly and in a loud tone of voice states that he became "quite annoyed" when hearing the report which he claims includes incorrect details.
>
> (Flower 2019b, 100)

We see the defence lawyer displays anger by using posture, eye contact, and voice intonation, however in relatively unobtrusive and muted ways. There is no jumping up from the chair and roar of objection and outrage to denounce the testimony of the expert and to expound the innocence of his client. Instead, there is a low-key performance of emotion aimed at conveying to the client that he – the defence lawyer – is loyally representing him, as the lawyer's performance of outrage is based on the account of events his client has provided – that the car was not left in the sun. It is also aimed at conveying to the judge that he is critical to the testimony of the expert witness. It is a performance in line with the rules of the courtroom. However, it is a subtle performance that risks going unseen in a digital setting. This is problematic for several reasons. It risks leading to uncertainty or confusion as to how roles should be performed appropriately and hence may lead to defence lawyers feeling they have not fulfilled their legal obligations properly. It also leads to a risk that defendants feel they have not been suitably defended if the subtle protestations of their defence lawyer go unseen by both the judge and the defendants themselves.

Eyework

Of particular note in the excerpt is the use of directed "eyework" (Flower 2019b) – making and avoiding eye contact to achieve a specific purpose, which is impossible in a digital setting due to the misalignment of sightlines (Flower, Klosterkamp, and Rowden 2023; Rowden 2018). Interactants are unable to engage in direct eye-to-eye contact when communicating via a screen which may be further impeded by low bandwidth, lagging, and poor audio-video quality (Wegge 2006; Bruce 1996; Mierke et al. 2011; Legg and Song 2021; Bohannon et al. 2013). Indeed, an early ethnographic study focusing on interactions via video link in France explored the impact of camera placement on on-screen impressions. The study found, for instance, that a lawyer's greeting may not be visible on screen due to the camera positioning (Licoppe, Verdier, and Dumoulin 2013; see also Mulcahy, Rowden, and Teeder 2021). This, in turn, can shape how participants perceive the trial and how they have been treated.

We can see the importance of eyework in the following excerpt taken from my fieldnotes of a trial for assault. Although the defendant and defence lawyer have spoken in whispers to each other when the defendant has leaned over towards the defence lawyer, I have not observed eye contact being made. At the end of the trial, when the defence lawyer is summing up the case, I note the following:

> The defence lawyer states that it is a modified truth that his client had a relapse into using drugs again as he has been clean for several years. He then asks his client to clarify this. He turns his head to face his client whilst keeping is body nearly completely turned towards the desk and says "you consider yourself to have an addiction and you want to be drug-free." When he says this there is direct eye contact. The defendant nods. The remaining questions he asks the defendant are done with his eyes facing down at the papers in front of him.
>
> (Fieldnote)

In another trial where the defendant is accused of breaking into and stealing some cans of drink and snacks from a shop, we join proceedings where the defence lawyer is questioning his client. Again, eye contact has been largely absent between defendant and defence lawyer prior to the following interaction:

> The defence lawyer asks his client if it could be the case that he did not steal the items. The defence lawyer looks directly at his client when he says this, and their eyes meet. The defendant replies, "yes." The defence lawyer then asks, "you were not there, is that correct?" Again, direct eye contact is made, and the question is delivered in a slightly sterner voice. The defendant replies, that this is indeed correct.
>
> (Fieldnote)

And in a drug smuggling trial:

> There is direct eye contact between the defence lawyer and his client when the defence lawyer asks, "if you had known that the drugs were illegal would you have done this?" He continues looking at him for the answer. The defendant replies "no, absolutely not." The defence lawyer is silent for a few moments after this.
>
> (Fieldnote)

In all three of these excerpts, taken from different trials and with different defence lawyers, the defence lawyer makes eye contact with the client in order to produce a particular impression to the courtroom: in the first, sympathy for the defendant is produced, in the second, an impression of innocence is constructed, and in the final excerpt, the defence lawyer is attempting to show the moral values of the defendant. The absence of previous eye contact between defence lawyer and defendant in all these trials makes the use of eye contact stand out, indicating its strategicness. Eyework is also used here as a form of moral work, constructing the defendant as someone of moral integrity: as someone who knows they have done wrong but that it is beyond their control, or as someone who has not committed an illegal act, or as someone who would not have committed an act if he had known it was illegal. All of these strategies become problematic when the possibility of eye contact is disrupted, such as when defence lawyer and defendant are not sitting next to each other as may be the case if one or both are present via video link.

Eyework is also used by prosecutors and defence lawyers to ensure they have not broken an emotion rule. This can be in the form of quick glances towards the judge who will indicate if a rule has been transgressed or is close to transgression by, for instance, slightly frowning or placing a pencil on the desk in front of them (Flower 2019b; Bergman Blix and Wettergren 2018; see also Johansen 2019) – small strategies that can easily be missed if they are viewed on a screen rather than face-to-face, or if they occur outside the camera shot.

Eyework is thus used for several purposes: a defence lawyer uses it to convey social information to their client, the judge uses it to indicate when the rules of interaction have been broken, and all parties use it to produce emotional displays such as sympathy and productions of remorse (Flower 2019b). The absence of this currently vital tool in courtroom interactions and how it relates to online settings is, as yet, unknown and the focus of my forthcoming research project "VIRTUTRIALS – The elusive role of physicality in virtual trials: Towards a new understanding of legal participation" funded by the European Research Council and running between 2025 and 2029.

Digital impression management

The sociological findings outlined thus far are backed by research in other disciplines, which show the importance of nonverbal cues, for instance, in ensuring understanding, comprehension, appropriate turn-taking, and intimacy (Driskell and Radtke 2003; Derks, Bos, and Von Grumbkow 2007; see Haas 2006 for an excellent overview) with eye contact of particular weight in face-to-face interactions (Kendon 1967; Yokoyama and Daibo 2012) as already noted.

Beyond eyework, the close physical proximity between defence lawyer and defendant is also key for being able to direct clients into appropriate performances. The use of gestures which I call "bodywork" (Flower 2019b) – a particular form of facework that focuses on the use of the body to convey social information in various ways – is particularly important when the scope for verbal interchange is limited, as is the case in large parts of many legal proceedings where turn-taking is often clearly ordered. During my fieldwork I have observed such strategies as defence lawyers placing a calming hand on the leg of a client, out of sight of the rest of the court, glasses of water poured to relax clients, notes written to each other in which – as many defence lawyers I have interviewed tell me – the lawyer writes "poker face" or "calm down." We see this also in the following excerpt from a drug smuggling trial where a translator is being used to translate for the defendant:

> The defendant suddenly begins to react to something that has been said. He lashes out with his hand and raises his voice. "It wasn't like that!" he says loudly. His lawyer immediately reacts with his whole body, turning towards his client and saying "shh, shh, shh!" The defence lawyer holds his hand in front of his client's face. The defendant quietens down and the lawyer leans in so that they can talk. The lawyer then says to the judge that he wants to point out that his client was reacting to a mistranslation saying, "it was the translation that was wrong."
>
> (Fieldnote)

Here we see that the defence lawyer can calm his client down immediately with the help of gestures that are directly visible and understandable for his client. In this manner the defence lawyer can mitigate any potential escalation of distress in his client which would risk further disrupting proceedings. Although the emotion and interaction rules for defendants are not the same as for the defence lawyer, their performance should still fall within the framework of what is permitted within the emotional regime of the court, that is, it should nevertheless remain fairly toned down in order to ensure that the flow of the trial is not interrupted which also, importantly, means that the trial can continue to run on schedule.[17] Once again, the absence of close physical presence if one or both participate virtually removes the opportunity for directing one's client, which may have vital consequences for the final outcome.

Furthermore, props can be used in order to convey a certain impression to the courtroom (Flower 2019b; Waldron 2000) – a performance which Goffman (1959) describes as taking place on the "personal front." Props are used to draw attention to certain things or, indeed, to divert attention away from unwanted focus – producing or reducing attention and focus (see Flower 2019b for a deeper discussion on "dramatic reductions"). For instance, in one criminal trial I observed, lawyers drew attention to the bountiful evidence they had collected by bringing forth piles of documents, which were colour-coded to also signal diligence and attention to detail. These documents were handed

17 This is an important factor, not only due to the cramped schedules of the courts and legal professionals but also, for instance, because witnesses are asked to give evidence during a certain timeframe, for instance, in the morning or the afternoon. A delay could therefore lead to a witness having to return the next day instead.

out in the courtroom by a smartly dressed lawyer, one of several representing the defendant.[18] All of this gave the impression of a solid case, built by a team of highly expert lawyers, all of whom oozed professionalism and all of whom sat together with the defendant in a squad. This impression management strategy is not possible when the courtroom is distributed over several spaces and when all participants are not sitting together, or, at the very least, the ways in which it can shape interactions may be altered. Here it is important to note that this does not necessarily need to be a negative development, rather such theatrical aspects may be considered by some to be outside the realms of acceptability in the drama of the courtroom. However, it remains that upholding a professional impression in the courtroom – conveying lawyer face and a united defence team is altered in digital settings. Indeed, the current ambiguity regarding how to perform one's role appropriately can lead to uncertainty and stress (Flower 2019b).

When interactions take place via video link, the absence of nonverbal indicators impacts perceptions as the spatial separation this mediation entails disrupts reciprocal communication. This means that interactants may be unable to see a clear or complete image of each other's gestures and facial expressions which, in turn, disrupts the possibility for interactants to manage the impression they are making on others, for instance, emphasising potential strengths and downplaying weaknesses using eye contact, smiling, nodding, and body posture (Bauer et al. 2011). It is thus apparent that video links risk changing how actors perceive each other and how they make impressions on others – factors which may be particularly challenging for the "digitally disadvantaged" (Mulcahy and Tsalapatanis 2022) who lack skills in digital technologies.[19]

There is also concern amongst defence lawyers and prosecutors that remote participation reduces the emotional impact of evidence on juries (see e.g. Carline, Gunby, and Murray 2021), despite experimental research drawing on mock juries indicating otherwise (Davies 1999; Ellison and Munro 2013).

18 In interviews I have conducted with defence lawyers, they say that they tell defendants to dress as they usually would (although perhaps without any provocative statements or logos on their clothing). One lawyer said that he had a client who turned up to court wearing a "typical English banker's suit that was black. Way too big of course. With a shaved head," which the lawyer thought gave a very odd impression as it was clear to the court that this was not how the defendant would typically present himself. Other clients turn up "in work clothes, straight from a paint job or some come in ripped jeans and t-shirts," but clothing is not considered to make an impact on the court according to the lawyers I interviewed.

19 The digital interaction order can be presented at the onset of a trial so that all participants are at least aware of the order of events, how proceedings will proceed, and so on. In terms of formal requirements, the digital interaction order follows that of the face-to-face interaction order with regards to turn taking, ordering, etiquette, and so on. For instance, the judge entering the virtual courtroom after the other parties have already joined, and leaving before the online link is broken, follows the same ordering of events as in the physical courtroom (see Mulcahy 2010, 170). Similarly, introducing all parties in the court is another way to align with physical courtroom orderings (see for instance Licoppe 2004).

Again, more recent studies appear to contradict previous work, indicating that we need to dig deeper.

It is therefore apparent that new strategies of digital impression management are needed, and that more knowledge regarding how digital participation shapes perceptions and interactions is also in demand. One way of understanding this new interactional sphere is by focusing on the concept of co-presence.

Co-presence

Traditional justice rituals centre on the fundamentality of physical co-presence. For instance, Collins (2004) writes that physically being together is a key component of successful interaction rituals, hence virtual rituals, or "technology-mediated interaction rituals" (Johannessen 2023), will be less successful. Likewise, successful interactions – reaching each other and acting accordingly – have traditionally been understood as demanding physical co-presence. However, some of the problems described in this chapter can be assuaged by working towards the construction of virtual co-presence in trials. For instance, studies indicate that virtual rituals are possible (Ling 2008; DiMaggio et al. 2019; Maloney 2013; Törnberg and Törnberg 2022; Nexø and Strandell 2020; Jodén and Strandell 2022) if there are "shared knowledge and conventions." This means that by enabling "culturally shared cognitive schemas" (Nexø and Strandell 2020), consisting of shared expectations, interpretive frameworks, and guidelines for appropriate behaviour guidelines, virtual participation could be successful. Mutual synchronisation, which Collins (2004) claims demands bodily presence, *can* therefore be replaced with other strategies. In Nexø and Strandell's (2020) study, they show how the use of emojis can generate attunement and, whilst the use of emojis in court is perhaps a little far-fetched, their finding nevertheless takes us one step further away from the presumption that attunement, and hence a successful interaction ritual, is impossible without bodily co-presence.

Another important step towards ensuring successful virtual justice rituals is by temporally constructing co-presence by ensuring immediate feedback or "response presence" (Cetina 2009, 74) whereby respondents should respond "without inappropriate delay to an incoming attention or interaction request." Again, this can contribute towards enabling coordinated action and mutual focus.

A key to understanding the possible frictions or problems with successfully enabling virtual justice rituals is that they are often compared to face-to-face rituals with studies indicating that when such mediated interactions replace face-to-face interactions they are less intense, as with online raves (Vandenberg, Berghman, and Schaap 2021). DiMaggio and colleagues suggest that virtual rituals are most likely to work if they entail:

> ongoing interaction, in real time; among people with a history of face-to-face interaction or, at least, biographical knowledge of one

> another; about topics in which participants are intensely interested; accompanied by visual information as well as text; supported by complementary offline communications; and bounded with a beginning and an end.
>
> (DiMaggio et al. 2019, 109)

There is therefore a risk that those working in courts, with shared cognitive schemas and expectations, may experience the interactions differently. Moving forward, we therefore need to work towards ensuring "perception of mutual entrainment" (Campos-Castillo and Hitlin 2013) online by initiating all parties into the interaction order of the courtroom. So, whilst some scholars argue that we need to understand online rituals "in their own right," rather than mere substitutes for face-to-face interactions (Osler 2024), moving forwards, we need to draw inspiration from more traditional theories but with a contemporary spin.

Final reflections

We need to start reflecting on what happens to the spectacle of justice when courthouses – previously located in prime, central positions to signify their central role in society – become redundant. How does this impact our understandings of justice not only being done, but also justice being *seen* to be done if the very courthouse vanishes or, at least, is no longer a necessary requirement (see also Mulcahy 2010, 162, 170)?

Understanding this is central for ensuring that in particular plaintiffs and defendants, but also victim's families, witnesses, and the wider public, feel they have experienced justice and *their day in court*, a key component in the continued legitimacy of the legal system (Tyler 2003). Understanding the spatiality and physicality of justice can thus help us to understand whether it is possible to successfully reconfigure court rituals into an online setting, without the loss of their essential meaning, flow, and intent.

Jones and colleagues (2023, 210) warn, with regards to expert witnesses, that more research is needed and therefore "remote testimony may not be desirable in higher-stakes legal cases (e.g. high-profile or highly publicized trials, competency for execution hearings)." I would like to perhaps draw this beyond expert witnesses to encompass all witnesses and, indeed, perhaps even all lay participants: the stakes of a trial can be extraordinarily high in low-profile, mundane trials. Losing custody of one's child, being found guilty of an offence that leads to loss of livelihood, being forced to pay legal costs after a loss – all of these, and more, can be life changing. I fear that we have swept video links into courts in our rush to digitalise and modernise, without fully reflecting on the consequences and implications for the hundreds of thousands of people who pass through the courts. A more nuanced reflection regarding when, where, how, and for whom video links are suitable is needed before we can fully embrace this form of participation.

In this way it will also be possible to ensure that procedural fairness is achieved. This refers to the safeguarding of "practical injustice" (Legg and Song 2021, 137) and ensuring that all parties in a trial are treated with respect and dignity, decisions are made in a neutral and transparent manner, and that there is opportunity to examine witnesses (i.e. the right to confrontation). All of this is essential for upholding rule of law and upholding public confidence in the legal system (Legg and Song 2021).

References

11 KHOU. 2021. "Doctor Makes Court Appearance While Performing Surgery." YouTube, Last Modified 2nd March 2021. Retrieved from https://youtu.be/Knfrv49Lmf0?si=Ye6aLxfn3iBys6Ag, accessed 23rd January 2024.

A&E. 2023. "Man Caught Red-Handed Smoking Weed in Virtual Courtroom." YouTube. Retrieved from www.youtube.com/watch?v=3J0zLmzYpyU, accessed 23rd January 2024.

A&E. 2024. "Court Cam: Top 5 Greatest Escapes." Retrieved from www.youtube.com/watch?v=pjDS578FROw, accessed 31st January.

Anderson, Ben. 2009. "Affective Atmospheres." *Emotion, Space and Society* 2 (1):77–81.

Anderson, Kay, and Susan J. Smith. 2001. "Editorial: Emotional Geographies." *Transactions of the Institute of British Geographers* 26 (1):7–10.

Ariturk, Deniz, William E. Crozier, and Brandon L. Garrett. 2020. "Virtual Criminal Courts." *University of Chicago Law Review Online* 2020:57–69.

Atkinson, J. Maxwell, and Paul Drew. 1979. *Order in Court.* Springer.

Bandes, Susan A., ed. 1999. *The Passions of Law.* New York: New York University Press.

Bandes, Susan A. 2009. "Empathetic Judging and the Rule of Law." *Cardozo Law Review De Novo* 1 (1):133–148.

Bandes, Susan A., and Jeremy Blumenthal. 2012. "Emotion and the Law." *Annual Review of Law and Social Science* 8:161–181.

Bauer, Talya, Donald Truxillo, Kyle Mack, and Ana Costa. 2011. "Applicant Reactions to Technology-Based Selection: What We Know So Far." *Technology-Enhanced Assessment of Talent*:190–223. https://doi.org/10.1002/9781118256022.ch6.

Bens, Jonas. 2018. "The Courtroom as an Affective Arrangement: Analysing Atmospheres in Courtroom Ethnography." *The Journal of Legal Pluralism and Unofficial Law* 50 (3):336–355. https://doi.org/10.1080/07329113.2018.1550313.

Bergman Blix, Stina, and Åsa Wettergren. 2018. *Professional Emotions in Court.* Abingdon: Routledge.

Bermant, Gordon, and Winton D. Woods. 1994. "Real Questions about the Virtual Courthouse Viewpoint." *Judicature* 78 (2):64–67.

Bohannon, Leanne S., Andrew M. Herbert, Jeff B. Pelz, and Esa M. Rantanen. 2013. "Eye Contact and Video-Mediated Communication: A Review." *Displays* 34 (2):177–185. https://doi.org/10.1016/j.displa.2012.10.009.

Böhme, Gernot. 1993. "Atmosphere as the Fundamental Concept of a New Aesthetics." *Thesis Eleven* 36 (1):113–126.

Böhme, Gernot. 2017. *The Aesthetics of Atmospheres.* New York: Routledge.

Brehm, Katie, Momori Hirabayashi, Clara Langevin, Bernardo Rivera Muñozcano, Katsuma Sekizawa, and Jiayi Zhu. 2020. *The Future of AI in the Brazilian Judicial System.* The National Council of Justice: Institute for Technology and Society of Rio de Janeiro.

Brennan, Teresa. 2004. *The Transmission of Affect.* Cornell University Press.

Bruce, Vicki. 1996. "The Role of the Face in Communication: Implications for Videophone Design." *Interacting with Computers* 8 (2):166–176. https://doi.org/10.1016/0953-5438(96)01026-0.

Burton, Mandy, Roger Evans, and Andrew Sanders. 2007. "Vulnerable and Intimidated Witnesses and the Adversarial Process in England and Wales." *The International Journal of Evidence & Proof* 11 (1):1–23. https://doi.org/10.1350/ijep.2006.11.1.1.
Bylander, Eric. 2006. "Muntlighetsprincipen: En rättsvetenskaplig studie av processuella handläggningsformer i svensk rätt." Doctoral thesis, monograph, Skrifter från Juridiska fakulteten i Uppsala, Iustus Förlag AB (102).
Campos-Castillo, Celeste, and Steven Hitlin. 2013. "Copresence: Revisiting a Building Block for Social Interaction Theories." *Sociological Theory* 31 (2):168–192. https://doi.org/10.1177/0735275113489811.
Carline, Anna, Clare Gunby, and Jamie Murray. 2021. "'And That's Why Street-Wise Complainants Now Always Give Evidence Behind Screens, Live': Exploring the Intensive Affects of the Courtroom." In *Courthouse Architecture, Design and Social Justice*, 169–189. London: Routledege.
Cetina, Karin Knorr. 2009. "The Synthetic Situation: Interactionism for a Global World." *Symbolic Interaction* 32 (1):61–87.
Collins, Randall. 2004. *Interaction Ritual Chains*. Princeton: Princeton University Press.
Conley, J. M., and W. M. O'Barr. 1990. *Rules Versus Relationships: The Ethnography of Legal Discourse*. Chicago: The University of Chicago Press.
Courts, National Center for State. 1995. "Briefing Papers: Videoconferencing." Retrieved from https://cdm16501.contentdm.oclc.org/digital/collection/tech/id/532: National Center for State Courts.
CourtTV. 2024. "'Free Thug Mistrial' Outburst in #YoungThug's RICO Trial as Someone on Zoom Yelled Inside the Court." YouTube. Retrieved from www.youtube.com/shorts/cIH9fM00MVw, accessed 23rd January 2024.
Daftary-Kapur, Tarika, Kelsey S. Henderson, and Tina M. Zottoli. 2021. "COVID-19 Exacerbates Existing System Factors That Disadvantage Defendants: Findings from a National Survey of Defense Attorneys." *Law and Human Behavior* 45 (2):81–96.
Dale, Milfred D., and Desiree Smith. 2021. "Making the Case for Videoconferencing and Remote Child Custody Evaluations (RCCEs): The Empirical, Ethical, and Evidentiary Arguments for Accepting New Technology." *Psychology, Public Policy, and Law* 27 (1):30.
Davies, G. 1999. "The Impact of Television on the Presentation and Reception of Children's Testimony." *International Journal of Law and Psychiatry* 22 (3–4):241–256.
Davies, G., and E. Noon. 1991. *An Evaluation of the Live Link for Child Witnesses*. London: Home Office.
Davis, Robin, Billie Jo Matelevich-Hoang, Alexandra Barton, Sara Debus-Sherrill, and Emily Niedzwiecki. 2015. *Research on Videoconferencing at Post-Arraingment Release Hearings: Phase I Final Report*. Fairfax: ICF International.
Delgado, Richard, and Jean Stefancic. 2019. "Do Judges Cry? An Essay on Empathy and Fellow-Feeling." *Case Western Reserve Law Review* 70:23.
Derks, Daantje, Arjan E. R. Bos, and Jasper Von Grumbkow. 2007. "Emoticons and Social Interaction on the Internet: The Importance of Social Context." *Computers in Human Behavior* 23 (1):842–849.
DiMaggio, Paul, Clark Bernier, Charles Heckscher, and David Mimno. 2019. "Interaction Ritual Threads: Does IRC Theory Apply Online?" In *Ritual, Emotion, Violence*, edited by Elliot B. Weininger, Annette Lareau, and Omar Lizardo, 81–124. New York: Routledge.
Douglas, Mary. 2002. *Purity and Danger: An Analysis of Concept of Pollution and Taboo*. Vol. 2. Psychology Press.
Driskell, James E., and Paul H. Radtke. 2003. "The Effect of Gesture on Speech Production and Comprehension." *Human Factors* 45 (3):445–454.

e-Justice, European. 2020. "Impact of COVID-19 on the Justice Field." *European Justice*. Retrieved from https://e-justice.europa.eu/content_impact_of_the_covid19_virus_on_the_justice_field-37147-en.do#tocHeader2, accessed 1st October 2023.
Ellison, Louise, and Vanessa E. Munro. 2013. "A 'Special' Delivery? Exploring the Impact of Screens, Live-Links and Video-Recorded Evidence on Mock Juror Deliberation in Rape Trials." *Social & Legal Studies* 23 (1):3–29. https://doi.org/10.1177/0964663913496676.
Flower, Lisa. 2014a. "Doing Objectivity: Professional Emotions." Conference paper Sociologidagarna, Gothenburg.
Flower, Lisa. 2014b. "The (Un)Emotional Law Student." *International Journal of Work Organisation and Emotion* 6 (3):295–309.
Flower, Lisa. 2016a. "Doing Loyalty: Defense Lawyers' Subtle Dramas in the Courtroom." *Journal of Contemporary Ethnography* 47 (2):226–254.
Flower, Lisa. 2016b. "Dramatic Subtlety: Exploring Anger and Strategic Niceness in the Courtroom." *Scandinavian Research Council for Criminology*, Bifröst, Iceland, 1–4 May.
Flower, Lisa. 2018. "Loyalty Work: Emotional Interactions of Defence Lawyers in Swedish Courtrooms." Doctorate, Sociology, Lund University (120).
Flower, Lisa. 2019a. "Emotional Defence Lawyers." *History, Culture, Society (Special Issue)* 3 (2):282–299.
Flower, Lisa. 2019b. *Interactional Justice: The Role of Emotions in the Performance of Loyalty*. Abingdon: Routledge.
Flower, Lisa. 2020. "Emotion Work, Cooling the Client Out and Lawyer Face: The Emotional Labour of Defence Lawyers in the Subtle Swedish Criminal Trial." In *Emotional Labour in Criminal Justice and Criminology*, edited by Jake Phillips, Jaime Waters, Chalen Westaby, and Andrew Fowler. London: Routledge.
Flower, Lisa. 2021. "Rumbling Stomachs and Silent Crying: Mapping and Reflecting Emotion in the Sensory Landscape of the Courthouse." In *Sensorial Penalities*, edited by Kate Herrity, Bethany E. Schmidt, and Jason Warr, 159–174. Bingley: Emerald Publishing.
Flower, Lisa. 2023. "Constructing Clickable Criminal Trials: Framing Trials and Legal Professionals in Digital News Reports." *Emotions and Society* 5 (1):48–66.
Flower, Lisa, Sarah Klosterkamp, and Emma Rowden. 2023. "Video Links and Eyework." In *Courtroom Ethnography*, edited by Lisa Flower and Sarah Klosterkamp, 111–128. Palgrave.
Foucault, Michel. 1975/1991. *Discipline and Punish: The Birth of the Prison*. Translated by Alan Sheridan. New York: Random House.
Frazier, Annabelle, Kaleigh Mulligan, Melissa Dipano, and Katelyn Turner. 2021. "Courts of the Future? Quantifying the Impact of Technical Problems on Virtual Court Hearings." *Psychology and Law Research Lab*. https://doi.org/10.13140/RG.2.2.35973.27361/1
Godfrey, Barry, Jane C. Richardson, and Sandra Walklate. 2022. "The Crisis in the Courts: Before and Beyond Covid." *The British Journal of Criminology* 62 (4):1036–1053. https://doi.org/10.1093/bjc/azab110.
Goffman, Erving. 1959. *The Presentation of Self in Everyday Life*. Harmondsworth: Penguin Books Ltd.
Goffman, Erving. 1963. *Behavior in Public Places: Notes on the Social Organization of Gatherings*. New York: The Free Press.
Goodman, Gail S., Ann E. Tobey, Jennifer M. Batterman-Faunce, Holly Orcutt, Sherry Thomas, Cheryl Shapiro, and Toby Sachsenmaier. 1998. "Face-to-Face Confrontation: Effects of Closed-Circuit Technology on Children's Eyewitness Testimony and Jurors' Decisions." *Law and Human Behavior* 22:165–203.

Government, Scottish. 1995. "Live Television Link: An Evaluation of Its Use by Child Witnesses in Scottish Criminal Trials." In *Crime and Criminal Justice Research Findings*. Scottish Office Central Research Unit.

Griffero, Tonino. 2014. *Atmospheres: Aesthetics of Emotional Spaces*. Dorchester: Ashgate.

Group, Pandemic Practices Working. 2023. *New York Courts' Response to the Pandemic: Observations, Perspectives, and Recommendations*. New York: State of New York.

Haas, Aaron. 2006. "Videoconferencing in Immigration Proceedings." *Pierce Law Review* 5 (1):59–90.

Hall, Matthew. 2007. "The Use and Abuse of Special Measures: Giving Victims the Choice?" *Journal of Scandinavian Studies in Criminology and Crime Prevention* 8 (S1):33–53.

Hamlyn, Becky, Andrew Phelps, and Ghazala Sattar. 2004. *Key Findings from the Survey of Vulnerable and Intimadated Witnesses*. UK Home Office: Research Development and Statistics Directorate.

Hastrup, Kirsten, and Peter Hervik. 1994. "Introduction." In *Social Experience and Anthropological Knowledge*, edited by Kirsten Hastrup and Peter Hervik, 1–12. London: Routledge.

Helsper, Ellen J., and Bianca C. Reisdorf. 2016. "The Emergence of a 'Digital Underclass' in Great Britain and Sweden: Changing Reasons for Digital Exclusion." *New Media & Society* 19 (8):1253–1270. https://doi.org/10.1177/1461444816634676.

Hendy, David. 2014. *Noise: A Human History of Sound and Listening*. 1. Ecco paperback ed. New York: Ecco. Book.

Herrity, Kate, Bethany E. Schmidt, and Jason Warr, eds. 2021. *Sensory Penalities: Exploring the Senses in Spaces of Punishment and Social Control*. Bingley: Emerald Publishing.

Hochschild, Arlie Russel. 1983. *The Managed Heart: The Commercialization of Human Feeling*. 2nd ed. Berkeley: University of California Press.

Hyde, John. 2020. "Nightingale Courts Are Like Taking a Bucket to a House Fire." Last Modified 20 July 2020. Retrieved from www.lawgazette.co.uk/commentary-and-opinion/nightingale-courts-are-like-taking-a-bucket-to-a-house-fire/5105073.article#commentsJump, accessed 1st February.

Jodén, Henrik, and Jacob Strandell. 2022. "Building Viewer Engagement Through Interaction Rituals on Twitch.tv." *Information, Communication & Society* 25 (13):1969–1986. https://doi.org/10.1080/1369118X.2021.1913211.

Johannessen, Lars E. F. 2023. "Interaction Rituals and Technology: A Review Essay." *Poetics* 98:101765.

Johansen, Louise Victoria. 2019. "Lay Participation in Danish Crime Trials: On the Interaction between Lay and Professional Judges during Deliberation." *Journal of Law and Society* 46 (4):586–611. https://doi.org/10.1111/jols.12189.

Johnson, Molly Treadway, and Elizabeth C. Wiggins. 2006. "Videoconferencing in Criminal Proceedings: Legal and Empirical Issues and Directions for Research." *Law & Policy* 28 (2):211–227.

Jones, Ashley C. T., Ashley B. Batastini, Meera B. Patel, Donald F. Sacco, and Craig A. Warlick. 2023. "Does Convenience Come with a Price? The Impact of Remote Testimony on Perceptions of Expert Credibility." *Criminal Justice and Behavior* 50 (2):197–215.

Judiciary, Courts and Tribunals. 2022. "Live Links in Criminal Courts Guidance." *Courts and Tribunals Judiciary*. Retrieved from www.judiciary.uk/wp-content/uploads/2022/07/Live-links-Guidance-for-criminal-courts-July-2022.pdf, accessed 13th February 2023.

Jurva, Gina. 2021. *The Impacts of the COVID-19 Pandemi on State & Local Courts Study 2021: A Look at Remote Hearings, Legal Technology, Case Backlogs, and Access to Justie*. Thomson Reuters.

Justice, Ministry of. 2016. "Transforming Our Justice System." In *Ministry of Justice*. London: Ministry of Justice.
Kendon, A. 1967. "Some Functions of Gaze-Direction in Social Interation." *Acta Psychologica* 26 (1):22–63.
Landström, Sara, Karl Ask, and Charlotte Sommar. 2015. "The Emotional Male Victim: Effects of Presentation Mode on Judged Credibility." *Scandinavian Journal of Psychology* 56 (1):99–104.
Landström, Sara, Karl Ask, and Charlotte Sommar. 2019. "Credibility Judgments in Context: Effects of Emotional Expression, Presentation Mode, and Statement Consistency." *Psychology, Crime & Law* 25 (3):279–297. https://doi.org/10.1080/1068316X.2018.1519828.
Landström, Sara, Pär Anders Granhag, and Maria Hartwig. 2005. "Witnesses Appearing Live Versus on Video: Effects on Observers' Perception, Veracity Assessments and Memory." *Applied Cognitive Psychology* 19 (7):913–933. https://doi.org/10.1002/acp.1131.
Landström, Sara, Pär Anders Granhag, and Maria Hartwig. 2007. "Children's Live and Videotaped Testimonies: How Presentation Mode Affects Observers' Perception, Assessment and Memory." *Legal and Criminological Psychology* 12 (2):333–348. https://doi.org/10.1348/135532506X133607.
Landström, Sara, Rebecca M. Willén, and Eric Bylander. 2012. "Rättspraktikers inställning till modern ljud- och bildteknik i rättssalen: En rättspsykologisk studie." *Svensk Juristtidning* (3):197–218.
Leader, Kate. 2018. "The Trial's the Thing: Performance and Legitimacy in International Criminal Trials." *Theoretical Criminology* 24 (2):241–257. https://doi.org/10.1177/1362480618806923.
Lederer, Fredric I. 1998. "The Road to the Virtual Courtroom – A Consideration of Today's – And Tomorrow's – High-Technology Courtrooms Art of Advocacy." *South Carolina Law Review* 50 (3):799–844.
Legg, Michael, and Anthony Song. 2021. "The Courts, the Remote Hearing and the Pandemic: From Action to Reflection." *University of New South Wales Law School* 44 (1):126–166.
Levén, Staffan, and Fredrik Wesäll. 2011. "En modernare rättegång – hur har det gått?" *Svensk Juristtidning* 1:18–31.
Licoppe, Christian. 2004. "'Connected' Presence: The Emergence of a New Repertoire for Managing Social Relationships in a Changing Communication Technoscape." *Society and Space* 22 (1):135–156.
Licoppe, Christian, Maud Verdier, and Laurence Dumoulin. 2013. "Courtroom Interaction as a Multimedia Event: The Work of Producing Relevant Videoconference Frames in French Pre-Trial Hearings." *The Electronic Journal of Communication* 23 (1&2):1–20.
Ling, Rich. 2008. *New Tech, New Ties: How Mobile Communication Is Reshaping Social Cohesion*. Cambridge, MA: MIT Press.
Macdonald, Ros, and Anne Wallace. 2004. "Review of the Extent of Courtroom Technology in Australia." *William & Mary Bill of Rights Journal* 12 (3):649.
Madani, Doha. 2021. "Video Shows Suspect Attack Judge in Mississippi Courtroom." *NBC News*, 2 February. Retrieved from www.nbcnews.com/news/us-news/video-shows-suspect-attack-judge-mississippi-courtroom-n1256512, accessed 12th April 2023.
Maloney, Patricia. 2013. "Online Networks and Emotional Energy." *Information, Communication & Society* 16 (1):105–124. https://doi.org/10.1080/1369118X.2012.659197.
Maroney, Terry A. 2006. "Law and Emotion: A Proposed Taxonomy of an Emerging Field." *Law and Human Behavior* 30 (2):119–142.

Maroney, Terry A. 2011. "The Persistent Cultural Script of Judicial Dispassion." *California Law Review* 99:629–681.
Maroney, Terry A. 2016. "The Emotionally Intelligent Judge: A New (and Realistic) Ideal." *Revista Forumul Judecatorilor* 61 (1):61–83.
Mayer, Chloe. 2022. "Huge Fight in Courtroom as Murder Suspect Walks Out, Video Shows." *Newsweek*, 25 October. Retrieved from www.newsweek.com/court-fight-brawl-murder-louisville-1754444, accessed 12th April 2023.
McKay, Carolyn. 2018. *The Pixelated Prisoner*. Abingdon: Routledge.
McKay, Carolyn. 2021. "Digital Justice and Video Links: Connecting and Conflating Courtroom and Carceral Places." In *Courthouse Architecture, Design and Social Justice*, edited by Kirsty Duncanson and Emma Henderson, 191–212. London: Routledge.
McKay, Carolyn, and Kristin Macintosh. 2023. "Digital Criminal Courts: The Place or Space of (Post) Pandemic Justice." In *Cybercrime in the Pandemic Digital Age and Beyond*, edited by Russell G. Smith, Rick Sarre, Lennon Yao-Chung Chang, and Laurie Yiu-Chung Lau, 193–208. Springer Link: Palgrave.
Mierke, Katja, Wera Aretz, Anna Nowack, Roland Wilmsen, and Tim Heinemann. 2011. "Impression Formation in Online-Dating-Situations: Effects of Media Richness and Physical Attractiveness Information." *Journal of Business and Media Psychology* 2:49–56.
Mike, Law Talk With. 2023. "All Kinds of Crazy from All Kinds of Courts." *YouTube*. Retrieved from www.youtube.com/watch?v=XinEe_NRxHs&t=307s, accessed 23rd January 2024.
Moore, Sarah. 2023. "Reimagining the Open Court in the Time of Pandemic: Towards 'Portal Justice' and 'Broadcast Justice'." In *Crime, Justice and COVID-19*, edited by Christopher Kay and Stephen Case, 31–49. Bristol University Press.
Mulcahy, Linda. 2008. "The Unbearable Lightness of Being: Shifts Towards the Virtual Trial." *Journal of Law and Society* 35 (4):464–489.
Mulcahy, Linda. 2010. *Legal Architecture: Justice, Due Process and the Place of Law*. London: Routledge.
Mulcahy, Linda, and Anna Tsalapatanis. 2022. "Exclusion in the Interests of Inclusion: Who Should Stay Offline in the Emerging World of Online Justice?" *Journal of Social Welfare and Family Law*:1–22. https://doi.org/10.1080/09649069.2022.2136713.
Mulcahy, Linda, Emma Rowden, and Wend Teeder. 2021. "Exploring the Case for Virtual Jury Trials During the COVID-19 Crisis: An Evaluation of a Pilot Study Conducted by JUSTICE." Retrieved from https://papers.ssrn.com/sol3/papers.cfm?abstract_id=3876199.
Munro, Vanessa E. 2018. "The Impact of the Use of Pre-Recorded Evidence on Juror Decision-Making: An Evidence Review." In *Crime and Justice*. Scottish Government.
Nexø, Louise Anker, and Jacob Strandell. 2020. "Testing, Filtering, and Insinuating: Matching and Attunement of Emoji Use Patterns as Non-Verbal Flirting in Online Dating." *Poetics* 83:101477.
Orcutt, Holly K., Gail S. Goodman, Ann E. Tobey, Jennifer M. Batterman-Faunce, and Sherry Thomas. 2001. "Detecting Deception in Children's Testimony: Factfinders' Abilities to Reach the Truth in Open Court and Closed-Circuit Trials." *Law and Human Behavior* 25 (4):339–372.
Osler, Lucy. 2024. "Belonging Online: Rituals, Sacred Objects, and Mediated Interactions." In *The Phenomenology of Belonging*, edited by Luna Dolezal and Danielle Petherbridge. SUNY Press.
Parker, James. 2011. "The Soundscape of Justice." *Griffith Law Review* 20 (4):962–993. https://doi.org/10.1080/10383441.2011.10854727.
Patrizio, Andy. 2021. "The History and Evolution of Video Conferencing." Retrieved from https://www.techtarget.com/whatis/feature/The-history-and-evolution-of-video-conferencing, accessed 12th February 2023.

Pink, Sarah. 2015. *Doing Sensory Ethnography.* 2nd ed. London: Sage. Non-fiction.

Pink, Sarah, and Kerstin Leder Mackley. 2016. "Moving, Making and Atmosphere: Routines of Home as Sites for Mundane Improvisation." *Mobilities* 11 (2):171–187.

Prescott, James J. 2017. "Improving Access to Justice in State Courts with Platform Technology." *Vanderbilt Law Review* 70:1993.

Puddister, Kate, and Tamara A. Small. 2020. "Trial by Zoom? The Response to COVID-19 by Canada's Courts." *Canadian Journal of Political Science/Revue Canadienne de Science Politique* 53 (2):373–377. https://doi.org/10.1017/S0008423920000505.

Reddy, William M. 2001. *The Navigation of Feeling: A Framework for the History of Emotions.* Cambridge: Cambridge University Press.

Roberts, Paul, and Adrian Zuckerman. 2022. *Roberts & Zuckerman's Criminal Evidence.* Oxford University Press. https://doi.org/10.1093/oso/9780198824480.001.0001.

Robins, Jon. 2021. "Courts Backlog Increasing Before Pandemic and Will Be a Problem 'for Years to Come'." *The Justice Gap.* Retrieved from https://www.thejusticegap.com/courts-backlog-increasing-before-pandemic-and-will-be-a-problem-for-years-to-come/.

Rossner, Meredith. 2021. "Remote Rituals in Virtual Courts." *Journal of Law and Society* 48 (3):334–361.

Rossner, Meredith, and Martha McCurdy. 2018. *Implementing Video Hearings (Party-to-State): A Process Evaluation.* London: Ministry of Justice.

Rossner, Meredith, and Martha McCurdy. 2020. *Video Hearings Process Evaluation (Phase 2).* London: Ministry of Justice.

Rossner, Meredith, and David Tait. 2021. "Presence and Participation in a Virtual Court." *Criminology & Criminal Justice* 23:135–157.

Rossner, Meredith, David Tait, and Martha McCurdy. 2021. "Justice Reimagined: Challenges and Opportunities with Implementing Virtual Courts." *Current Issues in Criminal Justice* 33 (1):94–110. https://doi.org/10.1080/10345329.2020.1859968.

Rowden, Emma. 2018. "Distributed Courts and Legitimacy: What Do We Lose When We Lose the Courthouse?" *Law, Culture and the Humanities* 14 (2):263–281.

Rowden, Emma, Anne Wallace, and Jane Goodman-Delahunty. 2010. "Sentencing by Videolink in Australia: Up in the Air." *Criminal Law Journal* 34:1–22.

Rowden, Emma, Anne Wallace, David Tait, Mark Hanson, and Diane Jones. 2013. *Gateways to Justice: Design and Operational Guidelines for Remote Participation in Court Proceedings.* Penrith, NSW: Western Sydney University.

Russell, Emma K., and Bree Carlton. 2018. "Counter-Carceral Acoustemologies: Sound, Permeability and Feminist Protest at the Prison Boundary." *Theoretical Criminology* 24 (2):296–313. https://doi.org/10.1177/1362480618769862.

Sanders, Anne. 2021. "Video-Hearings in Europe before, During and after the COVID-19 Pandemic the COVID-19 Crisis – Lessons for the Courts: Academic Article." *International Journal for Court Administration* 12 (2):1–21.

Schnaars, Steve, and Cliff Wymbs. 2004. "On the Persistence of Lackluster Demand – The History of the Video Telephone." *Technological Forecasting and Social Change* 71 (3):197–216. https://doi.org/10.1016/S0040-1625(02)00410-9.

Sela, Ayelet. 2017. "The Effect of Online Technologies on Dispute Resolution System Design: Antecedents, Current Trends and Future Directions." *Lewis & Clark Law Review* 21 (3):633–682.

SFS. 1942:740. *Rättegångsbalken.* Stockholm: Swedish Ministry of Justice.

Slaby, Jan, Rainer Mühlhoff, and Philipp Wüschner. 2017. "Affective Arrangements." *Emotion Review* 11 (1):3–12. https://doi.org/10.1177/1754073917722214.

Smith, Russell G., Rebecca Savage, and Catherine Emami. 2021. "Audiovisual Link Technologies in Australian Criminal Courts: Practical and Legal Considerations." In *AIC Research Reports*, edited by Australian Government. Canberra: Australian Institute of Criminology.

SOU. 2012:93. "En modernare rättegång II – en uppföljning." In *2012:93*, edited by Statens Offentliga Utredningar. Stockholm: Regeringenskansliet.

Sourdin, Tania, and John Zeleznikow. 2020. "Courts, Mediation and COVID-19." *Australian Business Law Review* 48 (2):138–158.

Steinbuch, Yaron. 2023. "Lawyer Attacked by Client Who Allegedly Decapitated Lover Withdraws From Case." *NY Post*, 28 February. Retrieved from https://nypost.com/2023/02/28/lawyer-attacked-by-killer-client-withdraws-from-case/, accessed 12th April 2023.

Tait, David, Blake McKimmie, Rick Sarre, Diane Jones, Laura W. McDonald, and Karen Gelb. 2017. *Towards a Distributed Court.* Western Sydney University.

Tait, David, and Vincent Tay. 2019. "Virtual Court Study: Report of a Pilot Test 2018." https://doi.org/10.26183/5d01d1418d757.

Taylor, Natalie, and Jacqueline Joudo. 2005. *The Impact of Pre-Recorded Video and Closed Circuit Television Testimony by Adult Sexual Assault Complainants on Jury Decision-Making: An Experimental Study, Research and Public Policy Series No. 68.* Online: Australian Institute of Criminology.

Temkin, Jennifer. 2000. "Prosecuting and Defending Rape: Perspectives from the Bar." *Journal of Law and Society* 27 (2):219–248.

Terry, Matthew, Steve Johnson, and Peter Thompson. 2010. "Virtual Court Pilot Outcome Evaluation." In *Ministry of Justice Research Series.* London: Ministry of Justice.

Thakur, Pradeep. 2021. "Pending Cases in India Cross 4.4 Crore, Up 19% Since Last Year." *The Times of India*, 15 April. Retrieved from https://timesofindia.indiatimes.com/india/pending-cases-in-india-cross-4-4-crore-up-19-since-last-year/articleshow/82088407.cms.

Tomlinson, Joe. 2019. *Justice in the Digital State: Assessing the Next Revolution in Administrative Justice.* Bristol: Polity Press.

Törnberg, Petter, and Anton Törnberg. 2022. "Inside a White Power Echo Chamber: Why Fringe Digital Spaces Are Polarizing Politics." *New Media & Society*:14614448221122915.

Tutenges, Sébastien, and Frederik Bøhling. 2019. "Designing Drunkenness: How Pubs, Bars and Nightclubs Increase Alcohol Sales." *International Journal of Drug Policy* 70:15–21. https://doi.org/10.1016/j.drugpo.2019.04.009.

Tyler, T. R. 1988. "What Is Procedural Justice?: Criteria Used by Citizens to Assess the Fairness of Legal Procedures." *Law & Society Review* 22 (1):103–136.

Tyler, T. R. 2003. "Procedural Justice, Legitimacy, and the Effective Rule of Law." *Crime and Justice* 30 (1):283–357.

Tyler, T. R. 2006. *Why People Obey the Law.* Princeton, NJ: Princeton University Press.

Tyler, T. R. 2007. "Court Review: Procedural Justice and the Courts." *Court Review: The Journal of the American Judges Association* 44 (1/2):26–31.

Van Dijk, Jan. 2019. *The Digital Divide.* Cambridge: Polity Press.

Vandenberg, Femke, Michaël Berghman, and Julian Schaap. 2021. "The 'Lonely Raver': Music Livestreams During COVID-19 as a Hotline to Collective Consciousness?" *European Societies* 23 (sup1):S141–S152. https://doi.org/10.1080/14616696.2020.1818271.

Viglione, Jill, Jennifer H. Peck, and Joanna D. Frazier. 2023. "COVID-19 and Courts: An Exploration of the Impacts of the Pandemic on Case Processing and Operations." *Victims & Offenders* 18 (5):818–841. https://doi.org/10.1080/15564886.2022.2133034.

Waldron, Vincent R. 2000. "Relational Experiences and Emotion at Work." In *Emotion in Organizations*, edited by S. Fineman, 64–82. London: SAGE Publications.

Walenta, Jayme. 2020. "Courtroom Ethnography: Researching the Intersection of Law, Space, and Everyday Practices." *The Professional Geographer* 72 (1):131–138. https://doi.org/10.1080/00330124.2019.1622427.

Wallace, Anne. 2008. "Virtual Justice in the Bush: The Use of Court Technology in Remote and Regional Australia." *Journal of Law, Information and Science* 2 (1).

Wallace, Anne, Sharyn Roach Anleu, and Kathy Mack. 2017. "Judicial Work and AV Use: Perceptions from Australian Courts." *Oñati Socio-Legal Series* 7 (4).
Walsh, Kieran. 2020. "How Skype Lost Its Crown to Zoom." Retrieved from https://www.wired.co.uk/article/skype-coronavirus-pandemic, accessed 12th February 2023.
Wästerfors, David. 2018. "Observations." In *The SAGE Handbook of Qualitative Data Collection*, edited by U. Flick, 314–326. Los Angeles: SAGE Publications Ltd.
Watch, Court. 2021. "Suspended Driver DRIVES into Judge Middleton's Courtroom." YouTube, Last Modified 2 April 2022. Retrieved from www.youtube.com/results?search_query=suspended+driver+in+zoom+trial, accessed 23rd January 2024.
Wegge, Jurgen. 2006. "Communication via Videoconference: Emotional and Cognitive Consequences of Affective Personality Dispositions, Seeing One's Own Picture, and Disturbing Events." *Human–Computer Interaction* 21 (3):273–318. https://doi.org/10.1207/s15327051hci2103_1.
Wiggins, Elizabeth C. 2003. "What We Know and What We Need to Know about the Effects of Courtroom Technology Symposium: International Conference on the Legal and Policy Implications of Courtroom Technology." *William & Mary Bill of Rights Journal* 12 (3):731–744.
Worldwide, Remote Courts. 2023. Retrieved from https://remotecourts.org, accessed 25th January 2023.
Wright, Ashlyn. 2023. "Courtroom Brawl Breaks Out Between Uncle and Grandmoter During Paternity Suit Hearing." *WRTV Indianapolis*, 10 March. Retrieved from www.wrtv.com/news/local-news/crime/courtroom-brawl-breaks-out-between-uncle-and-grandmother-during-paternity-suit-hearing, accessed 12th April 2023.
Yokoyama, Hitomi, and Ikuo Daibo. 2012. "Effects of Gaze and Speech Rate on Receivers' Evaluations of Persuasive Speech." *Psychological Reports* 110 (2):663–676. https://doi.org/10.2466/07.11.21.28.PR0.110.2.663-676.
Young, Alison. 2023. "Listening Criminologically: On the Materiality and Relationality of Sound." *Criminolocial Encounters* 6 (1):147–156.
Zahra, Noor. 2017. "Divorce Hearing Ends in First Fight." *GDN Online*, 23 March. Retrieved from www.gdnonline.com/Details/195829/Divorce-hearing-ends-in-fist-fight, accessed 12th April 2023.

3 Attendance

The International Military Tribunal held at the Palace of Justice in Nuremberg between November 1945 and October 1946 dealt with the 21 surviving high-ranking members of the Nazi state. It thus constitutes one of the most significant trials in history and is one of the first major trials where the public gallery reached far beyond the physical courtroom.[1] The rear wall of the courtroom was moved to make the courtroom larger to enable the technology of the day – news cameras – to expand the trial beyond the physical confines of the courtroom, enabling over 250 members of the international press to attend and with many parts of the trial filmed for newsreels to be shown later in the day on news broadcasts. This renovation also enabled nearly 400 visitors each day to observe the trial from the public gallery (Museum 2020).

The attendance of visitors and journalists and, in particular, the dissemination of the recorded news material was expected to fulfil demands of transparency and openness and educate the world on the horrors that occurred during World War II. However, the protracted nature of the trial, the relative absence of first-hand accounts by witnesses, and the fact that many already considered the defendants to be guilty, led many to consider the trial to be a waste of money (Douglas 1995; Ross 1995; Sharples 2013).

It therefore appears that although technological advances aimed at opening proceedings to a wider public enabled a greater audience to keep abreast with the goings on of the Nuremberg trials, this widespread coverage led to more unexpected consequences. Rather than educating the public as to the legal underpinnings and thus need for an extensive examination of the facts given the severity of the charges, public opinion of the defendants' guilt appeared to shape how they interacted with the trials, deeming them unnecessary; an opinion that was reinforced by the level of coverage which served to further remind how exhaustively the evidence was examined. The coverage did not lead to increased trust in the courts, instead it jeopardised this trust.

1 Prior to this, the 1935 US trial of Bruno Hauptman, accused of murdering the child of Charles and Anne Lindbergh, is considered to be one of the first media circus trials in the US (Bock and Araiza 2015).

DOI: 10.4324/9781003344643-3

Today's digitalisation enables even greater reach with trials de-spatialised, freed of the necessity of physically attending on-site (indeed, trials are also freed of temporal constraints, hence trials can be attended synchronously or asynchronously). Livestreamed trials available on YouTube, court websites, or other such online platforms and news reports blogged directly from the courtroom and published on news websites are two ways in which digitalisation has changed how we can attend trials, removing the need of physical presence. These new forms of attendance are ways of fulfilling goals of open justice, however in this chapter I will explore and problematise the implications of opening the courts to a far wider public than ever before via digital attendance, by asking and answering, "how much access is really in the public interest?"

Attending trials and open justice in the digital age

Open justice, as already introduced in Chapter 1, had three central tenets in its original form: education, truth, and discipline, all of which can be achieved by increasing *publicity* to use Bentham's (1843a) terminology. The first of these refers to the function of opening the courts to act as a school, educating people with regards to the law and the legal system. The second denotes the notion that the greater and wider the audience that can observe a witness's testimony, the greater the risk they will be caught in an untruth and thus the greater the chance they will tell the truth. The third tenet – discipline – refers to the need for the legal and moral responsibility of judges, prosecutors, and lawyers to be scrutinised and upheld. This was done by introducing observers who could write and distribute handwritten notes describing events taking place in the courtroom, a process serving to protect against unrighteous legal actors from executing acts of injustice such as sacrificing the interests of the public for those in power. Public opinion could therefore also serve a disciplinary function as the enforcer of moral sanctions against deviant legal professionals (Postema 2013; Resnik 2013; Twining 1985). In short, the surest way to safeguard against corruption and to ensure legal security was publicity and "exposure of the whole system of procedure – whatever is done by anybody, being done before the eyes of the universal public" (Bentham 1843a, 9). Bentham is implying that trials operate in a synopticon, with the many watching the few.

Open justice is perhaps most associated with the aphorism "justice must not only be done but must also be seen to be done" attributed to Lord Hewart, lord chief justice of England.[2] This has since had a twenty-first-century spin put on it as remarked by Lord Neuberger, president of the UK Supreme Court (UKSC 2015): "now justice can be seen to be done at a time which suits you" and to this I would now add, that justice can be seen to be done at a *place* which suits you, stemming from the de-spatialisation of attending

2 In the case *Rex v. Sussex Justices* (1924) 1KB 256.

trials with the entrance of live blogging and livestreaming meaning that "the same time" no longer presupposes "the same space" (J. B. Thompson 2005, 32; 2013).

So, whilst the central tenets of open justice remain fundamental in the democratic courts of today, open justice and its trinity of functions are changing in the digital age. The tenets of truth and education are shifting and the overall concept of open justice is largely focused on transparency, which has become the motto of liberal democracies (Moore 2018; Moore, Clayton, and Murphy 2019; Resnik 2013). This contemporary transparency is increasingly centring on the provision of online or virtual access to public sector data, including legal documents and proceedings, in order to open up the state, also known as "institutional transparency" (Moore 2018). There is thus a continuing quest for organised transparency, including within the legal institution, where amplified demands for scrutiny of legal processes prevail (Bogoch and Peleg 2014; Jaconelli 2002; Rodrick 2014; Townend and Welsh 2023). For instance, Moore and colleagues (2019, 6) suggest that contemporary public access is virtual, mediated, and "an altogether different form of openness." Here it should be highlighted that enabling publicity does not necessarily mean that the public will function as scrutinisers of the system, hence merely enabling the public to attend a trial via different means does not ensure active scrutiny, as I will return to later on (Moore 2018; Peters 2013).

The Nuremberg trial was one of the first trials that drew massive media attention and led to debate regarding the appropriateness of certain kinds of media coverage in court as a way of attending trials. Since then, digitalisation developments have enabled the possibility of trials being livestreamed and live blogged and thus attended by an audience far larger than ever before. Digitalisation has therefore played a fundamental role in increasing transparency, with the ways in which we are able to attend trials having undergone a vast transformation from the days of secretive proceedings behind closed doors, to television broadcasts, to contemporary technological and ideological developments which push the physical and temporal boundaries of attending legal proceedings wider and wider: beyond the four walls of the courtroom to the comfort of one's living room, the bus on the commute to work, in the same city, in the same state, or on a different continent.

In the next sections of this chapter, I will explore how live blogs, as a form of court reporting enabling digital attendance, and livestreaming, which I also present as a form of digitally attending trials, impact open justice. I also discuss how live blogs and livestreams shape the individuals working within courts to show that drives towards open justice can have unexpected consequences, such as changing the work practices of legal professionals.

Attending trials via live blogs and livestreams

Live blogs and livestreams are forms of court reporting that facilitate a way for people to digitally attend trials due to the level of detail and immediacy enabled. They can thus provide an essence of real-time "being-thereness" that is harder to attain in a news report published at the end of the day.

Live blogs entail a journalist sitting in the public gallery, writing short time-stamped descriptions of courtroom events that are instantly published on news website (Thurman and Walters 2013, 83). This reporting format embraces "radical immediacy" (Hall 2015, 120), allowing for the rapid distribution of extensive information to the public. It operates at a pace and level of immediacy that significantly exceeds traditional media formats (Allan 2006; Hall-Coates 2015; see also Karlsson 2011). A live blog of a trial thus consists of a continuum of descriptions which, pertaining to the legal rulings of each country, can include verbatim depictions of exchanges and highly detailed descriptions of evidence, actors, and interactions. This means that a journalist may be permitted to write word for word what a witness is saying in a trial and publish it immediately on a news website. This kind of journalistic live blog (as well as X) has rapidly become an important part of mainstream media (Goehler, Dias, and Bralow 2010, 14). Combined with the rising number in online news readerships (Barometer 2021; Palaces 2021) and falling numbers of people attending trials (Hans and Dee 1991; Mulcahy 2010; Rodrick 2014), this format has become an important source of information about trials for many (cf. Balbi and Magaudda 2018, Taneja et al. 2012, van Rees and van Eijck 2003).

Livestreamed trials are legal proceedings broadcast in real time over the internet, allowing the public to watch and follow courtroom events as they happen. Like live blogs, this form of broadcasting aims to promote transparency and public access to the judicial process, enabling viewers to observe legal arguments and witness testimonies without being physically present in the courtroom.

Both these forms of covering trials play a vital role in fulfilling the functions of open justice, by examining and making accessible court proceedings and constituting a way for the public to attend trials. Live blogs and livestreams are contemporary forms of court reporting and play a central role in modern states which are formally comprised of a tripartite, separating powers between three branches: an independent judiciary, a legislature, and an executive as is the case in, for instance, Australia, Denmark, United Kingdom, and the United States (with other systems in place in other jurisdictions, e.g. China). Court reporting thus serves an important monitoring function to ensure that the judiciary is functioning as it should. And, although accusations of *fake news* have hit the wider news media in recent years, court reporting continues to play an important function as scrutiniser of the remaining three estates – thereby holding each branch accountable – and as a provider of information to the public (Schultz 1998; Tandoc, Lim, and Ling 2018).

The roots of live blogs and livestreams can be found in Bentham's (1843a, 356) ideas on open justice. He wrote that the public should function as "auditors": watching trials, writing notes, and then distributing them to the wider public. These minutes, according to Bentham (1843a, 316), could serve not only as a way to protect against "unrighteous judges" from committing acts of injustice, but also as a way of ensuring that "Judge & Co" (Bentham 1843b, 7–63) – meaning all legal actors in the courtroom – behave appropriately.

Court reporting falls into a broader category of crime reporting which can be traced back to Britain and Germany from the middle of the sixteenth century up until the start of the eighteenth century (although representations of crime have been popular since the Greek and Roman dramatists (Turnbull 2010)) with an extraordinary number of publications reporting on capital crimes produced. In conjunction with rising literacy rates and the development of new technologies for printing, the production and circulation of crime pamphlets – short, unbound books, often detailing gruesome murders but also including notes taken from trials – began to rocket (Burger 2016).

One of the first trials with extensive media attention took place in 1859 in the US, for the abolitionist John Brown. Widespread dissemination of the trial via the national telegraph system washed over the country. Towards the end of the 1800s, the Lizzie Borden case hit the headlines in the US, leading to the original *trial of the century* garnering press coverage that perhaps even outweighed O.J. Simpson's proceedings a century later. Crime reporting has remained a constant presence in the news since this time (Pollack 2001; Reiner, Livingstone, and Allen 2000; Smolej and Kivivuori 2008).

So, livestreaming and live blogging can trace their lineage back to Bentham. They are both aimed at fulfilling ideals of open justice and can be seen as ways of people attending trials in the digital age. This is particularly pertinent in an age where public galleries are being designed out of courts thus reducing the amount of space available for public viewing, and in an age where people have less time to attend trials. They both enable the public to be digital auditors, watching the courts from afar and enabling the synopticon. Moreover, digitalisation has enabled a sense of being-thereness that provides the essence of attending a trial.

Before going any further, it is important to note that such portrayals of trials should not be understood as enabling a transparent window into legal life, rather akin to other forms of reporting, they are "prism[s], subtly bending and distorting the view of the world" (Jewkes 2015, 45). They are thus technological tools for seeing which are shaped by "cultural assumptions, frameworks, practices and organisational interests and priorities" (J. B. Thompson 2005, 36). This means that what we read about and who we read about are results of political, structural, and individual decisions all of which shape our understandings, public perceptions, and knowledge of the justice system, including the courts (Biressi and Nunn 2003; Ericson, Baranek, and Chan 1991; Hans and Dee 1991). For instance, as I will go into in more detail in this chapter, the emotionalisation of the court actors in live blogs is shifting our understandings of trials and legal professionals in new and exciting directions.

As already mentioned, livestreamed trials and live blogs have certain similarities. For instance, both have the capability to relay instantaneous and detailed information, possessing a sense of "liveness" (Flower and Ahlefeldt 2021) and being-thereness, transporting the reader into the courtroom. At first glance, both appear to fulfil the demands of open justice and both also reflect wider trends in society towards immediacy, connectivity, and direct access (Bauman 2007; Taylor 2004).

The crucial difference is the absence of an audio-visual component in live blogs: whilst photos of evidence may be published on live blogs, in many courtrooms where photographic or television cameras are not permitted, these photographs remains the only visual available. Likewise, audio broadcasting hearings live is also not allowed in many jurisdictions, also preventing the possibility of audio. For instance, in Sweden, it is not allowed to film or take photos in the courtroom, and broadcasting the audio from a trial is permitted in cases with high public interest (e.g. in 2015, the trial for the murder of a young woman, Lisa Holm, was audio broadcast with only a delay of a few minutes).

This raises the question of whether the audio-visual aspect is necessary with regards to ensuring open justice. Thompson (2011, 222) claims that the key reason for allowing cameras in court is to enable the public to see and thus judge appearance and demeanour for themselves, thereby making their own evaluations of credibility and reliability to gauge the quality of proceedings. However, as I will show in this chapter, in my studies of courtrooms, I have concluded that being able to see a trial is not a vital function of open justice and that good enough institutional transparency can be achieved with live blogs without the added intrusion of being filmed (Flower 2023; Flower and Ahlefeldt 2021; cf. Moore et al. 2019).

Moreover, although livestreamed trials and live blogs can both be effective tools for relaying immediate and detailed information of courtroom proceedings, they also both risk impinging on procedural integrity and the personal integrity of those taking part. Despite this, live blogs have garnered far less societal debate and academic attention than their camera counterpart. The reason for this could be that live blogs are not perceived as threatening due to the absence of audio-visual aspects: we cannot see or hear witnesses, plaintiffs, defendants, or legal professionals in live blogs. In the next section I will dive into these two forms of attending trials; however, due to the relative absence of critical work on live blogs, my focus will be largely on this format.

Livestreaming trials

The popularity of livestreaming court trials surged during the COVID-19 pandemic, as it allowed the principles of open justice to be maintained by enabling the public to observe legal proceedings remotely. Since then, the use of cameras in courtrooms for livestreaming has become more commonplace. Trials may be streamed on various platforms, including court websites, YouTube, and specialised services such as CourtTV. This is a practice that is employed by courts across the globe (Nasheri 2002) and transforms the court into a part of the synopticon with the many now able to watch the few in a livestream.

The International Criminal Court (ICC) and the International Court of Justice offer livestreams of public hearings,[3] while in the US, federal court judges may permit broadcasting under specific conditions, such as presenting evidence, ensuring security, or preserving a record of proceedings. However, livestreaming is currently not permitted in the US Supreme Court (Courts 2024).

In contrast, livestreaming has become common in China, where over 180 courts at various levels have adopted the practice since 2014, prioritising cases with significant social or educational value (Fan and Lap Fung Lee 2019). The Supreme Court in Canada and Kenya and Brazil's Supreme Federal Court also stream proceedings (Observer 2024; Stepniak 2008). In England, livestreaming began in 2011 on platforms like YouTube and, since 2015, via the Court's official website.[4] A milestone occurred in July 2022, when Judge Sarah Munro's sentencing of Ben Oliver at the Old Bailey was livestreamed for the first time.

New Zealand has permitted televised proceedings since 2000, while neighbouring Australia allows filming for cases of particular public interest – as is also the case in Norway – with recordings of High Court Hearings available on the website (Australia 2024). Conversely, other countries like Germany and Switzerland prohibit filming in courtrooms (Sanders 2021).

An example of a recent livestreamed trial is the 2022 trial of Darrell Brooks who was charged with six counts of first-degree intentional homicide, 61 counts of first-degree recklessly endangering safety, and six hit and runs causing death, and later convicted on all points, at a Christmas parade in Waukesha, Wisconsin, which was livestreamed on YouTube as well as other platforms. The first day of the trial had 287,339 views (as of June 2024) on CourtTV.

The livestream shows, among other things, Brooks being removed from the courtroom due to his consistently disruptive behaviour, leading the judge to state that he had "forfeited his right to be present." He is then placed in an adjacent courtroom which, as the judge notes, has the "functional equivalent of being present." In this adjacent courtroom, Brooks is seen pacing shirtless or sitting with his back to the court. At one point, when Brooks begins to disrupt again, the judge says, "Mr Brooks, the live stream is on," to which he replies, "I don't care if I'm on live stream, just like ya'll don't care." He holds up a sign reading "OBJECTION," protesting his removal and indicating that the judge has muted his microphone. The judge warns him that if he continues being disruptive, his microphone will be muted once again.

The subsequent sentencing hearing is also livestreamed, during which the son of one of the victims addresses Mr Brooks, saying, "I hope as I read my

3 The European Court of Human Rights broadcast hearings, but they are not live.

4 There is therefore a page for each appeal that includes these recordings along with the summary judgement video, full written judgement, and the press summary (Moran 2016). Photography, filming, and even sketching are not permitted, with courtroom sketchers working from memory.

statement you continue to roll your eyes. It's important that the world see that evil can be a tangible, living, breathing thing."

The livestreaming of the trial can be seen as a tool for ensuring that Brooks, who chose to represent himself, received a fair trial without the support of a defence lawyer. Brooks' disruptive behaviour, including interrupting, being rude, and not responding appropriately to questions, led the judge to not only remove him from the courtroom but also mute his microphone so that he was unable to be heard from the adjacent courtroom. Whilst these are strategies available to the judge to ensure proceedings run smoothly, there is a delicate balance between silencing a defendant who is disruptive and ensuring that their rights to be present in the trial are upheld. Livestreaming can serve to ensure that these rights are upheld and that a judge does not misuse these strategies for maintaining order in the courtroom, even without a lawyer present. Likewise, Brooks claimed that the trial should be dismissed, citing, amongst other reasons, the judge's conflict of interest and bias in the case, claims which the livestream captures and which show the judges' responses. Again, these are aspects that may have remained unknown if cameras were not present.

Livestreaming this trial is also a way for the families of the six people killed and the scores of injured victims and members of the local community and beyond to attend proceedings. A courtroom can only hold so many people and in trials with wide interest, livestreaming enables more interested parties to attend. The possibility of attending a trial in this way can constitute an important step in therapeutic jurisprudence as the trial can help those impacted to emotionally process a crime and its aftermath (Wexler 2000). It is the transformation of a trial into a part of the synopticon through livestreaming that enables widespread attendance and the possibility of greater access to therapeutic jurisprudence.

But this synopticisation can also lead to a broader forum emerging in which Brooks can be publicly shamed. The victim's son hints at this when he says that he hopes the world can see the evil that Brooks represents, clearly labelling Brooks as deviant. Moreover, Brooks' erratic behaviour in the courtroom, broadcast live into the homes of hundreds of thousands of people, can also serve to stigmatise him in the eyes of society. Being convicted of a crime can already be stigmatising, shaping how the convicted individual is perceived in the eyes of others. However, Brooks' presentation of self in the courtroom, removing clothing, shouting, and being disrespectful, can lead to further stigmatisation (Goffman 1963). Moreover, this behaviour, rather than functioning as a positive form of therapeutic jurisprudence, both for the victims and their families, but also for Brooks himself, may have a more detrimental effect.

Other trials that have been livestreamed have led to further issues. For instance, in 2021, a judge granted the media permission to livestream the trial of District Attorney Mark Jones, who was facing charges for defacing a car park whilst filming a music campaign video. It transpired that witnesses who had not yet given evidence were watching this livestream, leading to the judge calling a mistrial (Giles 2021).

Brooks' trial is an example of the lines of argument raised in the debate over livestreaming, which tends to divide public and legal opinion: the positive aspects of increased transparency from cameras in court are weighed against the increased risk of sensationalisation and negative impact on witnesses (see also Bernzen 2018; Cars 2021; Marder 2012; Strinäs 2021; Youm 2012). The discussion thus tends to centre on the quandary of increasing transparency in the judicial system versus the risk of justice becoming sensationalised (Garcia-Blanco and Bennett 2018). This first began to be discussed in conjunction with the 1935 trial of Bruno Hauptmann in the US, for the kidnapping and murder of Charles Lindberg's son, and later culminated in a court ruling that the televising of the 1965 trial of *Estes v State of Texas* (381 US 352) deprived Billie Sol Estes of his constitutional rights to due process.

So, although filming trials is now widely accepted, it has been in contention since the mid-1940s starting with the Nuremberg trials.

Early debates centred on concerns about their disruptive nature, as the technology at that time was bulky and obtrusive with television cameras constituting a novelty, all of this making them a potential distraction (Cohn and Dow 2002; Stepniak 2008). Today, these arguments have lost some of their strength due to the development of smaller, less intrusive filming equipment and the normalisation of cameras in everyday life. The increase in camera surveillance across many countries has further diminished the perception of cameras as a disruption in courtroom settings.

Critics argue that cameras may make witnesses nervous, causing difficulty recalling events or leading to hesitancy (French 2006; Packer 2013; Stepniak 2008; E. Thompson 2011). However, the extent of these effects is debated, with some research suggesting that the claims are based on judicial assumptions rather than empirical evidence (Stepniak 2008).

Moreover, with regards to livestreaming specifically, Nelson (2023) notes that livestreamed trials in Australia became more prevalent during the COVID-19 lockdowns, yet there remains a scarcity of research on the practice, despite its growing use. This increase in livestreaming has occurred alongside changes in the media landscape that have further weakened the traditional watchdog role of the media. As a result, coverage has increasingly focused on high-profile or celebrity cases, often at the expense of smaller cases, especially those from lower tier courts (Chamberlain et al. 2019).

Studies provide mixed results regarding the impact of cameras. Research from the 1980s and 1990s indicated that while witnesses reported increased nervousness and media awareness, this did not impair their performance (e.g. Borgida, DeBono, and Buckman 1990; Kassin 1984). More recent studies have produced similar findings, with some suggesting that cameras might even improve testimony by discouraging dishonesty (E. Thompson 2011) – in line with Bentham's original tenet of the truth function of open justice. In a recent Chinese study, livestreaming causes participants to speak more cautiously and judges to adopt a more formal tone, but there was no evidence that cameras led to distraction or "playing to the cameras" (Liu and Tang 2024). These findings suggest that while cameras may subtly shape courtroom behaviour, they do not significantly disrupt trial proceedings.

The arguments in favour of livestreaming can draw on the literature on cameras in court more broadly, which argues that it can emphasise enhancing accessibility, public education, and transparency in the justice system (Mason 2000; E. Thompson 2011). Yet, some scholars challenge the educational benefits, arguing that there is little evidence showing cameras improve public understandings of legal proceedings (Stepniak 2007). Despite these disagreements, Stepniak's (2008) review of studies across several countries concluded that the risks associated with cameras could be minimised through proper regulation of courtroom access and broadcasting.

The effects of livestreaming are less studied, with existing research often focusing on privacy and dignity (Bernzen 2018; Biber 2018). Fenn (2022) discusses potential risks to fair trials, analysing the 2021 trial of Derek Chauvin – the Minneapolis police officer accused and later found guilty of murdering George Floyd, an event that spurred global protests – where livestreaming allowed the jurors, who were not sequestered to access these livestreams, including the bounty of comments made in chat and commenting functions, all of which potentially influenced their impartiality. This highlights the need for measures to balance open justice with safeguarding defendants' rights.

The impact of livestreaming on audience perception also varies depending on how trials are filmed. Moore and colleagues (2019) found that different filming techniques could shape how viewers engage with courtroom events, influencing their judgements about the participants. As livestreaming becomes more common, nuanced approaches to its regulation will be crucial, considering its potential to subtly influence both courtroom behaviour, public understanding, and public shaming processes.

Overall, while technological advances have alleviated some initial concerns about cameras, the debate continues to evolve. Cameras have become an ingrained part of the surveillance society, and, as research indicates that practitioners reshape their practices when new technologies are integrated, making them a part of their everyday work tools (Lanzara 2009), we may find that livestreaming leaves a lesser imprint going forwards. However, questions remain regarding the impact the synopticonisation of trials has on the individuals depicted.

Live blogs

As is now evident, livestreaming trials is a contemporary phenomenon that has been and continues to be a widely discussed issue, albeit one that is generally accepted. In contrast, societal debate surrounding live blogs is largely absent. Research on live blogs is also limited with most studies focusing on live blogging on social media platforms such as X rather than news websites. Studies typically compare live blogs to traditional print reporting, rather than livestreaming, and find that live blogs do not present a "greater risk of prejudice than with traditional media reports" (Barrett 2011, 21; Commission 2009). Despite that this apparent lack of comparison with livestreaming is interesting, there are similar lines of argument that emerge in the literature and that I have also found in my own research.

Whilst X is seen to facilitate open justice by enabling larger amounts of information to be related to a vaster audience than newspaper reports (Findlay 2015), and live blogs are shown to give a more accurate description of proceedings (Krawitz 2013), overviews of judicial rulings in the US also find problematic issues. For instance, some courts have reasoned that live blogs fulfil the demands of the public's right to information and thus outweigh prejudice to other parties, whilst others highlight the threat posed by live blogs to the sanctity of the courtroom (Goehler et al. 2010; Lambert 2011) as well as the negative impact on witnesses (Goehler et al. 2010; Keyzer et al. 2013; Lambert 2011; Rodrick 2014). Further problematic implications include inaccurate and prejudicial reporting, as well as issues stemming from the dissemination of information online (Bartels and Lee 2013; Findlay 2015; Johnston and Wallace 2015).

In the cross-cultural study I conducted, comparing live blogging in Denmark and Sweden, in which judges, prosecutors, and defence lawyers in both countries were interviewed, I found that live blogging is generally perceived by the respondents in both countries as beneficial for promoting open justice, but that this digital court reporting also introduces complexities and risks in legal proceedings.

Live blogs are understood by the respondents in the study as a "sign of the times" as Dan (SWE), a defence lawyer I interviewed, worded it, in line with wider societal trends of digitalisation whereby transparency and immediacy are valued. This form of digitally attending trials enables the public to get a picture of "what's going on in a courtroom" as David (DK), a defence lawyer, states, and that live blogging can contribute to "demystifying" trials as judge Mette (DK) says. Live blogs are also seen as a helpful tool; for instance, when asked about the advantages of live blogs, defence lawyer Lina (DK) answered:

> The advantages are that people they can follow, I mean, you can't film from here like you can in American courtrooms, so this is something that comes as close as possible in a Danish system right? And I think it gives the public a picture of what's going on in a courtroom, so in that way I think it's fine.

Thus, for many of the respondents, open justice is presented as an important pillar of legal security and integral to the principle of public access to official records with live blogs accepted as a reporting practice to achieve this. Additionally, live blogs enable people who are unable to attend proceedings on site but who are interested in a trial to follow it, as defence lawyer Oliver (SWE) and judge Mikael (SWE) tell me in interviews. Live blogs also mean that the court can extend to an "audience that it doesn't otherwise reach," as judge Tomas (SWE) tells me.

An example of this is given by prosecutor Sebastien (DK) who draws on a high-profile trial in 2019 against a woman charged with defrauding the Danish National Board of Health and Welfare by transferring over 113,000,00 Danish crowns (€15,000,000), a case which garnered massive national and international attention. Many, many people were interested in attending the trial but were unable to due to limited seating. Live blogging thus provided a suitable solution for enabling digital attendance. Similarly, the trial against Rakhmat Akilov in Sweden in 2018 gained widespread Swedish interest, as did the trial against the rapper A$AP Rocky in 2019 with extensive live blogging by all major and many minor news outlets.

It is thus clear that live blogs facilitate the de-spatialisation of trials, given their capability of directly and immediately relaying events taking place in the courtroom which enables readers to attend a trial from the bus on their daily commute, from their kitchen table, or from their office desk on their lunchbreak. Attendance is no longer confined by physical restraints, rather live blogging becomes a part of the synopticon with live blogging journalists functioning, not only to reverse Foucault's (1975/1991, 201) "see/being seen dyad" to enable the many to watch the few, but also to disconnect from physical presence on the part of the watchers. Here the journalist functions as a conduit or mediator, enabling the many to watch from afar.

Live blogging also enables the de-temporalisation of attending trials, as live blogs can be scrolled through in their entirety at the end of the day or used to catch up with events if joining the trial mid-way through. This digitally enabled de-coupling of time and space dissolves the necessity of synchronous physical presence in attendance, much like livestreams. We see again that justice can now be seen to be done, at a time and place of one's choosing.

The benefits of opening courts should, however, be weighed against the inherent disadvantages. For instance, defence lawyer Linus (DK) says:

> Well, I am in favour of openness in the legal system, so I actually think that it's excellent that trials are being covered and I actually think it's also fine that it gives a more vivid picture of what's going on here and now, and you don't have to wait to read about it until the next day. So as a starting point, I don't mind live blogging. Where I see the problem, and that is also what is reflected in that Supreme Court ruling, from that home robbery case, it is that we have a rule in the Code of Civil Procedure that witnesses should not know what the witness before them has explained, and it is clear that it is, of course, undermined, if it's the case that the witnesses can sit at home and read what all the witnesses in the courtroom yesterday said, and the witness doesn't testify before the day after, that is the problem of live blogging.

Likewise, defence lawyer Marie (DK) was also critical of live blogs, going so far as to describe them as "devastating" for ensuring procedural correctness. Here it should be noted that the legal framework regarding live blogging is different in Sweden and Denmark. Whilst both countries permit live blogging from trials, in Denmark there are restrictions in place prohibiting journalists from publishing direct reproductions of what has been said in the courtroom. This change in the law after a Supreme Court ruling – as Linus refers to – was introduced following a case where a witness in a home robbery case changed their version of events after reading a live blog before they themselves had witnessed.

Live blogs are also discussed in more problematic terms in the Swedish material, but it is important to note that such reflections tend not to appear unsolicited in the Swedish interviews, rather they arise in response to direct interviewer questions regarding the negative impact of live blogs; in particular, how live blogs affect the administration of justice with regards to witness testimony. For most respondents in Sweden, their initial reflections reveal a somewhat fatalistic approach to live blogs with judges, prosecutors, and defence lawyers considering live blogs to be an inevitable and unavoidable consequence of Sweden's generous laws regarding public access to legal documents and proceedings, as well as the media's central role in this process. For instance, regarding access to legal documents and proceedings, defence lawyer Elsa (SWE) says that as the preliminary investigation – containing all evidence and witness testimony making up the prosecution's case – is available to the public in Sweden, live blogs do not constitute a problematic form of reporting because the information that could be published in a live blog is already available. With regards to live blogging journalists, prosecutor Rikard (SWE) voices a position presented by many other Swedish respondents in the interviews, saying, "it's part of our job – they have the right to report like this."

However, deeper examination finds tensions between the rhetoric and practice of open justice also in the Swedish material. For instance, prosecutor Jimmie (SWE) says of the Prosecution Authority and live blogging, "we don't think it's great, but at the same time, it isn't anything you can really prevent as the legal process is public," again a somewhat fatalistic approach to the principle of public access to information. When I ask judge Roland, an experienced Swedish judge, what he thinks about the fact that a journalist can publish a verbatim reproduction of courtroom testimony directly on a news website that could be read by witnesses before they have been questioned, he replies,

> I hadn't thought about that part, but of course, now when you say it, then I could imagine that it's completely crazy really, that they can sit there and listen.

A handful of respondents also had a similar response, such as prosecutor Carolyn (SWE), who discusses the importance of insight and the role that live blogs play in this.

> We're supposed to have as much insight as possible and so we have the lay judges who already have insight, but I think that it's totally enough

> to have a journalist listening and writing in the newspaper after the trial. Perhaps not word-for-word what a witness has said, I don't know how it should be arranged, but to not ruin witnesses' testimony. I understand that it can be very difficult in today's situation . . . But to [report] word-for-word in a blog, in a newspaper . . . I think that's a little bit insane actually.

We therefore begin to see some conflicts between the rhetoric of open justice and its practice. Whilst defence lawyer Elsa (SWE) and prosecutor Rikard (SWE) draw on the principle of public access to legal documents and proceedings to shape their understandings of live blogs as *not* constituting an added level of openness and thus *not* constituting a threat to the administration of justice, for others, such as prosecutor Carolyn (SWE) and judge Roland (SWE), the jurisdictional context is drawn on to present live blogs as more problematic. For them, the jurisdictional context serves to protect the administration of justice by enabling insight, but simultaneously also serves to constrain by enabling too much insight. Thus, whilst Carolyn and Roland accept the insight afforded by the principle of public access to official records, they appear ambivalent to the practice of live blogs for achieving this openness. Indeed, Carolyn extends her critique to include newspapers more generally reporting verbatim accounts of courtroom events. Whilst traditional newspaper reports could also constitute an important observer, for Carolyn this capacity should be constrained to avoid word-for-word reproductions in order to achieve the appropriate administration of justice without impacting on the credibility of witness testimony, more in line with Danish approach. What makes live blogs more of a perceived risk is the immediacy with which testimony can be published, accessible by witnesses sitting in the waiting room. Carolyn also draws on the specific jurisdictional context of Sweden where the bench comprises a legally trained judge and (usually) three lay judges who are politically appointed representatives and who are supposed to represent the voice of the public. She thus reasons that lay judges function as external observers providing insight into legal processes indicating a superfluousness to live blogs.

For others, the merit of live blogs was questioned even more explicitly. For instance, judge Cristina (SWE) also talks about how witnesses may change their testimony based on what they have read in a live blog. She says,

> you can't help but wonder – especially if they change what they say – why this is the case, it can be because of other things but you can't help but wonder. So, I'm not sure about what the added value of live blogs provides for the actual trial.

Cristina worries about the uncertainty of knowing whether a witness has changed their testimony based on what they have read in a live blog and questions their merit. Just as acceptance may be grounded in the specific Swedish context with its generous rules around public access to legal documents and proceedings, so too is resistance. We have already seen that prosecutor Carolyn (SWE) draws on this reasoning, as does defence lawyer Dan (SWE) who says of the Swedish context,

> There is a principle of access to public documents, and open trials, and we should be enormously grateful that we have this – it's a question of legal security and democracy – but I don't really know, I mean, why does Svensson need to sit in front of his computer and follow direct reports from questionings? It must be better if – I mean [you read] a summary or go there yourself.

It is therefore the specific jurisdictional context that shapes how live blogs as a tool for enabling open justice are understood, including their, as judge Cristina (SWE) said, "added value." Whilst this judge is resisting live blogs as a form of court reporting, she balances her resistance with appeals to the legal framework in place regarding open courts and documents. She is thus presenting an ambivalent resistance – both for and against.

The legal framework in place regarding the use of communication technologies in the courtroom is also drawn upon as a basis of ambivalent resistance. For instance, Cristina goes on to say that the Code of Judicial Procedure that regulates the courtroom came into effect in the 1940s. She points out that society has transformed enormously since then, saying,

> It's changed, I mean, the possibility of fast communication and transmission has changed a great deal since then. I don't think that they had thought about that you can access what someone else is saying at a trial, but at the moment it's nothing we can do anything about and then I think that there's no point – that's the reality we are in. Then whether it's good or not, that can be discussed, but that's something else.

Cristina perceives the legal framework to have lagged behind technological developments and indicates that such a failure may have repercussions for the administration of justice, however, her fatalistic approach – "it's nothing we can do anything about" – shades her resistance into one of ambivalence. Changing the current state of play and amending the law would require, as judge Mikael (SWE) points out, "an encroachment on the principle of public access to official records." This demands a complex process requiring rigorous and widespread attention and discussion and in the legal community which this study indicates is currently largely lacking. Moreover, as this judge points out, changing the laws regarding court reporting would also be an encroachment on "the purpose of the public trials so it has to be weighed against how big this problem really is and it's a question of if it's big enough." Like Cristina, Mikael is unsure as to the scale of the problem of witnesses accessing others' testimony in live blogs, which may account for the hesitancy in more explicitly resisting live blogs. Prosecutor Jan (SWE) presents a similar view, suggesting, "sure, it can be good with live blogs but there has to be a possibility of deciding when it should happen and as a judge or prosecutor, or other party, limit it." For him, a more nuanced legal framework needs to be in place to ensure that openness remains appropriate.

The truth function of open justice has therefore undergone a fundamental shift given the possibility of live blogging journalists immediately publishing exact details of witness testimony, which can be read by witnesses sitting outside the courtroom, waiting to give evidence, witnesses that, by law, are not permitted to attend hearings before giving evidence themselves. This development means that, rather than the open courts increasing the likelihood of being caught in a lie, live blogging from courts can instead increase the risk of witnesses changing their truth – either consciously or unconsciously – in line with the testimony of others they have read about in the live blog.

This threatens the very principle of fair trials. It is particularly problematic in Sweden which currently has a rapidly growing number of trials linked to organised crime. The prosecution authority is already struggling to find witnesses willing to give evidence in such trials, a challenge which becomes even more arduous if we consider, for instance, that gang members may be able to read the evidence given in court in real time, and hence know not only what a witness has said, but also their exact location, constituting a threat to their safety.

We therefore see that the legal professionals interviewed perceive the capabilities of live blogs as constituting a level of immediacy and detail – of institutional transparency (Moore 2018) – that current law does not fully consider. It is also apparent that the voices of legal professionals echo the tensions found in the previous research drawing on legal rulings wherein the balance of openness should be weighed against procedural integrity (e.g. Bosland and Townend 2018; Goehler et al. 2010; Lambert 2011; Small and Puddister 2020). Hence, we begin to glimpse the "surveillance politics" of the courtroom, with legal professionals beginning to resist scrutiny (Haggerty 2006). It thus also seems apparent that whilst some legal professionals are starting to attend to live blogging as a day-to-day reporting practice as Johnston (2018) suggested would be the case, this is a topic still in its nascent stages for many within the legal profession which may lead to new developments in the future.

Overall, the general agreement as to live blogs being permitted in courts, but with certain restrictions in place in the Danish context, suggests that live blogs and the notion of the see/being seen dyad are such mundane and integral aspects of open justice and courtroom work that they are not actively reflected upon, or indeed resisted in day-to-day life, and require detailed unpacking to reveal.

Conclusions

The digitalisation of court attendance has further uncoupled the observer role from spatial considerations. The public can now watch filmed proceedings from a distance, unseen by those in the courtroom. This has been described by Moore and colleagues as "a distinctly one-way form of access, where the public can see, but their presence is no longer felt" (Moore et al. 2019). Drawing on the qualitative interviews I have conducted with judges, prosecutors, and lawyers, I would nuance this claim, as my findings indicate that the presence of court reporters changes the practices of these legal professionals in subtle ways. Hence, I suggest that the public's presence continues to be felt, irrespective of proximity or virtuality. What does remain is the seeing-without-being-seen dyad. The extension of the public gallery into the virtual domain enables this dyad and entails a convoluted relationship between what is deemed worthy and not worthy of seeing, and how this is framed (Moore et al. 2019; Moran 2016). All of these choices have crucial implications for how the public makes sense of court proceedings and those within. This extends to which types of trial, which actors, which parts of trials, and so on. Livestreaming and live blogging expand the public's access to courtroom proceedings by creating a virtual gallery. However, this digital extension of the courtroom blurs the lines between physical and virtual participation, extending the scope of insight.

The legal professionals interviewed in this study consider open justice to have continuing importance for a functioning and legally secure legal system, however these current understandings of the functions of open justice appear to have shifted. Bentham's disciplinary function has thus shifted to a surveillance function. This shift entails a step away from punitive motivations for monitoring morally deficient legal professionals towards both a broader observation of actions and events and a more focused attention on individuals. Whilst this shift is accepted by some, for others, the surveilling gaze on lay participants is problematic. Thus, whilst synopticism may lead to the enablement of a broader public to access trials via live blogs, there are also more troubling aspects at stake. The politics of live blogs as a surveillance practice are thus beginning to bloom with resistance slowly growing unheard. There are therefore tensions present between the rhetoric of open justice and its practice.

Despite providing valuable insights into legal proceedings, live blogs also pose challenges, particularly concerning their impact on legal professionals and the development of new practices. Therefore, policymakers need to consider these issues carefully when determining the continued acceptance of live blogging and the potential introduction of television cameras into courtrooms. We need to stop and reflect on whether all publicity is good publicity or whether we need to limit open justice in a nuanced manner. Being able to see a trial is not a vital function of open justice; instead, good enough institutional transparency can be achieved with live blogs without the added intrusion of being filmed (Flower 2023; Flower and Ahlefeldt 2021; cf. Moore et al. 2019).

Moving forwards, we not only need to reflect on how much access is reasonable, but also take a penetrating look at whether we need to re-assess how evidence is gathered and presented in courts. Moreover, as Townend and Welsh (2023, 12) argue, transparency should be aimed at enabling scrutiny and education, rather than serving as a form of deterrent or punishment.

References

Allan, S. 2006. *Online News: Journalism and the Internet.* Open University Press.

Australia, H. C. O. 2024. "Recent AV Recordings." Retrieved from www.hcourt.gov.au/cases/recent-av-recordings.

Balbi, Gabriele, and Paolo Magaudda. 2018. *A History of Digital Media: An Intermedia and Global Perspective.* New York: Routledge.

Barometer. 2021. "The Media Barometer 2020." Retrieved from https://www.nordicom.gu.se/en/publications/mediebarometern-2020.

Barrett, J. 2011. "Open Justice or Open Season? Developments in Judicial Engagement with Social Media." *Queensland University of Technology Law and Justice Journal* 11:1–8.

Bartels, L., and J. Lee. 2013. "Jurors Using Social Media in Our Courts: Challenges and Responses." *Journal of Judicial Administration* 23:35–57.

Bauman, Z. 2007. *Konsumtionsliv.* Translated by S.-E. Torhell. Göteborg: Daidalos.

Bentham, J. 1843a. "Bentham's Draught for the Organization of Judicial Establishments, Compared with That of the National Assembly." In *Works of Jeremy Bentham*, edited by J. Bowring. Vol. 4. Edinburgh: William Tait.

Bentham, J. 1843b. "Principles of Judicial Procedure." In *The Works of Jeremy Bentham.* Vol. 2, edited by J. Bowring. Edinburgh: William Tait.

Bernzen, A. K. 2018. "The Court and the Camera: Should Privacy Be a Concern in Court Reporting?" *Journal of Media Law* 10 (1):37–48. https://doi.org/10.1080/17577632.2018.1466442

Biber, K. 2018. "Dignity in the Digital Age: Broadcasting the Oscar Pistorius Trial." *Crime, Media, Culture* 15 (3):401–422. https://doi.org/10.1177/1741659018780191.

Biressi, A., and H. Nunn. 2003. "Video Justice: Crimes of Violence in Social/Media Space." *Space and Culture* 6 (3):276–291. https://doi.org/10.1177/1206331203251659.

Bock, M. A., and J. A. Araiza. 2015. "Facing the Death Penalty While Facing the Cameras: A Case Study of Television Journalism Work Routines." *Journalism Practice* 9 (3):314–331. https://doi.org/10.1080/17512786.2014.964496.

Bogoch, B., and A. Peleg. 2014. "Law in the Age of Media Logic." In *Mediatization of Communication*, edited by K. Lundby, 443–462. Berlin: De Gruyter.

Borgida, E., K. G. DeBono, and L. A. Buckman. 1990. "Cameras in the Courtroom: The Effects of Media Coverage on Witness Testimony and Juror Perceptions." *Law and Human Behavior* 14 (5):489. Retrieved from http://ludwig.lub.lu.se/login?url=https://search.ebscohost.com/login.aspx?direct=true&db=edsjsr&AN=edsjsr.1393937&site=eds-live&scope=site.

Bosland, J., and J. Townend. 2018. "Open Justice, Transparency and the Media: Representing the Public Interest in the Physical and Virtual Courtroom." *Communications Law* 23 (4):183–202.

Burger, P. 2016. "The Bloody History of the True Crime Genre." *JSTOR Daily.* Retrieved from https://daily.jstor.org/bloody-history-of-true-crime-genre/.

Cars, T. 2021. "TV-sända rättegångar – transparens eller spektakel." *Nordsteds Juridik.* Retrieved from www.nj.se/nyheter/tv-sanda-rattegangar-efterstravansvard-transparens-eller-integritetskrankande-spektakel.

Chamberlain, P., M. Keppel-Palmer, S. Reardon, and T. Smith. 2019. "It Is Criminal: The State of Magistrates' Court Reporting in England and Wales." *Journalism* 22 (9):2404–2420. https://doi.org/10.1177/1464884919868049.

Cohn, M., and D. Dow. 2002. *Cameras in the Courtroom: Television and the Pursuit of Justice.* Lanham, MD and Oxford: Rowman & Littlefield.

Commission, N. Z. 2009. *Suppressing Names and Evidence.* Wellington.

Courts, U. 2024. "History of Cameras, Broadcasing, and Remote Public Access in Courts." Retrieved from www.uscourts.gov/about-federal-courts/judicial-administration/cameras-courts/history-cameras-broadcasting-and-remote#a1.

Douglas, L. 1995. "Film as Witness: Screening Nazi Concentration Camps before the Nuremberg Tribunal." *Yale Law Journal* 105:449–482.
Ericson, R. V., P. M. Baranek, and J. B. L. Chan, eds. 1991. *Representing Order: Crime, Law, and Justice in the News Media*. Milton Keynes: Open University Press.
Fan, H., and F. Lap Fung Lee. 2019. "Judicial Visibility Under Responsive Authoritarianism: A Study of the Live Broadcasting of Court Trials in China." *Media, Culture & Society* 41 (8):1088–1106. https://doi.org/10.1177/0163443718807377.
Fenn, Ryan. 2022. "This Isn't a Reality Show: How Social Media Livestreams of High-Profile Criminal Trials May Violate One's Right to a Fair Trial Notes." *St. John's Law Review* 96 (3):789–814.
Findlay, L. 2015. "Courting Social Media in Australia's Criminal Courtrooms: The Continuing Tension between Promoting Open Justice and Protecting Procedural Integrity." *Current Issues in Criminal Justice* 27 (2):237–246. Retrieved from http://ludwig.lub.lu.se/login?url=https://search.ebscohost.com/login.aspx?direct=true&db=edshol&AN=edshol.hein.journals.cicj27.22&site=eds-live&scope=site.
Flower, L. 2023. "Live Blogs Can't Handle the Truth? A Contemporary Cross-Cultural Consideration of Transparency and Procedural Justice." *Oñati Socio-Legal Series* 13 (5): 1690–1710. Retrieved from https://opo.iisj.net/index.php/osls/article/view/1674.
Flower, L., and M.-S. Ahlefeldt. 2021. "The Criminal Trial as a Live Event: Exploring How and Why Live Blogs Change the Professional Practices of Judges, Defence Lawyers and Prosecutors." *Media, Culture & Society* 43 (8):1480–1496. https://doi.org/10.1177/01634437211022730.
Foucault, Michel. 1975/1991. *Discipline and Punish: The Birth of the Prison*. Translated by Alan Sheridan. New York: Random House.
French, J. R. 2006. "Radio and Television Broadcasting in the Magistrates' Courts – Is There a Future?" *Federal Judicial Scholarship* 3:6–21.
Garcia-Blanco, I., and L. Bennett. 2018. "Between a 'Media Circus' and 'Seeing Justice Being Done': Metajournalistic Discourse and the Transparency of Justice in the Debate on Filming Trials in British Newspapers." *Journalism*. https://doi.org/10.1177/1464884918760025
Giles, J. 2021. "Judge Declares Mistrial After Witness Reveals She Shared Live Stream on Facebook." 16 September. Retrieved from www.wtvm.com/2021/09/16/judge-declares-mistrial-after-witness-reveals-she-shared-live-stream-facebook/.
Goehler, R. M., M. L. Dias, and D. Bralow. 2010. "The Legal Case for Twitter in the Courtroom." *Communications Lawyer* 27 (1):14–17. Retrieved from https://heinonline.org/HOL/P?h=hein.journals/comlaw27&i=14.
Goffman, E. 1963. *Stigma: Notes on the Management of Spoiled Identity*. NJ: Prentice-Hall Inc.
Haggerty, K. 2006. "Tear Down the Walls: On Demolishing the Panopticon." In *Theorizing Surveillance: The Panopticon and Beyond*, edited by David Lyon, 23–45. Cullompton: Willan.
Hall-Coates, S. 2015. "Following Digital Media into the Courtroom: Publicity and the Open Court Principle in the Information Age." *Dalhousie Journal of Legal Studies* 24:101–139. Retrieved from http://ludwig.lub.lu.se/login?url=https://search.ebscohost.com/login.aspx?direct=true&db=a9h&AN=114122814&site=eds-live&scope=site.
Hans, V. P., and J. L. Dee. 1991. "Media Coverage of Law: Its Impact on Juries and the Public." *American Behavioral Scientist* 35 (2):136–149. https://doi.org/10.1177/0002764291035002005
Jaconelli, J. 2002. *Open Justice: A Critique of the Public Trial*. Oxford: Oxford University Press.
Jewkes, Y. 2015. *Media and Crime*. 3rd ed. London: Sage Publications Ltd.
Johnston, A., and A. Wallace. 2015. "Tweeting from Court: New Guidelines for Modern Media." *Media Arts Law Review* 20 (1):15–32.

Johnston, J. 2018. "Three phases of courts' publicity: reconfiguring Bentham's open justice in the twenty-first century." *International Journal of Law in Context* 14 (4):525–538.

Karlsson, M. 2011. "The Immediacy of Online News, the Visibility of Journalistic Processes and a Restructuring of Journalistic Authority." *Journalism* 12 (3):279–295.

Kassin, S. 1984. "TV Cameras, Public Self-Consciousness, and Mock Juror Performance." *Journal of Experimental Social Psychology* 20:336–349. https://doi.org/10.1016/0022-1031(84)90030-1

Keyzer, P., J. Johnston, M. L. Pearson, S. Rodrick, and A. Wallace. 2013. "The Courts and Social Media: What Do Judges and Court Workers Think." *Judicial Officers' Bulletin* 25 (6):47–51.

Krawitz, M. 2013. "Stop the Presses, But Not the Tweets: Why Australian Judicial Officials Should Permit Journalists to Use Social Media in the Courtroom." *Flinders Law Journal* 15 (1):1–39.

Lambert, P. 2011. *Courting Publicity: Twitter and Television Cameras in Court.* West Sussex: Bloomsbury Professional.

Lanzara, G. F. 2009. "Reshaping Practice Across Media: Material Mediation, Medium Specificity and Practical Knowledge in Judicial Work." *Organization Studies* 30 (12):1369–1390. https://doi.org/10.1177/0170840609349873.

Liu, Z., and Y. Tang. 2024. "Live Broadcasting the Courtroom: A Field Experiment in Real Trials." *SSRN.* Retrieved from https://papers.ssrn.com/sol3/papers.cfm?abstract_id=4778348.

Marder, N. S. 2012. "The Conundrum of Cameras in the Courtroom." *Arizona State Law Journal* 44 (4):1489–1574. Retrieved from https://heinonline.org/HOL/P?h=hein.journals/arzjl44&i=1525; https://heinonline.org/HOL/PrintRequest?handle=hein.journals/arzjl44&collection=journals&div=60&id=1525&print=section&sction=60.

Mason, P. 2000. "Lights, Camera, Justice? Cameras in the Courtroom: An Outline of the Issues." *Crime Prevention and Community Safety* 2 (3):23–34. https://doi.org/10.1057/palgrave.cpcs.8140063.

Moore, S. 2018. "Towards a Sociology of Institutional Transparency: Openness, Deception and the Problem of Public Trust." *Sociology* 52 (2):416–430. https://doi.org/10.1177/0038038516686530.

Moore, S., A. Clayton, and H. Murphy. 2019. "Seeing Justice Done: Courtroom Filming and the Deceptions of Transparency." *Crime, Media, Culture*, 1741659019883764. https://doi.org/10.1177/1741659019883764.

Moran, L. J. 2016. "Visible Justice: YouTube and the UK Supreme Court." *The Annual Review of Interdisciplinary Justice Research* 5:223–263.

Mulcahy, L. 2010. *Legal Architecture: Justice, Due Process and the Place of Law*. London: Routledge.

Museum, N. W. 2020. "Curactor's Choice: Nuremberg Trial Visitor." Retrieved from www.nationalww2museum.org/war/articles/nuremberg-trial-tickets.

Nasheri, H. 2002. *Crime and Justice in the Age of Court TV.* LFB Scholarly Pub.

Nelson, Camilla. 2023. "The 'Most Maligned' Witness in the Christopher Dawson Case: Gender, Power, Media and Legal Culture in the Digitally Distributed Live-Streamed Court." *Crime, Media, Culture.* 20 (1):83–106.

Observer, S. C. 2024. "How Courts Across the World Broadcast Proceedings." 25 January 2021. Retrieved from www.scobserver.in/journal/how-courts-across-the-world-broadcast-proceedings/.

Packer, C. 2013. "Should Courtroom Observers Be Allowed to Use Their Smartphones and Computers in Court? An Examination of the Arguments." *American Journal of Trial Advocacy* 36 (3):573–595. Retrieved from http://ludwig.lub.lu.se/login?url=https://search.ebscohost.com/login.aspx?direct=true&db=a9h&AN=110609492&site=eds-live&scope=site.

Palaces, T. D. A. F. C. A. 2021. "Media Development in Denmark: Summary and Discourse." Retrieved from https://mediernesudvikling.kum.dk/fileadmin/user_upload/dokumenter/medier/Mediernes_udvikling/2020/Overblik_og_perspektivering/Summary_and_discourse_2020.pdf.

Peters, A. 2013. "Towards Transparency as a Global Norm." In *Transparency in International Law*, edited by A. Bianchi and A. Peters, 534–607. Cambridge: Cambridge University Press.

Pollack, E. 2001. *En Studie i Medier och Brott*. Stockholm: Stockholms Universitet.

Postema, G. J. 2013. "The Soul of Justice: Bentham on Publicity, Law, and the Rule of Law." In *Bentham's Theory of Law & Public Opinion*, edited by X. Zhai and M. Quinn, 40–62. Cambridge: Cambridge University Press.

Reiner, R., S. Livingstone, and J. Allen. 2000. "No More Happy Endings? The Media and Popular Concern About Crime Since the Second World War." In *Crime, Risk and Insecurity: Law and Order in Everyday Life and Political Discourse*, edited by T. Hope and R. Sparks, 107–126. London: Routledge.

Resnik, J. 2013. "The Democracy in Courts: Jeremy Bentham, 'Publicity', and the Privatization of Process in the Twenty-First Century." *NoFo: An Interdisciplinary Journal or Law and Justice* 10 (1):77–119.

Rodrick, S. 2014. "Achieving the Aims of Open Justice – The Relationship between the Courts, the Media and the Public." *Deakin Law Review* 19 (1):123–162. Retrieved from http://ludwig.lub.lu.se/login?url=https://search.ebscohost.com/login.aspx?direct=true&db=edshol&AN=edshol.hein.journals.deakin19.8&site=eds-live&scope=site.

Ross, A. 1995. "Television View; Watching for a Judgment of Real Evil." *New York Times*, 12 November.

Sanders, A. 2021. "Video-Hearings in Europe Before, During and after the COVID-19 Pandemic The COVID-19 Crisis – Lessons for the Courts: Academic Article." *International Journal for Court Administration* 12 (2):1–21. Retrieved from https://heinonline.org/HOL/P?h=hein.journals/ijca12&i=124; https://heinonline.org/HOL/PrintRequest?handle=hein.journals/ijca12&collection=journals&div=14&id=124&print=section&sction=14.

Schultz, J. 1998. *Reviving the Fourth Estate: Democracy, Accountability & The Media*. Cambridge: Cambridge Unviersity Press.

Sharples, C. 2013. "Holocaust on Trial: Mass Observation and British Media Responses to the Nuremberg Tribunal, 1945–1946." In *Britain and the Holocaust: Remembering and Representing War and Genocide*, edited by C. Sharples and O. Jensen, 31–50. London: Palgrave Macmillan UK.

Small, T. A., and K. Puddister. 2020. "Play-by-Play Justice: Tweeting Criminal Trials in the Digital Age." *Canadian Journal of Law and Society/Revue Canadienne Droit et Société* 35 (1):1–22. https://doi.org/10.1017/cls.2019.21.

Smolej, M., and J. Kivivuori. 2008. "Crime News Trends in Finland: A Review of Recent Research." *Journal of Scandinavian Studies in Criminology and Crime Prevention* 9 (1):202–219.

Stepniak, D. 2007. "Cameras in Court: Reluctant Admission to Proactive Collaboration." In *The Courts and the Media*, edited by P. Keyzer, A. Johnston, and M. Pearson, 66–78. Braddon: Halstead Press.

Stepniak, D. 2008. *Audio-visual Coverage of Courts: A Comparative Analysis*. Cambridge: Cambridge University Press.

Strinäs, L. 2021. "De stora farorna med tv-sända rättegångar." *Expressen*. Retrieved from www.expressen.se/debatt/de-stora-farorna-med-tv-sanda-rattegangar/.

Tandoc, E. C., Z. W. Lim, and R. Ling. 2018. "Defining 'Fake News'." *Digital Journalism* 6 (2):137–153. https://doi.org/10.1080/21670811.2017.1360143.

Taneja, Harsh, James G. Webster, Edward C. Malthouse, and Thomas B. Ksiazek. 2012. "Media Consumption Across Platforms: Identifying User-Defined Repertoires." *New Media and Society* 14 (6):951–968.

Taylor, C. 2004. *Modern Social Imaginaries*. Duke University Press.
Thompson, E. 2011. "Does the Open Justice Principle Require Cameras to Be Permitted in the Courtroom and the Broadcasting of Legal Proceedings." *Journal of Media Law* 3 (2):211–236. Retrieved from http://ludwig.lub.lu.se/login?url=https://search.ebscohost.com/login.aspx?direct=true&AuthType=ip,uid&db=edshol&AN=edshol.hein.journals.joomaw3.17&site=eds-live&scope=site.
Thompson, J. B. 2005. "The New Visibility." *Theory, Culture & Society* 22 (6):31–51. https://doi.org/10.1177/0263276405059413.
Thompson, J. B. 2013. *Media and Modernity: A Social Theory of the Media*. Hoboken: Polity.
Thurman, N., and A. Walters. 2013. "Live Blogging – Digital Journalism's Pivotal Platform? A Case Study of the Production, Consumption and Form of Live Blogs at Guardian.co.uk." *Digitial Journalism* 1 (1):82–101.
Townend, J., and L. Welsh. 2023. *Observing Justice: Digital Transparency, Openness and Accountability in Criminal Courts*. Policy Press.
Turnbull, S. 2010. "Crime as Entertainment: The Case of the TV Crime Drama." *Continuum* 24 (6):819–827.
Twining, W. 1985. *Theories of Evidence. Bentham and Wigmore*. Palo Alto, CA: Stanford University Press.
UKSC, C. O. 2015. "Catch-Up on Court Action: Supreme Court Laugnes 'Video on Demand' Service [Press release]." Retrieved from www.supremecourt.uk/docs/news-release-150505.pdf.
van Rees, Kees, and Koen van Eijck. 2003. "Media Repertoires of Selective Audiences: The Impact of Status, Gender, and Age on Media Use." *Poetics* 31 (5):465–490.
Wexler, D. 2000. "Therapeutic Jurisprudence: An Overview." *Thomas M. Cooley Law Review* 17:125.
Youm, K. H. 2012. "Cameras in the Courtroom in the Twenty-First Century: The U.S. Supreme Court Learning from Abroad." *Brigham Young University Law Review* 2012 (6):1989–2032. Retrieved from https://heinonline.org/HOL/P?h=hein.journals/byulr2012&i=2042; https://heinonline.org/HOL/PrintRequest?handle=hein.journals/byulr2012&collection=journals&div=73&id=2042&print=section&sction=73.

4 Engagement

The adoption of social media by courts represents a relatively recent phenomenon in the progression of court publicity, evolving from traditional press coverage, to the introduction of media liaison officers, and now to digital platforms (see Johnston 2018).[1] Initially, courts were cautious about engaging with social media due to concerns over privacy and security. However, as social media has become increasingly prevalent, many courts have begun to utilise these platforms to communicate with the public and share information about court proceedings. Today, most courts maintain a social media presence on platforms like X and Facebook.

Social media can therefore be an effective means for courts to engage with the public and is thought to enhance transparency, accessibility, and understanding of judicial processes. By disseminating information about court decisions, updates on cases, and educational posts about their work, courts can demystify legal proceedings and foster public trust.

However, this approach is fraught with significant challenges. Risks include the potential misinterpretation of legal information, breaches of confidentiality, and threats to judicial impartiality. Whilst social media provides valuable opportunities for public outreach and legal education, it also presents notable legal and ethical issues, including issues related to privacy, potential bias, and the implications for the fairness of court proceedings. It therefore carries risks that could undermine the integrity and credibility of the judicial system.

In this chapter, I examine how the courts and legal professionals utilise social media to engage with the broader society, highlighting both the advantages and challenges of this trend. The central theme revolves around the duality of social media: while it serves as a tool for enhancing transparency and educating the public about legal processes, its role as a common communication medium also introduces the risk of misuse by judges, jurors, and others. This raises an important question: where do we draw the line between appropriate use and potential abuse?

1 For a discussion on the problem of upholding the disciplinary function when courts are privatized, see (Resnik 2013).

DOI: 10.4324/9781003344643-4

I begin with an overview of various social media platforms, then trace their use within the judicial system with concrete examples of how courts have adopted these tools. Finally, I discuss the benefits, challenges, and considerations associated with this integration, highlighting the delicate balance that courts and legal professionals must negotiate between ensuring judicial impartiality and exercising their right to communicate, and between ensuring open justice whilst protecting the personal integrity of all trial participants.

What is social media?

Before diving into social media and engagement, I would like to give a concise overview of the subject at hand, namely social media. The term *social media* was first used in the mid-1990s to describe the evolution of the internet from a static document archive into a dynamic network of users, actively participating and interacting with each other (Bercovici 2010; see also Aichner et al. 2020). It is generally used as an umbrella term for a range of digital platforms such as social networks, forums, social gaming, blogs, business networks, and virtual words (boyd and Ellison 2007; Aichner et al. 2020) which are "built around the convergence of content sharing, public communication, and interpersonal connection" (Burgess, Marwick, and Poell 2018, 1). Social media platforms are thus used for job seeking, socialising, romance, interacting with companies, doing business, and more. From platforms such as Facebook and X (formerly known as Twitter) being a source of youth distraction, these have become embedded into public institutions, societal organisations, and corporations.[2]

There are different types of social media platforms which van Dijck (2013) divides into four categories but notes that their boundaries are fairly fluid: (1) social network sites, used foremostly to promote interpersonal contact, such as Facebook, LinkedIn, and X; (2) user-generated content sites, which support creativity and encourage the exchange of content, such as YouTube and Wikipedia; (3) trading and marketing sites, aimed at selling or exchanging products, such as eBay and Amazon; and (4) play and game sites such as Minecraft and Fortnite. My focus in this book is on social network sites and user-generated content sites (although in 2004 a New York woman who was being evicted from her flat placed a listing on eBay selling the judge presiding over her case. The "judge for sale" garnered 21 bids with a top price of

2 In some parts of the world, access to the internet is considered so important that laws are in place to limit the state's ability to restrict internet access (e.g. Costa Rica, Estonia, Finland, France, Greece), whilst in other areas (such as China and Egypt), the opposite has occurred with governments curbing unrestricted internet access due to the perceived damaging effects such access could have on political, social, or economic order (Dutton and Graham 2019). As mentioned in chapter one, the digital divide separating those with the means, capability, and experience of accessing the internet continues to prevail with the digitally disadvantage becoming more prevalent.

$127,50 – including shipping – before the listing was removed for violating eBay's policy prohibiting the sale of humans (CNN 2004)).

Figures from March 2024 indicate that 5.17 billion people use social media, constituting over 63 percent of the world's population (Demandsage 2024). Facebook remains the biggest social media platform with 3.05 billion users (followed by WhatsApp and YouTube) (Demandsage 2024)[3] and is particularly strong in middle-income countries (Center 2024). LinkedIn is also a strong contender with over 1 billion members (LinkedIn 2024).

The original roots of Facebook saw its founder, Mark Zuckerberg, professing a desire to "make the world more transparent" (as quoted in van Dijck 2013, 14). Buzzwords such as transparency, sociality, openness, and sharing were key. The rise of social media has, however, faced a standoff between supporters and critics. Enthusiasts see it as a tool for connection, creation, and the development of new spheres whereby the space between private and public becomes fuzzy, thereby enabling new identity formation (Papacharissi 2010). In contrast, critics see social media platforms as tools of surveillance and attacks on privacy. These are issues that remain central in the current debate around social media.

Over the past recent decades, social media has nevertheless become an integral part of everyday life for many across the globe, with online and offline interactions amalgamated into their daily lives (Hine 2000). The courts also picked up on this trend, with a *Future Trends* report written by the National Center for State Courts stating in 2011: "courts must now decide not if we will embrace social media but when and to what degree" (Slayton 2011, 24, cited in Johnston 2017, 671). From the early 2010s, courts in jurisdictions such as Australia, England, and the US began to reorient their external communication practices towards social media (Johnston 2017), and it is now used by courts across the globe, including France, Philippines, Denmark, and Costa Rica. For instance, a recent study of Ghanese judges finds that social media usage is on the rise, particularly amongst younger judges (Adu 2022).

Thus as the internet has evolved from a place of networked communication via weblogs and email to one of platformed sociality, where everyday social practices shape day-to-day life and are becoming a "part of society's institutional fabric" (van Dijck 2013, 5–6), the courts are increasingly opening up to the use of social media as a vital tool. So, how has social media usage evolved in the judicial sphere?

The evolution of courts' use of social media

Courts' strategies towards publicity have evolved through three phases: "the press, media liaison, and media management" (Johnston 2018, 526). The first

3 Although a typical social media user interacts with 6 or 7 social platforms every month with the widespread penetration of smartphones accounting for this user growth (Demandsage 2024).

of these centred on press coverage with the news media relating trials and the justice system more generally first with the use of newspaper reports, and most recently with live blogging trials and livestreamed trials. The second phase entailed the appointment of court information officers or judicial press officers, whose role entails dealing with media communications and enquiries. In some jurisdictions, such as in Sweden, this also includes a "Media Team" – a list of judges who are designated media contacts, who may be contacted for specific enquiries regarding law and questions relating to courts. The final phase is the internet, which includes the use of court websites to inform about legal happenings such as decisions, rulings, and appeals, along with official appointments and about public access to courts and legal proceedings more generally, as well as social media. This final phase has shaped "contemporary practices of court-generated media" (Johnston 2018, 525), including the use of social media.

Social media has the opportunity for enabling a more "dialogic" (Johnston 2018, 532) form of interaction, facilitating the courts to proactively manage the message and the impression they are attempting to make. Hence, the courts are no longer as reliant on the media for this, rather they can rely on their internally driven media channels, including livestreaming trials, and, of relevance for the current chapter, social media channels. Whether such an exchange-oriented interaction is enabled, thus allowing two-way communication between the courts and society, or remains a one-way channel of information is tied to whether the courts enable commenting functions (Keyzer et al. 2013). This is important, not least in those jurisdictions battling with low levels of trust in courts, as one of the goals of transparency is for people to have faith in the accountability, competence, and integrity of courts which, in turn, leads to the placement of trust. Social media can thus be used by courts to expose people to information and news, which can contribute to raising awareness and knowledge of these issues (see Boulianne 2019 for a more developed overview).

A range of social media platforms are currently used by courts across the globe. For instance, according to the website for the National Center for State Courts in the US, X and YouTube are the most widely used social media platforms used by state courts, followed by LinkedIn and Facebook, with Instagram used only by a handful of courts (NCSC 2024).

We can take the International Criminal Court (ICC) as an illustrative example of how other courts are also using platforms. During 2024, the ICC used Instagram, X, Facebook, YouTube, LinkedIn, and Flickr. There are slight variations in how each of these platforms were used, and significant differences in their apparent reach. For instance, their X page was used for a wider range of information conveyance including policies on, for instance, gender-based crime, information about upcoming trials including links to webstreams, and information about ongoing trials, including details regarding which witness was testifying, verdicts, and more. In August 2024, the page had over 790,000 followers, with posts tending to gain around 10,000 viewings. Over 16,000 tweets and retweets were posted, with certain ones gaining significantly more viewings, such as a video calling for information and cooperation in relation to allegations of international crimes committed in Darfur, which gained over 336,000 views.

The ICC's Instagram page is used for education and informing about the process of legal proceedings, their outreach work, official visits, and new appointments. It is also used for disseminating information regarding charges against defendants who have not been located. This account has over 140,000 followers and over 1600 posts.

Their Facebook page has over 312,000 followers and, again, follows a similar type of communication strategy as the X page with a wider range of information conveyed, including information about their outreach activities and the work they do, along with information about trials, including links to livestreams.

The court also has a YouTube channel with over 108,000 subscribers and hosts over 2400 videos, including informational films regarding their work, together with calls for information in relation to crimes (for instance in Darfur, Sudan), rulings, and recordings from proceedings.

There is also a LinkedIn page with over 236,000 followers. This page is primarily used for disseminating information about recruitment opportunities, together with information on how the ICC works, as well as sharing relevant posts from, for instance, Trust Fund for Victims at the ICC.

And finally, the ICC also has a Flickr page with photos from various proceedings, moot courts, and suchlike. This has only 696 followers, despite being updated on a regular basis since 2008.

The ICC uses social media platforms to provide information about proceedings, including schedules and information about witnesses, in real time to many followers. Although it appears that only a small fraction of the followers sees the majority of posts, in high-profile cases they gain widespread attention. This can help to ensure that the public is informed. There are also educational films and posts explaining what the ICC does, such as explaining which crimes lie under the ICC's jurisdiction. Interestingly, there are also calls for help in finding suspects, as in the case with the call for information regarding the whereabouts of Joseph Kony, accused of numerous war crimes and crimes against humanity. The ICC thus uses social media to push beyond the original boundaries of publicity to include a type of surveillance approach – asking for information regarding the whereabouts of suspects. Finally, LinkedIn is used to advertise employment positions available, again serving to spread information about the court as a possible employer.

Why do courts engage via social media?

I suggest there are two central driving forces discernible behind the ICC's – and other courts' – use of social media engagement, two aspects which together constitute a form of impression management. The first is that social media is regarded as an unavoidable facet of twenty-first century life: contemporary society is a digital society. The second is the continued drive towards increased transparency. Courts thus use social media to fulfil open justice functions: communication, education, and transparency. For instance, the ICC thus uses social media to present an impression of itself as a legal institution aimed at actively upholding justice, with the help of international citizens. Social media is not only a tool for the courts to ensure open justice, but also a strategy for conveying an impression – a way of constructing a certain understanding of the courts, its actors, and the work within. This means that social media is a powerful means of presenting the courts to society. However, the case for social media is not as clear cut as it first appears . . .

In a comparative study of Canada, Ireland, and Australia, Townend and Wiener (2021) find that public confidence in the justice system may increase if the public has "access to materials, data and educational tools – they are able to have more confidence in the justice system and observe for themselves if justice is being done fairly" (Townend and Wiener 2021, 117) and that less transparent systems may dissuade people from engaging in the justice system or, indeed, pursue other forms of justice that may have risky outcomes. Courts in Ireland, Canada, and Australia all actively worked with reach-out programs to increase public confidence, including the use of social media. This is a trend seen in many other jurisdictions. Upon first glance, social media contributes to achieving the goals of open justice.

However, the impact of new social media on the judicial system and the people within is multitudinous and oftentimes ambiguous. For instance, whilst social media has enabled a spotlight to be placed on legal proceedings, such as in lower courts which work with the everyday mundane events and which tend to gather less news media coverage (Chamberlain et al. 2019), it has also increased the difficulty of insulating jurors, witnesses, and other participants from outside influences (Surette 2015). Surette (2015) argues further that social media has also increased the challenge of conducting high-profile trials by transforming small, local proceedings into national events, thereby placing greater demands on court infrastructures (e.g. Wi-Fi networks, seating, and such).

This duality can therefore see social media platforms being used to support open justice, but simultaneously, have more damaging consequences. This has been shown in studies by Bosland and Townend (2018) and Hall-Coates (2015), who both present legal reviews of US rulings. The aforementioned explores tensions between legal and ethical considerations of open justice finding that, on the one hand, these forms of reporting can enable direct communication with the public, but on the other hand, limited judicial understandings of digital technologies and the risks associated with online publication may impact more negatively on open justice (see also Janoski-Haehlen 2011).

The second of these law reviews by Hall-Coates (2015) also finds a balance at play. Social media usage is found to have the potential to improve accessibility, judicial accountability, and freedom of speech, thereby increasing transparency by demystifying the judicial process (Hall-Coates 2015). However, digital media platforms also enable anonymous citizens to construct and spread courtroom narratives that may border on misinformation and impinge on the personal integrity of those depicted. Digital media technology can thus act to "both complement and complicate the administration of justice in novel ways" (Hall-Coates 2015).

Likewise, a qualitative study by Small and Puddister (2020) which analyses journalist tweets from trials in Canada finds that whilst live blogging may improve access to court, it does little to increase engagement with, or understanding of, the legal system.

Moving to the Australasian context, a law review conducted by Barrett (2011) explores the tension between the judiciary and social media with a particular focus on the balance between jurors' use of social media and freedom of expression versus open justice and privacy,[4] as I will return to shortly. Both Barrett (2011) and Bosland and Townend (2018) find that suppression orders are used and, at times, abused to restrict social media usage. In line with one of the central arguments in this book, Barrett concludes that the law has not kept abreast of digital developments (Barrett 2011, 30).

Turning to the voices of those working within the judicial system and how they view the use of social media, a study by Keyzer and colleagues in Australia surveyed 62 legal professionals (such as judges, magistrates, and court public information officers) regarding the impact and issues arising from the use of social media in court (Keyzer et al. 2013). This is one of the few studies that has highlighted the voices of judges and magistrates with regards to social media usage including X. The survey identified and ranked problems in order of importance with regards to the challenges and opportunities that social media poses for the courts (Keyzer et al. 2013). They found that juror misuse, the risk of suppressed information being inadvertently spread and "going viral," misrepresentation of court work and misinformation about trial processes, as well as disclosure of information to witnesses of others waiting outside court were ranked as problematic (Keyzer et al. 2013; see also Lambert 2011).

We therefore see that the goal of open justice is not necessarily fulfilled by engaging via social media. Moreover, despite the potential benefits, the court's use of social media also raises important legal and ethical issues. One of the main concerns is privacy. Courts need to ensure that they are not sharing confidential information on social media platforms and that they are complying with privacy laws and regulations.[5]

4 Whilst outside the scope of this article, it is important to note that a similar field of research regarding televised trials has also examined the interplay between the courts, media, and public, finding similar tensions (see e.g. Biber 2018; Mason 2000; Thompson 2011; Gerbner 1979; Garcia-Blanco and Bennett 2018; Marder 2012; Bernzen 2018).

5 Social media is also important in shaping the experience of fear of crime. For instance, Näsi and colleagues (2020) find that traditional media is still the foremost source of information regarding violent crime, however Facebook and Twitter were frequently used for sourcing such

In the next section, I zoom in on the use of social media by those actors within the courts: judges and jurors.

Judicial use of social media

Yet another vital balance to be drawn concerns the judicial use of social media. The backbone of the legal system is judicial impartiality. Judges are therefore expected to exercise restraint in making public pronouncements or statements. This stems not only from the demands on judges to maintain impartiality, but also from the authority of the judiciary more broadly. Judges speaking out on pending or ongoing cases may risk being perceived as biased and thus unable to make an impartial judgement (Seibert-Fohr 2019). Likewise, reading social media posts by others may also risk impinging on a judge's impartiality.

A more slippery area is judges who create, comment on, or share posts on other subjects, such as political parties or ideological debates, who may also be interpreted as having an opinion that impinges on their ability to maintain neutrality. For instance, in many European countries, judges may not participate actively in politics while in office and should not mix personal views with their judicial office (Seibert-Fohr 2019). In the UK, judges are not permitted to communicate about their judicial work or matters related to the judiciary via social media (Guide of Judicial Conduct 2023). Despite these restrictions, judicial officeholders in the UK are on social media, leading some scholars to claim that said limitations are "unjustified and useless" (Hazlehurst 2022, 253).

This shows that, in the digital age, where our social lives are played out in public in social network platforms, judicial use of social media such as posting on Facebook or X constitutes a major source of debate as it is considered to entail a clash between the right to freedom of expression and the risk of impinging upon judicial impartiality (Browning 2014b; Curry and Fix 2019; Mahmoud and Chiha 2020).

Another example of this is from April 2014, in Texas where a mistrial was called due to Judge Michelle M. Slaughter posting on Facebook about an ongoing trial she was presiding over. She was publicly admonished and ordered to attend and complete an educational course on proper and ethical use of social media by judges. The trial in question was known as the "Boy in the Box" trial and regarded a man accused of punishing his 9-year-old son by keeping

information. Furthermore, they found a link between the type of news consumed and fear of crime, for instance, high levels of violent crime news consumption were connected to a high fear of violent crime. Although causality is not shown, the authors of the study argue that factors such as prior victimization and interest towards crime news content are also consistent with such a link. Perceiving terrorism as a threat to oneself was particularly pertinently linked to the consumption of social media. Näsi and colleagues (2020) reason that fear of terrorism could be linked to more actively seeking out information on social media channels, in contrast to passive consumption of traditional formats.

him in a wooden crate. Judge Slaughter had started a Facebook page intended to be "the most efficient way to fulfil [h]er campaign promise and [h]er own goals of educating the public about our courts" (CJC no.14–0820-DI & 14–0838-DI, p. 1, point 3) as she described it. The page was open to anyone wishing to view it online.

Judge Slaughter began the trial by instructing the selected jurors regarding their use of social media, including using Facebook, as a form of communication and that these rules applied to all parties, including herself. She then posted comments on her Facebook page, describing events taking place during the trial and including evidence that had not yet been entered as such, as well as linking to news articles that contained evidence presented, including evidence that the jurors were asked to disregard.

Judge Slaughter was removed from the case and the defendant was granted a mistrial. She defended her public Facebook comments by arguing that her purpose was to promote "transparency" and to "encourage individuals to come watch the proceedings" (CJC no.14–0820-DI & 14–0838-DI, p. 4, point 21).

This, however, was not Judge Slaughter's first hiccup with social media. In February of the same year, she posted on Facebook, "Bless the jury for their service and especially bless the poor child victims" (CJC no.14–0820-DI & 14–0838-DI, p. 4, point 25) in an ongoing trial for child pornography. The Texas State Commission on Judicial Conduct condemned her actions, ruling,

> Judge Slaughter cast reasonable doubt upon her own impartiality and violated her own admonition to jurors by turning to social media to publicly discuss cases pending in her court, giving rise to a legitimate concern that she would not be fair or impartial.
>
> (CJC no.14–0820-DI & 14–0838-DI, p. 5)

However, the drama did not stop here as Judge Slaughter appealed the decision for her to attend social media classes, claiming that none of her statements expressed bias and all the information she published was publicly available (BBC 2015).

Another example is from 2016 regarding a German judge who posted photos of himself wearing a T-shirt printed with the words "We give your future a home – prison" along with the comment "this is my 'when you get out, I will have retired' look." According to the Federal Court of Justice in Germany, this statement endangered the judge's impartiality (as discussed in Jahn 2021, 145).

Also, in 2021, a mistrial was called in a Danish case based on the presiding judge's comments posted on Facebook (Reuters 2022). The case was held at district court and regarded Morten Messerschmidt, a former European Parliament member and leader of the Danish People's Party (a nationalist and right-wing populist party) who was accused and later sentenced to fraud using EU funds and document forgery. However, the judgement was later annulled after it was discovered that the presiding judge in the case had liked comments on Facebook that criticised the defendant and his party. The appeals court reasoned that, although a judge's generally held political and social beliefs are not in themselves cause for disqualification from presiding, statements about the defendant's person and, in particular, about the trial at hand could imply that the judge was not suitable to preside.

These cases show that the line between social media use and abuse is not always clear and risks leading to misinterpretation without clear laws for its appropriate usage in place.

Moreover, social media posts by judges risk damaging the public's perception of the judiciary for future cases she or he may preside over due to the long-standing "presence" of social media posts over time – constantly available (Jahn 2021). Jahn (2021) notes that it may be not only the wording of a post that indicates a lack of impartiality, but also the sheer number of posts. This pertains not only to posts made by the judge, but also on posts in discussion forums of social media sites where they engage in debate with others.

This can be understood as the blurring of boundaries between private and public, stemming from the "context collapse" (Marwick and boyd 2010) that arises when judges post on social media. Context collapse refers to the phenomenon whereby social media users must navigate the challenge of presenting themselves to different audiences simultaneously on the same platform. This can lead to issues regarding communication and self-presentation, as the content intended for one audience may be read by another, leading to potential misunderstandings or conflicts. This is of interest here as the blurring of legal professionals' boundaries, particularly judges who post in a private and/or professional role may have important consequences for how they, and the courts more broadly, are perceived (Liebler and Chaney 2014).

The use of social media by legal professionals may therefore create conflicts of interest, particularly if it is unclear. On the one hand lies judges' freedom of expression, on the other hand, the need for the judiciary to remain independent and impartial. A suitable solution is to shift focus away from restrictions and towards educating judges on how to use social media (see also Hazlehurst 2022).

This has triggered codes of conduct for judicial use of social media to be created (e.g. the European Network of Councils for the Judiciary) and with judiciaries drafting guidelines for judicial conduct, for instance as is done in Germany, England, and France (Jahn 2021, 146). The French code of conduct states that the individual is posting in an official role if they are publicly known to be a judge or if their judicial role is disclosed on their profile (Jahn 2021). This is an important distinction to draw as a judge's impartiality comes into conflict with her or his freedom of public expression. Social media is a central way in which people can exercise the right to freedom of expressions, yet as a judge, expressions could indicate an absence of impartiality. For instance, the European Court of Human Rights has a functional approach to this which means that judges are not sanctioned if their social media posts lack a negative impact on the performance of their judicial duties (Jahn 2021). The duty of judicial restraint can therefore encompass the use of social media, if posts are in an official role.

Google mistrials

Another important way in which the courts are impacted by social media is by juror use and abuse. The term "Google mistrials" (Schwartz 2009) was minted in an article in the *New York Times* in 2009 and used to refer to jurors, who have been instructed to not seek out information regarding a case, googling information and causing a mistrial to be called. The case which sparked awareness of this phenomenon was a US federal drug trial in Florida which was declared a mistrial when nine jurors were found to have been researching the case online (Nuzum 2019; McGee 2009).

Since then, cases have abounded. For instance, in Australia in 2022 the conviction of a tutor accused of child sexual offences was quashed after it was revealed a juror had done online searches regarding the case prior to handing down the final verdict, and in 2016 a jury was discharged after two jurors were found to have googled the names and backgrounds of the accused (LAWCPD 2022; see also Goodman-Delahunty and Tait 2022; Grossman and Lev-On 2023; Johnston et al. 2013a, 2013b; Nuzum 2019; McGee 2009; St Eve, Burns, and Zuckerman 2013; Hannaford-Agor, Rottman, and Waters 2012).[6]

TikTok trials

One central way in which social media platforms are changing the ways in which we interact with the courts is via so-called TikTok trials, which is a trial broadcast live on TikTok, as is permitted in certain courts in certain jurisdictions. TikTok trials refer to the ensuing unofficial trial that takes place online where the trial, the actors within, the evidence, and so on are assessed, judged, and criticised. Such trials can go viral, with content and opinions being rapidly spread with the ability to influence public perceptions and understandings, yet without any formal legal or ethical scrutiny.

One of the most well-known TikTok trials was the 2023 defamation case, brought to court by actor Johnny Depp against his ex-wife, actress Amber Heard. Depp sued Heard for $50 million over a 2018 op-ed she published which detailed her experiences as a domestic abuse survivor with the clear implication that Depp was the perpetrator. Heard counter-sued Depp for $100 million, claiming that she was defamed when Depp claimed her allegations were false.

6 Also worth noting is that social media can also be used for intimidating witnesses (Browning 2014a) and that evidence taken from social media is becoming increasingly common, seen as a way of building cases (Surette 2011, 359). This can be a problematic development as it may not consider these posts to be performances, rather it considers them to be a truth (Stuart 2020).

The case drew enormous media attention and, as of June 2023, had over 18 billion views on TikTok.[7] Viewers engaged with the content by commenting, reacting, and sharing. For instance, the hashtag used #justiceforjohnnydepp had nearly 20 billion views, while #justiceforamberheard had closer to 80 million views and the hashtag @amberheardisguilty had 900 million views. The overwhelming support for Johnny Depp in the online TikTok community was, however, coupled with widespread misogyny and online harassment aimed at Amber Heard. The decision of the judge to allow the trial to be televised and livestreamed, therefore, faced criticism that it would stop other victims of domestic violence (which this case included) from coming forwards. The viral nature of TikTok thus enables swift dissemination of information, a speed which can lead to misinformation and disproportionate reactions.

Beyond this, intimate details regarding Depp and Heard's abusive relationship were presented at trial and later discussed, probed, and mocked in TikTok comments and by commentators on TikTok, with thousands of TikTok users providing live commentary in real time. This widespread media attention can be understood as a public shaming process, with the trial becoming a public spectacle. TikTok, along with other social platforms, can thus be used not only for entertainment, but also for creating public discourse. Hence, whilst social media platforms can democratise justice and hold people accountable in ways that the traditional legal system may miss, there are clear dangers with regards to the lack of privacy and fairness and the potential harms caused by such widespread public scrutiny.

The impact of social media

The public's perception of the courts and the legal professionals within is shaped by the posts and comments made by legal institutions and the actors. Social media posts could affect the perception of a judge's competency and impartiality in presiding over a trial, a lawyer's ability to effectively defend a client, or a prosecutor's ability to impartially prosecute a defender. There is a therefore an overarching risk that social media as a tool for ensuring open justice and increasing confidence in the legal system instead serves to damage or diminish this confidence (Boothe-Perry 2014). This may be particularly pertinent if social media usage by the courts and legal professionals is unregulated, or if these actors lack training or education in how to effectively and appropriately use it as an efficient communication and information tool.

Detailed studies identifying the exact impact of social media on understandings are currently few and far between. One study examining the volume and

7 The Depp vs Heard trial was held at a county court in Virginia where cameras and recording devices are allowed if the judge permits.

content of Twitter commentary regarding a decision made by the High Court of Australia found that Twitter was neither well used nor persuasive as a platform for community engagement (Henderson 2018). Indeed,

> Advocating for courts to become actively involved in this "cocktail party from hell" as a means of becoming more responsive in its broader sense assumes that there is a waiting audience open to differing points of view on the work of the courts. This may, in part, be true. As a surrogate of the packed public galleries of bygone age, social media offers a potentially vast audience. However, the overwhelming choice of material available to users means that breaking through the background noise is challenging.
>
> (Henderson 2018, 17)

However, social media has an undeniable impact on trials and courts, leading to verdicts being challenged and overturned as well as juror misconduct leading to mistrials (Johnston et al. 2013). Furthermore, even though we currently do not know enough about the impact of social media, the courts and the legal professionals within "*think* there is an impact" (Hayes and Luther 2018, 64, emphasis added), which has led to the construction of guidelines and rules for social media usage, not only for legal professionals but also for jurors (Gibson 2017). These guidelines are aimed at ensuring that social media usage is ethical and appropriate.

Conclusion

It seems apparent that judges are no longer the "gatekeepers for the flow of information into a courtroom" (Hannaford-Agor, Rottman, and Waters 2012), and indeed, may be – at times –the unintended source of information flow in part stemming from the fuzzy boundaries between personal and professional posts online. The courts face challenges in shaping a public image that more closely reflects their traditional role as fair and impartial institutions dedicated to uncovering truth and administering justice in accordance with the rule of law.

With the growing integration of technology into society shifting us towards becoming "digital natives" (Coombs et al. 2015) who are digitally literate and able to navigate online norms and environments with competency, the courts need to ensure that social media is appropriately used as a vital tool for enabling democracy by enabling transparency and accountability (Nothhaft 2015).

Judicial independence is a cornerstone of legal systems and can coexist with effective communication practices by the courts. The challenge for courts is to find the right balance between maintaining independence and ensuring accountability through a thoughtful and strategic approach to adopting new technologies. Moving forwards, the courts need to continue to engage in social media as a vital tool of open justice, yet doing so in an ethical manner that maintains the integrity of the institution. However, the drive for increased transparency with the help of social media should nevertheless ensure that the rights of those taking part in a trial are protected, due process is upheld, and procedural fairness is maintained.

References

Adu, Kofi Koranteng. 2022. "The Use of Social Media by African Judges. The Ghanaian Experience." *Information Development* 38 (1):40–51.

Aichner, Thomas, Matthias Grünfelder, Oswin Maurer, and Deni Jegeni. 2020. "Twenty-Five Years of Social Media: A Review of Social Media Applications and Definitions from 1994 to 2019." *Cyberpsychology, Behavior, and Social Networking* 24 (4):215–222. https://doi.org/10.1089/cyber.2020.0134.

Barrett, Jonathan. 2011. "Open Justice or Open Season? Developments in Judicial Engagement with Social Media." *Queensland University of Technology Law and Justice Journal* 11:1–8.

BBC. 2015. "Judge Appeals Against Facebook Training Demand." *BBC*, 29 April. Retrieved from www.bbc.com/news/technology-32513074, accessed 19th June 2024.

Bercovici, Jejj. 2010. "Who Coined the Term 'Social Media'? Web Pioneers Compete for Credit." *Forbes*, 9 December.

Bernzen, Anna K. 2018. "The Court and the Camera: Should Privacy Be a Concern in Court Reporting?" *Journal of Media Law* 10 (1):37–48. https://doi.org/10.1080/17577632.2018.1466442.

Biber, Katherine. 2018. "Dignity in the Digital Age: Broadcasting the Oscar Pistorius Trial." *Crime, Media, Culture* 15 (3):401–422. https://doi.org/10.1177/1741659018780191.

Boothe-Perry, Nicola A. 2014. "Friends of Justice: Does Social Media Impact the Public Perception of the Justice System." *Pace Law Review* 35 (1):72–114.

Bosland, Jason, and Judith Townend. 2018. "Open Justice, Transparency and the Media: Representing the Public Interest in the Physical and Virtual Courtroom." *Communications Law* 23 (4):183–202.

Boulianne, Shelley. 2019. "Revolution in the Making? Social Media Effects Across the Globe." *Information, Communication & Society* 22 (1):39–54. https://doi.org/10.1080/1369118X.2017.1353641.

Boyd, Danah M., and Nicole B. Ellison. 2007. "Social Network Sites: Definition, History, and Scholarship." *Journal of Computer-Mediated Communication* 13 (1): 210–230. https://doi.org/10.1111/j.1083-6101.2007.00393.x.

Browning, John G. 2014b. "Why Can't We Be Friends? Judges' Use of Social Media." *University of Miami Law Review* 68 (2):487.

Browning, John. 2014a. "#Snitches Get Stitches: Witness Intimidation in the Age of Facebook and Twitter." *Pace Law Review* 35 (1):192–214.

Burgess, Jean, Alice E. Marwick, and Thomas Poell. 2018. "Editor's Introduction." In *The SAGE Handbook of Social Media*, edited by Jean Burgess, Alice E. Marwick and Thomas Poell, 1–10. London: Sage.

Center, Pew Research. 2024. "WhatsApp and Facebook Dominate the Social Media Landscape in Middle-Income Nations." Retrieved from www.pewresearch.org/short-reads/2024/03/22/whatsapp-and-facebook-dominate-the-social-media-landscape-in-middle-income-nations/, accessed 15th April 2024.

Chamberlain, Phil, Marcus Keppel-Palmer, Sally Reardon, and Thomas Smith. 2019. "It Is Criminal: The State of Magistrates' Court Reporting in England and Wales." *Journalism* 22 (9):2404–2420. https://doi.org/10.1177/1464884919868049.

CNN. 2004. "Judge for 'Sale' Sparks Questions." *CNN*, 13 December. Retrieved from https://money.cnn.com/2004/12/13/news/newsmakers/ebay_judge/, accessed 19th June 2024.

Coombs, W. Timothy, Jesper Falkheimer, Mats Heide, and Philip Young. 2015. *Strategic Communication, Social Media and Democracy: The Challenge of the Digital Naturals*. Milton: Taylor & Francis Group.

Curry, Todd A., and Michael P. Fix. 2019. "May It Please the Twitterverse: The Use of Twitter by State High Court Judges." *Journal of Information Technology & Politics* 16 (4):379–393. https://doi.org/10.1080/19331681.2019.1657048.

Demandsage. 2024. *Social Media Users 2024* (Global Data & Statistics). https://www.demandsage.com/social-media-users/.

Dutton, William H., and Mark Graham. 2019. "Introduction." In *Society and the Internet: How Networks of Information and Communication are Changing Our Lives*. Oxford University Press.

Garcia-Blanco, Iñaki, and Lucy Bennett. 2018. "Between a 'Media Circus' and 'Seeing Justice Being Done': Metajournalistic Discourse and the Transparency of Justice in the Debate on Filming Trials in British Newspapers." *Journalism*. https://doi.org/10.1177/1464884918760025.

Gerbner, George. 1979. "Trial by Television: Are We at the Point of No Return." *Judicature* 63 (9):416–426.

Gibson, Judith. 2017. "Social Media and the Electronic New World of Judges Attitudes." *Revista Forumul Judecatorilor (Judiciary Forum Review)* 2017 (1):26–38.

Goodman-Delahunty, Jane, and David Tait. 2022. "Juries in the Digital Age: Managing Juror Online and Social Media Use During Trial." In *Australian Courts: Controversies, Challenges and Change*, edited by Marg Camilleri and Alistair Harkness, 45–71. Cham: Springer International Publishing.

Grossman, Nerit, and Azi Lev-On. 2023. "Social Media Jurors: Conceptualizing and Analyzing Online Public Engagement in reference to Legal Cases." *Crime, Law and Social Change* 79 (3):223–240. https://doi.org/10.1007/s10611-022-10047-w.

GuidetoJudicialConduct.2023."CourtsandTribunalsJudiciary."Retrievedfromhttps://www.judiciary.uk/guidance-and-resources/guide-to-judicial-conduct-revised-july-2023/.

Hall-Coates, Shauna. 2015. "Following Digital Media into the Courtroom: Publicity and the Open Court Principle in the Information Age." *Dalhousie Journal of Legal Studies* 24:101–139.

Hannaford-Agor, Paula, David B. Rottman, and Nicole L. Waters. 2012. *Juror and Jury Use of New Media: A Baseline Exploration*. National Center for State Courts Williamsburg, VA.

Hayes, Rebecca M., and Kate Luther. 2018. *#crime: Social media, Crime, and the Criminal Legal System*. Cham: Palgrave MacMillan.

Hazlehurst, Lydia Jane. 2022. "Judicial Independence in the Digital Age: The Challenges and Opportunities of Social Media for Judges." Doctorate, School of Law and Social Justice, University of Liverpool.

Henderson, Andrew. 2018. "The High Court and the Cocktail Party from Hell: Can Social Media Improve Community Engagement with the Courts?" In *The Responsive Judge: International Perspectives*, edited by Tania Sourdin and Archie Zariski, 121–141. Singapore: Springer Singapore.

Hine, Christine. 2000. *Virtual Ethnography*. London: Sage publishing.

Jahn, Jannika. 2021. "Social Media Communication by Judges: Assessing Guidelines and New Challenges for Free Speech and Judicial Duties in the Light of the Convention." In *The Rule of Law in Europe: Recent Challenges and Judicial Responses*, edited by María Elósegui, Alina Miron and Iulia Motoc, 137–153. Cham: Springer International Publishing.

Janoski-Haehlen, Emily M. 2011. "The Courts Are All a Twitter: The Implications of Social Media Use in the Courts." *Valparaiso University Law Review* 46 (1):43–68.
Johnston, Jane. 2017. "Courts' Use of Social Media: A Community Practice Model." *International Journal of Communication* 11 (1):669–683.
Johnston, Jane. 2018. "Three Phases of Courts' Publicity: Reconfiguring Bentham's Open Justice in the Twenty-First Century." *International Journal of Law in Context* 14 (4):525–538. https://doi.org/10.1017/S1744552318000228.
Johnston, Jane, Patrick Keyzer, Geoffry Holland, Mark L. Pearson, and Sharon Rodrick. 2013. *Juries and Social Media: A Report Prepared for the Victorian Department of Justice*. Standing Council on Law and Justice.
Keyzer, Patrick, Jane Johnston, Mark L. Pearson, Sharon Rodrick, and Anne Wallace. 2013. "The Courts and Social Media: What Do Judges and Court Workers Think." *Judicial Officers' Bulletin* 25 (6):47–51.
Lambert, Paul. 2011. *Courting Publicity: Twitter and Television Cameras in Court*. West Sussex: Bloomsbury Professional.
LAWCPD. 2022. "Social Media and Its Impact on Trials." Retrieved from https://lawcpd.com.au/blog/social-media-and-its-impact-trials/, accessed 19th June 2024.
Liebler, Raizel, and Keidra Chaney. 2014. "Here We Are Now, Entertain Us: Defining the Line between Personal and Professional Context on Social Media." *Pace Law Review* 35 (1):[i]–454.
LinkedIn. 2024. "About Us." Retrieved from https://news.linkedin.com/about-us#Statistics, accessed 15th April 2024.
Mahmoud, Ahmed Sayed Ahmed, and Islam Ibrahim Abdelaziz Chiha. 2020. "The Judge and Social Media: A Balance between the Judge's Freedom of Expression and His Independence and Impartiality." *International Review of Law* 2020 (1):97–162.
Marder, Nancy S. 2012. "The Conundrum of Cameras in the Courtroom." *Arizona State Law Journal* 44 (4):1489–1574.
Marwick, Alice E., and Danah Boyd. 2010. "I Tweet Honestly, I Tweet Passionately: Twitter Users, Context Collapse, and the Imagined Audience." *New Media & Society* 13 (1):114–133. https://doi.org/10.1177/1461444810365313.
Mason, Paul. 2000. "Lights, Camera, Justice? Cameras in the Courtroom: An Outline of the Issues." *Crime Prevention and Community Safety* 2 (3):23–34. https://doi.org/10.1057/palgrave.cpcs.8140063.
McGee, Amanda. 2009. "Juror Misconduct in the Twenty-First Century: The Prevalence of the Internet and Its Effect on American Courtrooms." *Loyola of Los Angeles Entertainment Law Review* 30:301.
Näsi, Matti, Maiju Tanskanen, Janne Kivivuori, Paula Haara, and Esa Reunanen. 2020. "Crime News Consumption and Fear of Violence: The Role of Traditional Media, Social Media, and Alternative Information Sources." *Crime & Delinquency* 67 (4):574–600. https://doi.org/10.1177/0011128720922539.
NCSC, National Center for State Courts. 2024. "Court and Social Media Accounts." October2023.Retrievedfromwww.ncsc.org/consulting-and-research/areas-of-expertise/communications,-civics-and-disinformation/social-media-and-courts/Courts-and-social-media-accounts, accessed 15th April 2024.
Nothhaft, Howard. 2015. "The Dream of Enlightenment Within Digital Reach?" In *Strategic Communication, Social Media and Democracy*, edited by Timothy W. Coombs, Jesper Falkheimer, Mats Heide, and Philip Young, 65–82. London: Routledge.
Nuzum, Krislin C. 2019. "Letting Google into the Jury Room a Proposed Study on the Effect of Abolishing the Juror Research Admonition." *Jurimetrics* 60 (1):105–123.
Papacharissi, Zizi. 2010. *A Private Sphere: Democracy in a Digital Age*. Polity.
Resnik, Judith. 2013. "The Democracy in Courts: Jeremy Bentham, 'Publicity', and the Privatization of Process in the Twenty-First Century." *NoFo: An Interdisciplinary Journal or Law and Justice* 10 (1):77–119.

Reuters. 2022. "Danish Eurosceptic Lawmaker Acquitted in EU Fraud Case." Retrieved from www.reuters.com/article/world/danish-eurosceptic-lawmaker-acquitted-in-eu-fraud-case-idUSKBN2T50P6/, accessed 1st June 2024.

Schwartz, John. 2009. "As Jurors Turn to Web, Mistrials are Popping Up." Last Modified 17 March 2009. Retrieved from www.nytimes.com/2009/03/18/us/18juries.html, accessed 19th June 2024.

Seibert-Fohr, Anja. 2019. "The Independence of Judges and Their Freedom of Expression: An Ambivalent Relationship." In *The Rule of Law in Europe: Recent Challenges and Judicial Responses*, edited by María Elósegui, Alina Miron, and Iulia Motoc, 89–110. New York: Springer Cham.

Small, Tamara A., and Kate Puddister. 2020. "Play-by-Play Justice: Tweeting Criminal Trials in the Digital Age." *Canadian Journal of Law and Society/Revue Canadienne Droit et Société* 35 (1):1–22.

St Eve, Amy J., Charles P. Burns, and Michael A. Zuckerman. 2013. "More from the# Jury Box: The Latest on Juries and Social Media." *Duke Law & Technology Review* 12:64.

Stuart, Forrest. 2020. *Ballad of the Bullet: Gangs, Drill Music, and the Power of Online Infamy*. Princeton: Princeton University Press.

Surette, Ray. 2011. *Media, Crime, and Criminal Justice: Images, Realities, and Policies*. 4th ed. Belmont, CA: Wadsworth Cengage Learning.

Surette, Ray. 2015. *Media, Crime, and Criminal Justice*. 5th ed. Cengage Learning.

Thompson, Edward. 2011. "Does the Open Justice Principle Require Cameras to Be Permitted in the Courtroom and the Broadcasting of Legal Proceedings." *Journal of Media Law* 3 (2):211–236.

Townend, Judith, and Cassandra Wiener. 2021. *Justice System Data: A Comparative Study*. Sussex: Legal Education Foundation.

van Dijck, Jose. 2013. *The Culture of Connectivity: A Critical History of Social Media*. Oxford University Press. https://doi.org/10.1093/acprof:oso/9780199970773.001.0001.

5 Consumption

In the opening pages of Foucault's (1975/1991) *Discipline and Punish*, the reader is treated to three pages of an incredibly gruesome and detailed description of a public execution which took place in France in 1757 and which exemplified the spectacle of torture and punishment of that time:

> On 2 March 1757 Damiens the regicide was condemned "to make the *amende honorable* before the main door of the Church of Paris", where he was to be "taken and conveyed in a cart, wearing nothing but a shirt, holding a torch of burning wax weighing two pounds"; then, "in the said cart, to the Place de Grève, where, on a scaffold that will be erected there, the flesh will be torn from his breasts, arms, thighs and calves with red-hot pincers, his right hand, holding the knife with which he committed the said parricide, burnt with sulphur, and, on those places where the flesh will be torn away, poured molten lead, boiling oil, burning resin, wax and sulphur melted together and then his body drawn and quartered by four horses and his limbs and body consumed by fire, reduced to ashes and his ashes thrown to the winds" (*Pieces originales* . . . 372–4).
>
> (Foucault 1975/1991, 3)

Foucault then moves 80 years later and describes the rules for young prisoners in Paris, whose days were scheduled minute by minute. For Foucault, this indicated a shift from public execution to strict control of time as a form of punishment and, hence, "the disappearance of torture as a public spectacle" (Foucault 1975/1991, 7).

This transition from punishing the body to punishing the soul also denotes a transition from public punishment to punishment behind closed doors which is a characteristic of the "civilising process" (Elias 1994) whereby distasteful acts were moved from the public eye into more private settings. These developments took place alongside changes to legal proceedings which transformed from secretive events – with opaque judgements and sentencing – to public trials, in tandem with the drive towards open justice and increased legal security propounded by the founders of classical criminology. This means that

DOI: 10.4324/9781003344643-5

as punishment moved behind closed doors, trials became more open and publicity "shifted to the trial" (Foucault 1975/1991, 9).

In Chapter 3, I explored how news media has played a key role in transforming trials from routine institutional processes into public spectacles, with the Nuremberg trials serving as a prime example of how a trial captivated a global audience. More recently, the focus of interest in the legal system has continued to shift from the punishment phase to the trial itself, with mass communication through the media turning trials into cultural products. This phenomenon, rooted in historical practices, has been accelerated by digital technologies and the push for increased transparency, allowing trial information to be disseminated more widely and easily than ever before, even outpacing legal oversight.

In parallel, the rising public fascination with true crime has reignited trials as public spectacles, serving as platforms for public shaming. In essence, the digitalisation of legal documents and proceedings has made them readily accessible, coinciding with society's growing obsession with true crime. This convergence has led to the trial itself becoming a form of true crime entertainment as it becomes part of the synopticon, and once again transforming it into a public spectacle.

Depictions of trials tend to be examined within three categories: the entertainment media's construction of the courtroom, infotainment-style media trials, and concerns regarding pre-trial publicity and media access to government-held information, along with government access to media-held information (Surette 2011). The first refers to traditional films and television series. The second captures media trials and the third is self-explanatory. My contribution is to thus to examine a merging of these first two categories and how digitalisation has impacted on the "media-criminal justice industry" (Surette 2011). This is important because the sustained interest in trials indicates the continuing importance they play in society, serving as a sacred ritual around which society gathers.

What is true crime?

Before we go any further, it is important to define what I mean by "true crime." True crime scholars have suggested various definitions, however a common thread regarding the lasting and prominent popularity as a genre stems from its function of conveying the sociocultural issues of the time (Horeck 2019, 7). True crime is therefore not "a single, monolithic genre" (Biressi 2001), rather it is a "slippery" (Yardley, Kelly, and Robinson-Edwards 2018, 505) genre, distinguished by its starting point of taking a real crime and basing the subsequence content around "reconstructing the crime and engaging in sense-making around it." True crime thus entails presenting "crime fact that looks like crime fiction" (Seltzer 2006, 2) in order to entertain (Cecil 2020, 5). It distinguishes itself from journalistic endeavours by, at times, embellishing or fictionalising parts of the story (Punnett 2018).

Seltzer (2006, 2) describes true crime as a "wound culture," or "cult . . . of commiseration" which constitutes the "pathological public sphere" wherein we gather around crime, violence, terror, and trauma. In the "abnormal normality of the world of true crime" (Seltzer 2006, 2) everyday events turn sour, ordinary days become pathological. By coupling together violence and mass observation, "such that public violence and mass death are theater for the living" (Seltzer 2006, 3), true crime enables us to return to the scene of the crime, collecting around its re-enactment and the ensuing aftermath. For Seltzer (2006, 48), this "collective intimacy" is a form of social bonding, tying us together in the face of graphic horrors and mass-mediated violence.

Drawing on Clark's (1997, 21) theory of sympathy, I suggest that the appeal of the trial as true crime also lies in the fact that "getting involved in someone else's 'soap opera' can provide relief from the boredom of the mundane world." As the dramas that spark our sympathy tend to be moral in their nature, trials constitute a fantastic format, providing us with the possibility to rehearse our notions of morality (Clark 1997). Listening to podcasts and watching documentaries, films, and TV series of trials are ways for people to feel involved in a moral drama yet from a safe distance.

One of the earliest essays, which by today's reckoning would be classed as true crime, was written in 1827 by Thomas De Quincey and focused on the murder of seven people from two families, known as the *Ratcliff Highway* murders which took place in 1811. The essay invited readers to move beyond the crime itself and instead reflect upon how society interprets it (Burger 2016)[1] – much like many of the talk-show-based podcasts we see today, such as *My Favorite Murder*.

Moving forwards, the nineteenth century saw the proliferation in England of *penny dreadfuls,* fictional accounts of criminal actions and chases. These early accounts of crimes "were marked by their deliberate techniques designed to enhance the emotional impact of their contents" (Wiltenburg 2004, 1379) and were a form of sensationalism (see Halttunen 2000 for more on sensationalism).

This burgeoning interest in crime developed alongside the emergence of a new scientific discipline, namely criminology. Cesare Beccaria (1734–1794), a prominent proponent of rule of law with rational, humane, and fair punishment, kickstarted the field, which was further developed by Jeremy Bentham (1745–1832) who is often cited in the academic literature as giving birth to the notion of open justice.[2] By the end of the nineteenth century criminology

1 This crime took place prior to the establishment of a formal police department in London with the Metropolitan Police established in 1829; indeed, police departments were not yet established in every city in Europe and North America (1838 in Boston, US).

2 Classic criminological understandings of crime, criminals, and punishment were followed by a move towards positivism with the work of Cesare Lombroso (1836–1909), who presented a deterministic approach to criminal behaviour, thus moving away from classical criminology's focus on rationality and free will. For Lombroso, criminals are born bad. This was followed by

was firmly recognised, helped in part by the work of Charles Darwin's cousin, Francis Galton (1822–1911), who established the use of fingerprinting in police work (along with eugenics), cementing the public's interest in true crime in parts of Europe and North America. Indeed, by this time, many Americans were comfortable with the concept of forensic science and police officers (Burger 2016).

As already noted in Chapter 3, other key trials which created widespread media attention include the 1859 trial for the abolitionist John Brown, the Lizzie Borden[3] case, and O.J. Simpson's proceedings a century later (Hughes 2016). This growing interest in crime led to the birth of the media trial[4] – "the co-optation of a regional or national crime or justice event by the media, which is developed and marketed along entertainment-style storylines as a source of drama, entertainment, and profit" (Surette 2011, 23; see also Surette 1989).

The ensuing upsurge of media trials over the following centuries should be understood in light of developments in news organisations at the end of the twentieth century, wherein increased competition led to news becoming structured along entertainment lines: simplified, fast-moving, and dramatic (Surette 2011). The entrance of digitalisation has boosted this, due to the immediacy and level of detail afforded and the possibility of widespread dissemination. It seems that the media trial of yore is the podcast of today, with trials being co-opted for podcasts, documentaries, films, and a host of other forms of content.

As media trials continued to grow in popularity, a shift in popular culture also took place which has led to rising interest in crime as a source of entertainment more broadly, as reflected in the popularity of Nordic crime fiction such as *The Bridge* (*Bron*), American TV documentaries based on murder trials such as *Making a Murderer*,[5] and crime podcasts such as *My Favorite Murder*.

Research on true crime indicates that it examines themes such as victimhood, vulnerability, criminality, mortality, fear of crime, law and order, and more, constructing dangerous criminals, moral subjects, ideal victims, and

psychological positivism drawing on the work of social learning theories (such as Ivan Pavlov 1849–1936, B.F. Skinner 1904–1990, and Albert Banduro 1925–2021), wherein childhood and socialization are understood as shaping our criminal tendencies.

3 Lizzie Borden was tried and acquitted of the brutal axe murders of her father and stepmother in Massachusetts in 1892 with the trial receiving enormous media coverage and remains to this day a topic in American popular culture (Hughes 2016). Indeed, in 2020, a Showtime historical drama mini-series on John Brown entitled "The Good Lord Bird" starring Ethan Hawke was released and in 2018 a Hollywood film on Lizzie Borden entitled "Lizzie," starring Kerstin Stewart hit the screens.

4 Media trials are not to be confused with "trial by media" which are defined as a "market-driven form of multidimensional, interactive, populist justice in which individuals are exposed, tried, judged and sentences in the 'court of public opinion'" (Greer and McLaughlin 2012, 397; see also Greer and McLaughlin 2011).

5 And in 2020, a new journal was published: *Crime Fiction Studies.*

decent citizens (Christie 1986; Biressi 2001). However, the attention given to different actors in true crime is uneven. For instance, Greer (2007) describes how more attention is given to victims who can be portrayed as "ideal" and can be understood in terms of a "hierarchy of victimization," wherein those attributed legitimate status as victim tend to attract greater media attention. Others have argued that true crime is dominated by the murders of white middle-class women by white men and that the cases are solved by experts and heroes who are also male (Cavender, Bond-Maupin, and Jurik 1999). This raises an important point, that we remain cognizant not only of what true crime portrays, but also what it obscures (Yardley, Kelly, and Robinson-Edwards 2018, 507). Crimes such as male rape and domestic abuse, with victims from minority groups, are often absent (Jermyn 2006; Dowler, Fleming, and Muzzatti 2006; Murley 2008).

The trial as true crime

The entrance of digitalisation has meant that new forms of popular consumption such as podcasts have emerged, adding to the already established mix of narratives, accounts, and stories conveyed about the legal sphere (Surette 2015, 135). This is in tandem with the rise of streaming services. For instance, Netflix released more original productions in 2019 than the entire TV industry did in 2005 (Bridge 2019). This gives us an idea of the volume of content available. Digitalisation is thus a development which has turbo-boosted the now dizzying array of true crime documentaries, mini-series, films, and so on centring on trials.

We have also seen a shift in television and other screen cultures from focusing on the crime, the case, and the apprehension of the offender towards an increased interest in the trial and punishment phase (e.g. *Orange Is the New Black*, *Prison Break*, *Judge Judy*) (Biressi and Nunn 2003). And, in conjunction with the shift from the execution and investigation of the crime, many of these more recent true crime features are focusing on trials. For instance, beyond *Making a Murderer*, *The Staircase* gained international attention in 2018, and in 2024 the trial of the Menendez brothers is a Netflix documentary. Likewise, in Sweden, *Rättegångspodden* (*The Trial Podcast*) presents sound recordings from criminal trials in documentary format and is one of the most popular podcasts in the country.

Given the magnitude of the content we are now exposed to, it is also possible to glimpse the magnitude of ways in which our perceptions can be shaped – both in ways that accurately reflect legal proceedings and happenings and in ways that distort our understandings. Indeed, Smith (2022, 23) argues that, rather than being able to physically see and engage with criminality, punishment, and justice, the spectacle of criminality "is now mediated though the television screen, on the pages of newspapers, and in the tide of social media." This is a worrying development as the courts' ability to remain a legitimising social mechanism, defining unacceptable social actions and instilling cohesion around such norms is invariably impacted by anything that shapes the public image of courts.[6]

For instance, studies show that such is the omnipresence of North American and English trials depicted in films and TV series that public expectations of trials and legal professionals include lawyers leaping form their chair to shout "objection," judges wearing wigs, and the presence of a jury, even in jurisdictions where objections are conveyed using other means and wigs and juries are absent (Machura and Ulbrich 2001; Machura 2005; Asimow et al. 2005; Flower 2019; Greenfield and Osborn 1995). Likewise, in my research on Swedish courtrooms, many of the defence lawyers, prosecutors, and judges I interviewed have talked about the American expectations many people have when entering the courtroom for the first time, including wondering where the jury will sit. This speaks to the power of the media in shaping our expectations.

This is compounded by studies that indicate that fictional films and TV series tend to portray a distorted image of courts wherein lawyers are portrayed as fighting crime, rather than practicing law; when engaging in law, cases tend to be high-stake trials such as murder, and trials are usually highly adversarial and confrontative (Machura and Ulbrich 2001). Whilst there can be a grain of accuracy in such depictions, Surette (2011, 124) argues, "none of the medial judicial images you are likely to be exposed to represent the reality of the judicial system." For instance, portrayals of women as attorneys or, even more rarely, judges are often defeminised as career women or depicted as embroiled in sexual conflicts (Surette 2011).[7] Likewise, as I will show in Chapter 6, female legal professionals are largely missing in court reporting from legal trials.[8]

All of this means that the conveyances portrayed in fictional and – the focus of this chapter – true crime have become an ingrained perception of courts in the public and, in turn, form the expectations we have of, for instance, judicial demeanour, how defence lawyers defend clients, how prosecutors try cases, and who is a typical judge, defence lawyer, prosecutor, victim, and so on. They thus serve as a social construction arena for what a trial is, how it is done, which roles there are within, how these roles are performed and by whom, and much, much more. This social construction process continues with the

6 The cultural work of true crime contributes to the construction of institutions and criminals in particular ways, shaping how we should feel about crime (Yardley, Kelly, and Robinson-Edwards 2018), but it also shapes how we think about the courts.

7 Sticking with the portrayal of female legal professionals in law-related shows more broadly, Lovell Banks (2012) shows that women characters do not simply replace male characters, rather the behaviours of these women are "judged through a gendered lens. In other words, it is impossible to separate their gender from their characters" (Lovell Banks 2012, 136).

8 A trial lends itself to dramatization and sensationalisation as it often entails competing versions of reality (Flower 2019): the prosecution claims that the defendant is guilty, the defence – oftentimes – claims the defendant is innocent. Both sides attempt to construct these social realities in the courtroom.

public's perceptions in turn, circling back to shape the actual courts, to paraphrase Surette (2015, 124) true crime's portrait of the judicial system "constructs a reality that the public comes to expect, and the courts subsequently strive to fulfil."

However, the relationship between what is portrayed in trials as true crime and understandings of the courts is not straightforward. There are conflicting findings as to the relationship between television, crime, news viewing, and attitudes towards the criminal justice system and little research placing true crime in particular under the spotlight. Whilst some research finds no link between these aspects and attitudes towards police, others find that such depictions can, for instance, shape such attitudes (see Hayes and Luther 2018 for an overview).

Hayes and Luther (2018) discuss the challenges that fictional depictions of crime could pose for juries and have the potential to impact trial outcomes. For instance, they present an overview of mixed findings, some of which support and some of which refute the "CSI effect." The CSI effect states that the absence of forensic evidence leads jurors who watch the American show *CSI* to be more sceptical of testimony, and the presence of forensic evidence leads to other types of evidence being disregarded (Hayes and Luther 2018). One study found support for the effect; however, this was more focused on the amount of forensic evidence presented at trial and the number of crime show viewings the participant had (Hayes and Levett 2013). However, other research indicates that jurors with higher rates of crime fiction show viewing were more likely to acquit defendants (Mancini 2013); others found no such effect (Shelton, Kim, and Barak 2006). Yet another study, from 2002, conducted by the American Bar Association showed that the level of confidence people who watch law-related television programs such as *Law and Order*, *Court TV*, and *Judge Judy* was nearly the same as those who do not watch such programs (Association 2002).

The jury is thus still out regarding the extent to which podcasts and documentaries shape the courts, trials, and actors or goings on within. However, drawing on the wider research on how our understandings are shaped, and how we, in turn, shape society around us, it seems likely that the ubiquity of trials in true crime is likely to impact us in different ways. Indeed, "[s]ince the early modern murder pamphlet, true crime has asked us to consider how we, as a society, both contribute to and learn from the most shocking acts of our age" (Burger 2016).

Documentaries of trials

A point of contrast to true crime that is important to include in this chapter is the juridical documentary. Fuhs (2014, 784) writes that juridical documentaries which depict trials with evidence and a verdict that seems to be flawed serve as an alternative public trial and a "meta-trial on the legitimacy of the actual trials." For Fuhs, juridical documentaries are understood as non-fiction films primarily focused on legal proceedings or the administration of law which utilise the legal trial as both a platform and a structural device to challenge the credibility of testimonies, observe the enactment of law in our society, and participate in social discussions regarding flaws in contemporary jurisprudence. Due to the perceived authenticity of non-fiction films and their presumed connection to reality, these visual representations carry significant ethical and epistemological implications. Consequently, our expectations regarding truthfulness in juridical documentaries make them highly charged arenas for examining the ethical and epistemological obligations of documentary portrayal, as well as for uncovering truths about the legal system and the establishment of a just society (Fuhs 2014, 783).

Documentaries about trials can "shape the social legacy of trial narratives" (Fuhs 2014, 785), leaving an imprint that may or may not support the decision of the legal institution. Although the documentary and the trial share epistemological understandings of evidence, narrative, and argument, how the trial is framed in these documentaries will nevertheless shape how we come to understand law in action (Fuhs 2014). Both documentaries and trials are interested in accessing the truth via evidence; however, as Fuhs (2014) also notes, documentaries often make claims that the evidence presented in such films is more reliable than that presented in a court of law. This is because documentaries have fewer restrictions placed on them, despite retaining a deep investment in authenticity, and may therefore enable a more open exploration around a case.

Documentaries are therefore a form of exploring how the public comes to understand the power of the law, as well as the law's control of how we relate to, experience, and see the world around us (Fuhs 2014). These documentaries not only depict the functioning of the justice system but also challenge its portrayal as an institution proficient in impartially assessing evidence and determining objective truth. By highlighting the intricate link between evidence, understanding, and truth, trial documentaries reveal how historical narratives are shaped by the creation and dissemination of non-fiction legal accounts, as well as their interpretation within society (Fuhs 2014, 803).

Fuhs (2014, 804) suggests that documentaries are primarily interested in examining the process of justice, rather than exclusively focusing on the result. They challenge hierarchies of power, expose institutional flaws and ideological biases, and interrogate the institutional, social, and political factors that contribute to structural social division, thereby forcing us to confront our own stereotypes regarding criminality, class, and social identity (Fuhs 2014). To draw on Larke-Walsh's (2021) concept, Fuhs would probably argue that the media often constructs "injustice narratives" (Larke-Walsh 2021) which encourage audiences to question the notion of fair practice and which can also be understood as a central aspect of investigative journalism (Yardley, Wilson, and Kennedy 2017). Such narratives tend to characterise individuals as *good guys* or *bad guys*, a division which may be particularly problematic in cases where guilt has been found in a court of law but questioned in the documentary, inviting viewers to question the work and the motivations of those depicted in ways that may undermine their integrity. Moreover, the crime may be simplified in such documentaries (Larke-Walsh 2021; Horeck 2019). This is highly problematic as it can lead to inaccurate representations being constructed and conveyed.

Podcasts of trials

True crime podcasts have emerged as a particularly popular form of consuming trials and have breathed new life into traditional news and documentary formats (Yardley, Kelly, and Robinson-Edwards 2018; Pâquet 2018). The term "podcast" comes from a combination of the words "iPod" and "broadcasting." Podcasts are "digital audio files which can be downloaded by users to personal devices like MP3 players, smartphones or computers to listen to at their convenience" (Yardley, Kelly, and Robinson-Edwards 2018, 504). The roots of podcasting can be traced back to 2000 with software enabling the delivery of audio files in web feeds. In 2004, following technology developments, podcasting emerged as a viable technology as reflected in it becoming the "word of the year" in the US and Sweden in 2005 and in the UK in 2006. Little more than a decade later, in 2015, it became firmly established in the cultural mainstream as a new medium when Apple integrated podcast support in its software, making it possible to search for and subscribe to podcasts (Bottomley 2015). According to Listen Notes as of May 2023 there are 3,113,391 podcasts and 166,226,481 episodes available for listening (Notes 2023). The US is by far the biggest producer of podcasts, producing around two thirds of podcasts, followed by Brazil (around 200,000 podcasts), Indonesia (around 140,000), and Germany (around 80,000) (Notes 2023). In 2022, half of surveyed Americans said they consumed true crime content (YouGov 2022). With previous studies indicating that people listen to podcasts for different reasons such as entertainment, convenience, or timeshifting (being able to listen to podcasts whenever chosen), placeshifting (being able to listen to podcasts wherever), and boredom, to social aspects which entail interacting with the podcasts in various ways such as sharing and discussing with friends (McClung and Johnson 2010; Boling and Hull 2018).

True crime podcasts "'colour in' and extend beyond the news agenda" (McHugh 2014, 142) and are able to attract larger and more diverse audiences due to the lack of constraints they entail in contrast to regular news broadcasts. A contributing factor to the concretisation of podcasts as a part of the cultural consciousness was in 2015, and the podcast *Serial*,[9] a weekly true crime podcast consisting of 12 episodes. *Serial* details the 1999 Baltimore murder of Hae Min Lee and the conviction of her ex-boyfriend Adnan

9 The contemporaneity of *Serial* was central in its appeal (Horeck 2019). Viewers experienced that they could actively change the shape of the series, as with *Making a Murderer*.

Syed for her murder, along with robbery, kidnapping, and false imprisonment. In each episode, journalist Sarah Koenig presents her detailed investigative work, uncovering twists and turns, alibi witnesses, shifting statements, and meagre forensic evidence. The podcast gained enormous international attention, with over 100 million downloads in its first year (Victor 2023). It also led to reawakened interest in Syed's case which, in turn, ultimately resulted in his conviction being overturned in 2022, after serving 23 years in prison (see Bruzzi 2016 for a discussion on the direct impact of documentaries on actual cases; similarly, Fuhs 2014 discusses documentaries about the West Memphis Three which led to the negotiation of a plea deal and their release). Additionally, it led to fan-generated online forums such as *Serial Subreddit* where the case was discussed (Yardley, Wilson, and Kennedy 2017; Horeck 2019) and sparked interest in true crime podcasts on an academic front (e.g. Kelly, Lynes, and Hart 2022; Buozis 2017; Boling and Hull 2018). Indeed, the "*Serial* Effect" (Vogt 2016) led to an increase in the creation, growth, and monetary investment in podcasts. Serialised true crime podcasts are now an ingrained part of society and function as important indicators of how society views and understands crime (Yardley, Kelly, and Robinson-Edwards 2018).

Studies of podcasts and documentaries tend to focus on the crime itself, rather than the trial (e.g. Pâquet 2021). And, although Vitis (2023) claims there is limited research on true crime podcasts, there is a growing field. For instance, one study – albeit small scale – indicates that true crime podcast listeners prefer topics that "aligned with entrenched law-and-order discourses" (Vitis 2023). Other true crime podcast studies focus on, for instance, the victim (Slakoff, Boling, and Tadros 2024; O'Meara 2023), the host (Boling 2023), the audience (Hughes 2023), or the ethics of true crime podcasts (Haugtvedt 2017). Research has also shown that the online communities following podcasts, such as *My Favorite Murder*, have been transformed into subcultural spaces which advance discourses aimed at challenging women's victimisation and fear of violence (Rodgers 2023).

In Horeck's (2019) book exploring how different platforms for true crime are shaping our affective interactions with the genre, she analyses the *My Favorite Murder* podcast to show how the hosts privilege their emotional responses to crimes, rather than conducting rigorous research into them. Horeck (2019, 28) concludes that this reflects and spurs on a wider societal trend for trumping affect over knowledge: I feel something is true, therefore it is. If we return to the central theme of this chapter – trials as true crime – Horeck's (2019) work points to a worrying drift that could result in legal decisions covered in podcasts not valued as "true" or legitimate. This, in turn, can damage trust in the courts as a legal institution of justice. Horeck (2019) also takes Seltzer's work and shows how true crime functions in the digital age, to explore the ways in which true crime captures affective responses. She argues that it is the interactivity and engagement that digital platforms enable that has sparked true crime's rebirth in the digital age.

Podcasts and the communities associated with them can therefore constitute an arena for driving change regarding victimhood, amongst other things. For instance, other studies claim that "podcasts are impacting the criminal justice system in unprecedented ways" (Boling 2019, 161). And, whilst it is accurate that court decisions have begun to cite podcasts in their decisions, as was the case in the *Syed v Maryland* decision from 2016 linked to the *Serial* podcast, the specific ways in which podcasts are specifically impacting the criminal justice system, and, in particular, trials and the actors within, remain relatively unexplored. Yes, there is evidence that support for innocence projects has increased, but in the next chapter I will focus on more worrying aspects, drawing on the Swedish context.

The digitalisation of court proceedings

The boom in podcasts has been enabled by technologies which have enabled documents and other sources of legal information from proceedings to be accessed and disseminated. The rise of true crime has thus occurred in conjunction with digitalisation at a rapid rate, a rate at which the law has not always been able to keep up with.

As already discussed in this book, the goals of open justice have, for instance, previously been met by people physically visiting a courthouse to attend or observe a trial, or by journalists attending and reporting. However, another goal has centred on access to legal documents which are available for public access in accordance with the open justice principles followed in any given jurisdiction. This means that documents such as court judgements and orders issued by judges, case transcripts consisting of verbatim records of what was said during court proceedings (such as in the US), and preliminary investigation reports which gather the evidence sufficient to lead to trial (as in Sweden) could previously be obtained, but only as physical copies.

For instance, in the US, Public Access of Court Electronic Records (PACER) enables access to millions of case file documents as well as docket information, immediately after they have been electronically filed at all district, bankruptcy, and appellate courts (PACER 2024). Also in the US, the US Freedom of Information laws and First Amendment protection enable digital records including court documents to be acquired, posted, and reposted with little or no regulation (Corda 2016). In Denmark, the Domsdatabasen (the Rulings Database) contains rulings from civil and selected criminal cases; France has a similar database (Légifrance), as does, for instance, Germany, India, Malaysia, and Singapore.

The introduction of these kinds of digital technologies in courts has greatly facilitated the ability to submit, compile, access, and disseminate legal documents and proceedings digitally and, indeed, is often a key facet of courts' strategic plans for their long-term plans and ambitions. However, this leads to problems pertaining to the increased access to public documents it enables and challenges relating to the widespread dispersion, together with the longevity of the internet. The material used in podcasts, documentaries, and films that are accessible due to digitalisation mean that the impact on those depicted may be stronger and longer lasting. Stronger, in terms of the widespread coverage possible, and longer due to the notion that the internet never dies – that is, information posted online is available forever.

Here it should be noted that the idea that the internet never dies is not entirely accurate. In 2014, the first case for the "right to be forgotten" was heard at the European Court of Justice which found that there is a legitimate right to request having one's data delisted from Google's search engine (Case 131/12 2014). The case regarded the publication of an online notice regarding the recovery of social security debts, but it has significant relevance for the right to be forgotten with regards to criminal matters also. For instance, in England, even though previous convictions may not be necessary to disclose when applying for jobs or similar, if they are "spent," that is, after a certain period of time has passed (gov.uk 2024), a Google search could still reveal information from the media reporting of a trial, for instance. This means that one's right to "practical obscurity – the idea that privacy interest exists in information that is not secret but that is nonetheless difficult to obtain" (File 2017, 4) which was introduced in a US Supreme Court decision in 1989 and which animated the aforementioned Google Spain case – is in place. Ensuring practical obscurity in the digital context is, however, difficult and problematic and has become even more so given the ubiquity of true crime content drawing on material from trials.[10]

Easy digital access to legal documents and proceedings therefore has downsides. For instance, Lageson and Maruna (2017, 115–116) show that the internet has changed punishment in a fundamental way because of the possibility of easily accessing such things as criminal records, combined with the possibility of posting such documents on online forums for them to be discussed, commented on, evaluated, and critiqued. They write,

> Whereas the police and prosecutors (representing the state), and journalists (representing the public interest) have historically been key gatekeepers of punishment practices, the internet has profoundly changed this model by offering users easy access to criminal justice information and platforms to actively engage in the stigmatization process by republishing, commenting, and critiquing criminal records . . . online representations of criminality and "criminals" are rich contemporary examples

10 A comparative study by Townend and Wiener (2021, 3) explored the ways in which justice system data – "the information generated by the process of justice" – is accessed in Australia, Canada, and Ireland, including data collected by authorities for internal use and data that may be released publicly. They identified that a central challenge in each of these jurisdictions regarded a reluctance for people to use the court system due to concerns about the digital availability of personal data negatively impacting on the possibility of practical obscurity (Townend and Wiener 2021, 112).

> of the symbolic rituals of punishment, producing stigma that is increasingly diffuse and permanent in a new technological landscape.

For Lageson and Maruna (2017), the online publication of documents available through the digitalisation developments of courts can lead to a risk of individuals being stigmatised or labelled online, of being identified as deviating from societal norms and expectations, and being treated as a lesser individual accordingly (Goffman 1963). The trial as true crime podcast can therefore lead to those being depicted in podcasts as deviants. This pertains not only to defendants who may become "virtual stigma bearers" (Lageson and Maruna 2017, 117), placed in a "digital prison" (Lageson and Maruna 2017, 113) which inhibits reintegration into society. I suggest that other participants – plaintiffs, witnesses, but also legal professionals – also risk being labelled as deviating from the expected behaviours and actions associated with their specific role in a trial; for instance, a witness who does not display the expected emotion (cf. Porter and ten Brink 2009). Moreover, beyond such podcasts constituting a digital prison inhibiting the prisoner from reintegration, it also constitutes a digital waiting room preventing, for instance, family members from moving on from a loved one's murder due to the ever-presence of data. Podcasts thus extend the "crime complex" (Garland 2001) even more, further blurring the lines of where punishment begins and where it ends.

In short, opening the courts by digital means has enabled content to more easily be used in podcasts, documentaries, and films, which, in turn, creates greater risks for labelling and public shaming. As Lageson and Maruna (2017) also point out, the consequences of such online labelling can be damning (see also Lageson 2022). For instance, research indicates that formally labelling someone as criminal significantly increases the likelihood of recidivism (Chiricos et al. 2007).

The clash between open justice and digitalised materials

In this section I will use the case of Sweden to discuss the clash between open justice and digitalised materials. Sweden's principle of public access to information is rooted in the 1766 Freedom of the Press Act – the first of its kind – which promotes transparency by granting public access to official documents unless legally exempted. This principle means that all documents that are received by an authority, created by the authority, or stored there are public, meaning that anyone has the right to access them. Exceptions to this rule exist, for example, if a document is classified. This includes the courts.

In 2008, a modernisation reform was implemented in Sweden (*En modernare rättegång*) which enabled digital document management and introduced digital case management systems, allowing electronic storage and handling of investigation protocols. This digitalisation also made it not only feasible, but also easy and cheap, to distribute these documents electronically. This, combined with changes implemented regarding electronic communication, meant that documents could now be requested and sent via email. Together with the establishment of online portals providing a platform for individuals to request such documents as the preliminary investigation report (which contains the findings and evidence gathered during the preliminary investigation phase of a criminal case, conducted by the police and the prosecutor and which determines whether there is sufficient basis to prosecute a case), all of this means that it is possible for the preliminary investigation report to be obtained in a swift, low-cost manner. Similarly, all examinations and cross-examinations are also recorded (both audio and visual), with audio files available to the public for a relatively low fee (visual recordings can be requested but are only approved in certain circumstances). Importantly, there are no restrictions on disseminating these files, allowing their use in media, social platforms, podcasts, and more.

In this section I will focus on and problematise two ways in which this information is currently being disseminated: podcasts and online forums.

Spurred by the rise in podcasts and an increased interest in true crime, several podcasts have emerged in Sweden over the past few years such as *Rättegångspodden*, *Prime Crime*, *Krimofon*, *Rättegångsappen*, and *Krimfup*. The first of these to emerge on the market was *Rättegångspodden* in 2013, which quickly became a hit with listeners. With support in the principle of public access to documents, the creators of *Rättegångspodden*, and the others mentioned here, can access audio files of the examination and cross-examination of victims, defendants, and witnesses in trials, police interrogations, emergency services phone calls, and the prosecution's case file amongst other materials. This content is then clipped together to produce podcasts where the listeners can follow victims, family members, and perpetrators' own stories of murder and other violent crimes. Trials covered include several regarding the murder of teenage girls, the attempted murder of a baby, and an axe murder. All of this is done without the permission, or in many cases knowledge, of these involuntary podcast contributors. A defendant, witness, plaintiff, lawyer, judge, or prosecutor can therefore not refuse to have their voice included in the podcast. Here it should, once again, be pointed out that audio files from Swedish trials can be obtained by anyone and used in any way in accordance with the principle of public access to information.

The rapid rise in the number of podcasts led to hard competition between creators, with *Krimofon* recently closing due to the number of competitors currently on the market. The creator of *Krimofon* stated that his decision to quit was not only due to the number of competitors on the market, but also due to the criticism regarding the negative impact such podcasts can have on trials, with witnesses not daring to witness because of worries linked to appearing in the podcast (Pan 2024c). An example of this is in a recent trial for attempted murder which led to the defendant being sentenced to a long prison term. A witness later discovered that the audio file of the trial, including her full name, had been published on *Prime Crime*'s app, leading her to ask for her testimony to be removed from the podcast, which the podcasters refused (Pan and Avenäs 2024).[11] The witness stated that had she known she would be part of a podcast, she would never have agreed to witness in the trial.

These lines of critique, that podcasts impinge on the integrity of participants and can lead to people refusing to take part in trials, have followed such podcasts from their inception. For instance, when *Rättegångspodden* first emerged on the scene, the families of murder victims whose trials were covered in the podcast talked about the podcast as a form of re-traumatisation, saying, "We had no idea that *Rättegångspodden* had done an episode about the worst day of our lives. You are very exposed, without having any say in the matter" (Sundell and Erlandsson 2019).

This is a direct consequence of digitalisation, or as Swedish prosecutor and expert on digitalisation Lisa Dos Santos explains, "[b]efore the internet, we didn't send trial protocols home to everyone's postbox" (Sonn Lindell 2022). She further highlights that platforms such as *Prime Crime* can discourage individuals from witnessing at trials, or influence how they behave and what they say in court due to the risk of being featured in a podcast. This can ultimately affect the quality of the evidence provided. Dos Santos also underlines that criminal networks may exploit *Prime Crime* as a channel to broadcast their message in real time or apply pressure on individuals as anyone can easily access information about that is being said in court. The uncensored availability of trial material online in Sweden is therefore problematic on several levels. While the law has addressed some concerns by banning recording equipment in courtrooms, other crucial aspects have been overlooked.

It seems, however, as though change might be on the way. At the start of 2024, the creator of yet another podcast, *Brottmålspodden*, was denied access to 700 audio files with the court arguing that the EU data protection laws (GDPR) weigh heavier than the Swedish Freedom of Expression Act, and that "specific interests" needed to be in place in order for this kind of information to be accessible (Pan 2024b). And, in a recent interview, the chief of Stockholm District Court, Göran Lundahl, also states that it is harder to get people to come to court and witness if they know they can be part of a podcast later. He argues that it is a large step from trials being open to the public to being able to upload documents and audio recordings, a step which brings with it large risks (Pan 2024a).

It does seem that the tides are starting to turn in the Swedish context, with awareness and resistance growing towards the uninhibited distribution of digital legal documents, including audio recordings. I argue that the balance between integrity and publicity has not yet been found; indeed, the balance is

11 Representatives for *Prime Crime* chose instead to remove the witness' surname from the podcast, but otherwise the podcast remained published. *Prime Crime* now chooses to only include the full name of witnesses and plaintiffs if they are public figures. Despite this, names are still audible in the podcasts, which the creators argue is acceptable as this is not possible to find using a Google search.

tipped towards impinging on the integrity of those taking part in trials as the law has not kept up to speed with these digital developments.

I am not arguing that we should return to closed courts, as open justice offers significant advantages. For instance, in a 2023 murder trial in Sweden, two individuals from the popular podcast *Rättegångspodden* were removed from the courtroom after it was discovered that they were broadcasting sound from an adjacent courtroom, without permission from the judge (Erlandsson 2023). In the same trial, a well-known criminologist was also reprimanded by the judge for making inappropriate comments about a participant in the trial. These details only came to light through the release of the trial protocol, something that would not have been possible if the courts were closed institutions once again.

What I am instead arguing for is a more nuanced approach to accessing and distributing legal documents and materials. An approach that considers the reach of the internet and the long-term impact the dissemination of legal documents including personal details, intimate events, and private experiences can have for those depicted. This regards not only content created for podcasts, but also regarding online forums which also freely spread and examine such materials.

At the same time as we are experiencing a boom in true crime and new digital technologies are enabling increased access to legal proceedings to be included in podcasts, the turn towards a "culture of detection" (Andrejevic 2007, 38) has led to people attempting to solve crimes by sharing and discussing evidence, clues, and theories in online forums (Yardley, Kelly, and Robinson-Edwards 2018; Wästerfors, Burcar Alm, and Hannerz 2023; Horeck 2019).[12] Online sleuthing is thus the digital age's armchair detection and includes discussions on the evidence presented at trials, the tactics taken by legal parties, and suchlike.[13] Online sleuthing in forums such as Reddit, Flashback, and Darknet forums has thus become a central way in which understandings of courts and the actors within take shape[14] and constitutes another forum within which victims, family members, and others can experience re-traumatisation.

12 One particularly unfortunate example of such a crowd-sourced investigation what that following the Boston marathon bombing in 2013 when a university student named Sunil Tripathi was wrongly pointed out as a suspect in the case. Sunil had gone missing a month prior to the bombing and was later found to have died by suicide on the day he went missing; however, his body was not found until one week after the bombing. His family faced overwhelming media attention.

13 An example of this is a Flashback thread which discusses a trial regarding child abuse "50 grova övergrepp mot barn I Ulricehamn, Rättegång inledd." At the time of writing, the thread had been shown 165,604 times and included 259 comments including heated discussions regarding the judge's decision to place the entire preliminary investigation file as confidential, thus preventing the public from accessing the information within.

14 Moreover, beyond the drive for engaging in this online sleuthing that the internet enables by providing the rapid conveyance of information and 24/7 availability and strategies to grab and engross active users to construct collective identities and a sense of belonging (Wästerfors,

In Sweden, research has shown how Flashback, an online forum similar to Reddit, is used to investigate crimes and debate trials with legal documents, audio recordings, and suchlike uploaded, discussed, and investigated (Wästerfors, Burcar Alm, and Hannerz 2023; Hannerz, Burcar Alm, and Wästerfors 2023; Burcar Alm, Hannerz, and Wästerfors 2024).

Not only is Flashback a forum for discussing trials and the participants within, it is also a forum where the preliminary case file is regularly uploaded and discussed. As the case file includes details that are not necessarily presented as evidence in court – remember, in Sweden the principle of orality means all evidence to be evaluated by the judges must be orally presented in court – this means that Flashback users are privy to all the information gathered for the prosecution, not just that presented in court. This is problematic as it constitutes a further impingement on the privacy of those included in the file.

Conclusions

The advent of digital technology has revolutionised the dissemination and consumption of trial proceedings, enabling their broad circulation through true crime platforms and transforming trials into cultural products. Trials have now become public spectacles, enabled be digital advancements and a push for greater transparency which have allowed trial information to spread more widely and effortlessly than ever before. This evolution has outpaced lawmakers, who have struggled to keep up with these changes. Combined with a growing public fascination with true crime, trials have re-emerged as dramatic public spectacles and platforms for public shaming.

Consuming trials in the ways described in this chapter implies that a trial and the associated true crime content they create can be understood as a form of entertainment, rather than as an opportunity for educating the public. However, is this a binary relation: entertainment or education? Indeed, Bentham (1843, 313) wrote that education and entertainment are inextricably linked, writing that one of the advantages of publicity is "*the amusement which results from it.* I say amusement by itself, separate from instruction, though it be, in fact, not possible to separate them." This is a theme to be explored in the next chapter, along with the other major themes of this book thus far.

References

Andrejevic, Mark. 2007. *iSpy: Power and Surveillance in the Interactive Era.* Lawrence: University of Kansas Press.

Asimow, Michael, Steve Greenfield, Guillermo Jorge, Stefan Machura, Guy Osborn, Peter Robson, Cassandra Sharp, and Robert Sockloskie. 2005. "Perceptions of Lawyers – A Transnational Study of Student Views on the Image of Law and

Burcar Alm, and Hannerz 2023) may also lie the sense of drama that engaging in such sleuthing can spark.

Lawyers." *International Journal of the Legal Profession* 12 (3):407–436. https://doi.org/10.1080/09695950500420358.
Association, American Bar. 2002. "Public Perceptions of Lawyers: Consumer Research Findings." Retrieved from www.americanbar.org/groups/litigation/, accessed 29th June 2024.
Bentham, Jeremy. 1843. *The Works of Jeremy Bentham*. Edited by John Bowring. Vol. II. Edinburgh: William Tait.
Biressi, Anita. 2001. *Crime, Fear and the Law in True Crime Stories*. Springer.
Biressi, Anita, and Heather Nunn. 2003. "Video Justice: Crimes of Violence in Social/Media Space." *Space and Culture* 6 (3):276–291. https://doi.org/10.1177/1206331203251659.
Boling, Kelli S. 2019. "True Crime Podcasting: Journalism, Justice or Entertainment?" *Radio Journal: International Studies in Broadcast & Audio Media* 17 (2):161–178. https://doi.org/10.1386/rjao_00003_1.
Boling, Kelli S. 2023. "'We Can Do Better. We Can Be Better': Counter-Narratives in True Crime Podcasts on Domestic Violence." *Critical Studies in Media Communication* 40 (5):363–380. https://doi.org/10.1080/15295036.2023.2265982.
Boling, Kelli S., and Kevin Hull. 2018. "Undisclosed Information – Serial Is My Favorite Murder: Examining Motivations in the True Crime Podcast Audience." *Journal of Radio & Audio Media* 25 (1):92–108. https://doi.org/10.1080/19376529.2017.1370714.
Bottomley, Andrew J. 2015. "Podcasting: A Decade in the Life of a 'New' Audio Medium: Introduction." *Journal of Radio* & *Audio Media* 22 (2):164–169. https://doi.org/10.1080/19376529.2015.1082880.
Bridge, Gavin. 2019. "Netflix Released More Originals in 2019 Than the Entire TV Industry Did in 2005." Last Modified 17 December 2019. Retrieved from https://variety.com/2019/tv/news/netflix-more-2019-originals-than-entire-tv-industry-in-2005-1203441709/, accessed 23rd May 2023.
Bruzzi, Stella. 2016. "Making a Genre: The Case of the Contemporary True Crime Documentary." *Law and Humanities* 10 (2):249–280. https://doi.org/10.1080/17521483.2016.1233741.
Buozis, Michael. 2017. "Giving Voice to the Accused: Serial and the Critical Potential of True Crime." *Communication and Critical/Cultural Studies* 14 (3):254–270. https://doi.org/10.1080/14791420.2017.1287410.
Burcar Alm, Veronika, Erik Hannerz, and David Wästerfors. 2024. "Hard Work and Fun: Collective Online Interaction in a Case of Photo Fraud." *Symbolic Interaction* 47 (1):45–67.
Burger, Pamela. 2016. "The Bloody History of the True Crime Genre." *JSTOR Daily*. https://daily.jstor.org/bloody-history-of-true-crime-genre/.
Case 131/12, 2014. *Google Spain SL v Agencia Española de Protección de Datos (AEPD)*, edited by European Court of Justice.
Cavender, Gray, Lisa Bond-Maupin, and Nancy C. Jurik. 1999. "The Construction of Gender in Reality Crime TV." *Gender & Society* 13 (5):643–663.
Cecil, Dawn K. 2020. *Fear, Justice, and Modern True Crime*. Boulder: Lynne Rienner.
Chiricos, Ted, Kelle Barrick, William Bales, and Stephanie Bontrager. 2007. "The Labeling of Convicted Felons and Its Consequences for Recidivism." *Criminology* 45 (3):547–581.
Christie, N. 1986. "The Ideal Victim." In *From Crime Policy to Victim Policy*, edited by E. A. Fattah, 17–30. Basingstoke: Palgrave Macmillan.
Clark, Candace. 1997. *Misery and Company*. Chicago, IL: University of Chicago Press.
Corda, Alessandro. 2016. "More Justice and Less Harm: Reinventing Access to Criminal History Records." *Howard Law Journal* 60:1.
Dowler, Kenneth, Thomas Fleming, and Stephen Muzzatti. 2006. "Constructing Crime: Media, Crime, and Popular Culture." *Canadian Journal of Criminology and Criminal Justice/La Revue canadienne de criminologie et de justice pénale* 48:837–850. https://doi.org/10.3138/cjccj.48.6.837.

Elias, N. 1994. *The Civilizing Process*. Oxford: Blackwell Publishers Ltd.
Erlandsson, Åsa. 2023. "Domare gav Leif GW Persson tillsägelse 'en gräns hade passerats'." *Dagens Nyheter*, 10 May. Retrieved from www.dn.se/sverige/domare-gav-leif-gw-persson-tillsagelse-en-grans-hade-passerats/.
File, Patrick C. 2017. "A History of Practical Obscurity: Clarifying and Contemplating the Twentieth Century Roots of a Digital Age Concept of Privacy." *University of Baltimore Journal of Media Law & Ethics* 6 (1–2):4–21.
Flower, Lisa. 2019. *Interactional Justice: The Role of Emotions in the Performance of Loyalty*. Abingdon: Routledge.
Foucault, Michel. 1975/1991. *Discipline and Punish: The Birth of the Prison*. Translated by Alan Sheridan. New York: Random House.
Fuhs, Kristen. 2014. "The Legal Trial And/In Documentary Film." *Cultural Studies* 28 (5–6):781–808. https://doi.org/10.1080/09502386.2014.886484.
Garland, David. 2001. *The Culture of Control: Crime and Social Order in Contemporary Society*. Vol. 77. Clarendon Studies in Criminolo.
Goffman, Erving. 1963. *Stigma: Notes on the Management of Spoiled Identity*. NJ: Prentice-Hall Inc.
gov.uk. 2024. "Rehabilitation Periods." Retrieved from www.gov.uk/guidance/rehabilitation-periods.
Greenfield, S., and G. Osborn. 1995. "Where Cultures Collide: The Characterization of Law and Lawyers in Film." *International Journal of the Sociology of Law* 23 (2):107–130.
Greer, Chris. 2007. *Victims, Crime and Society*. London: SAGE Publications Ltd.
Greer, Chris, and Eugene McLaughlin. 2011. "Trial by Media: Policing, the 24–7 News Mediasphere and the Politics of Outrage." *Theoretical Criminology* 15 (1): 23–46.
Greer, Chris, and Eugene McLaughlin. 2012. "Media Justice: Madeleine McCann, Intermediatization and 'Trial by Media'in the British Press." *Theoretical Criminology* 16 (4):395–416.
Halttunen, Karen. 2000. *Murder Most Foul: The Killer and the American Gothic Imagniation*. Harvard: Harvard University Press.
Hannerz, Erik, Veronika Burcar Alm, and David Wästerfors. 2023. "Accomplishing Reality Media: The Affective Lure of Online Crime Discussions." *Cultural Sociology* 17 (4):476–492.
Haugtvedt, Erica. 2017. "The Ethics of Serialized True Crime: Fictionality in Serial Season One." In *The Serial Podcast and Storytelling in the Digital Age*, 7–23. Routledge.
Hayes, Rebecca M., and Lora M. Levett. 2013. "Community Members' Perceptions of the CSI Effect." *American Journal of Criminal Justice* 38:216–235.
Hayes, Rebecca M., and Kate Luther. 2018. *#crime: Social Media, Crime, and the Criminal Legal System*. Cham: Palgrave MacMillan.
Horeck, Tanya. 2019. *Justice on Demand: True Crime in the Digital Streaming Era*. Detroit: Wayne State University Press.
Hughes, Bella. 2023. "Murderinos: Examining the Female Audience of True Crime Podcasts with My Favorite Murder." *Digital Literature Review* 10 (1):121–132.
Hughes, Sarah. 2016. "'She Gave Her Mother 40 Whacks': The Lasting Fascination with Lizzie Borden." *The Guardian*, 4th December. Retrieved from www.theguardian.com/books/2016/dec/04/lizzie-borden-40-whacks-lasting-fascination, accessed 9th May 2023.
Jermyn, Deborah. 2006. *Crime Watching: Investigating Real Crime TV*. IB Tauris.
Kelly, Craig, Adam Lynes, and Max Hart. 2022. "'Graze Culture' and Serial Murder: Brushing Up Against 'Familiar Monsters' in the Wake of 9/11." In *Serial Killing on Screen*, edited by Sarah Fanning and Claire O'Callaghan, 295–321. Palgrave.
Lageson, Sarah E. 2022. "Criminal Record Stigma and Surveillance in the Digital Age." *Annual Review of Criminology* 5 (2022):67–90. https://doi.org/10.1146/annurev-criminol-030920-092833.

Lageson, Sarah E., and Shadd Maruna. 2017. "Digital Degradation: Stigma Management in the Internet Age." *Punishment & Society* 20 (1):113–133. https://doi.org/10.1177/1462474517737050.
Larke-Walsh, George S. 2021. "'Don't Let Netflic Tell You What to Think!": Debates on Getting to Know the Accused/Convicted in Making a Murderer and Other Injustice Narratives." In *Critiquing Violent Crime in the Media*, edited by Maria Mellins and Sarah Moore, 22–53. Cham: Palgrave Macmillan.
Lovell Banks, Taunya. 2012. "Dark Justice: Women Legal Actors on Basic Cable." In *Law and Justice on the Small Screen*, edited by Peter Robson and Jessica Silbey, 135–151. Oxford: Hart.
Machura, Stefan. 2005. "Procedural Unfairness in Real and Film Trials: Why Do Audiences Understand Stories Placed in Foreign Legal Systems?" In *Law and Popular Culture*. Oxford: Oxford University Press.
Machura, Stefan, and S. Ulbrich. 2001. "Law in Film: Globalizing the Hollywood Courtroom Drama." *Journal of Law and Society* 28 (1):117–132.
Mancini, Dante E. 2013. "The" CSI Effect" in an Actual Juror Sample: Why Crime Show Genre May Matter." *North American Journal of Psychology* 15 (3).
McClung, Steven, and Kristine Johnson. 2010. "Examining the Motives of Podcast Users." *Journal of Radio & Audio Media* 17 (1):82–95. https://doi.org/10.1080/19376521003719391.
McHugh, Siobhan. 2014. "Audio Storytelling: Unlocking the Power of Audio to Inform, Empower and Connect." *Asia Pacific Media Educator* 24 (2):141–156.
Murley, Jean. 2008. *The Rise of True Crime: 20th-Century Murder and American Popular Culture*. London: Praeger.
Notes, Listen. 2023. "Podcast Stats: How Many Podcasts Are There?" Retrieved from www.listennotes.com/podcast-stats/, accessed 26th May 2023.
O'Meara, Jennifer. 2023. "Mental Images and Emotive Voices in True Crime Podcasts Focused on Female Victims." In *The Routledge Companion to Gender, Media and Violence*, 222–231. Routledge.
PACER. 2024. "What Information Is Available Through PACER?". Retrieved from https://pacer.uscourts.gov/help/faqs/what-information-available-through-pacer, accessed 26th June 2024.
Pan, Ellen. 2024a. "Domstolschef varnar för riskterna med krimpoddar." *SVT Nyheter*, 30 August. Retrieved from www.svt.se/nyheter/lokalt/stockholm/domstolschefen-varnar-for-riskerna-med-krimpoddar-forutspar-nytt-regelverk.
Pan, Ellen. 2024b. "Han hänger ut brottsoffer och vittnen på nätet." *SVT Nyheter*, 29 August. Retrieved from www.svt.se/nyheter/lokalt/stockholm/han-hanger-ut-brottsoffer-och-vittnen-pa-natet.
Pan, Ellen. 2024c. "Populär krimpodd lägger ned – efter fajten mot konkurrenterna." *SVT Nyheter*, 30 August. Retrieved from www.svt.se/nyheter/lokalt/stockholm/popular-krimpodd-lagger-ned-efter-fajten-mot-konkurrenterna, accessed 12th September 2024.
Pan, Ellen, and Karin Avenäs. 2024. "Suzanne vittnade om mordförsök – hängdes ut i krimpodd." *SVT Nyheter*, 29 August. Retrieved from www.svt.se/nyheter/lokalt/stockholm/suzanne-vittnade-om-mordforsok-hangdes-ut-i-krimpodd.
Pâquet, Lili. 2018. "Literary Forensic Rhetoric: Maps, Emotional Assent, and Rhetorical Space in Serial and Making a Murderer." *Law and Humanities* 12 (1):71–92.
Pâquet, Lili. 2021. "Seeking Justice Elsewhere: Informal and Formal Justice in the True Crime Podcasts Trace and the Teacher's Pet." *Crime, Media, Culture* 17 (3):421–437.
Porter, S., and L. Ten Brink. 2009. "Dangerous Decisions: A Theoretical Framework for Understanding How Judges Assess Credibility in the Courtroom." *Legal and Criminal Psychology* 14 (1):119–134.
Punnett, Ian Case. 2018. *Toward a Theory of True Crime Narratives: A Textual Analysis*. Routledge.

Rodgers, Kathleen. 2023. "'F*cking Politeness' and 'Staying Sexy' While Doing It: Intimacy, Interactivity and the Feminist Politics of True Crime Podcasts." *Feminist Media Studies* 23 (6):3048–3063. https://doi.org/10.1080/14680777.2022.2098799.

Seltzer, Mark. 2006. "True Crime: Observations on Violence and Modernity." *True Crime: Observations on Violence and Modernity*. https://doi.org/10.4324/9780203944202.

Shelton, Donald E., Young S. Kim, and Gregg Barak. 2006. "A Study of Juror Expectations and Demands Concerning Scientific Evidence: Does the 'CSI Effect' Exist?" *Vanderbilt Journal of Entertainment and Technology* 9 (2):331–368.

Slakoff, Danielle C., Kelli S. Boling, and Eman Tadros. 2024. "'I Just Couldn't Cope with It, You Know? I Just Couldn't Believe That She Was Gone': The Portrayal of Co-victims' Grief in True Crime Podcasts about Missing (But Presumed Killed) Women." *Journal of Family Violence* 39 (2):303–313.

Smith, Rosie. 2022. *The Spectacle of Criminal Justice: Mass Media and the Criminal Trial*. Emerald Publishing Limited.

Sonn Lindell, Oskar. 2022. "Lisa Dos Santos: De kriminella nätverken kan nyttja kanalen." *Filter*, 22 November. https://magasinetfilter.se/samtal/lisa-dos-santos-prime-crime/.

Sundell, Joachim, and Åsa Erlandsson. 2019. "Hård kritik mot Rättegångspodden från anhöriga: 'En upprepning av traumat'." *SVT Nyheter*, 20 November. Retrieved from www.svt.se/kultur/hard-kritik-mot-rattegangspodden-fran-anhoriga-hur-kan-man-behandla-brottsoffer-sa.

Surette, Ray. 1989. "Media Trials." *Journal of Criminal Justice* 17 (4):293–308. https://doi.org/10.1016/0047-2352(89)90034-2.

Surette, Ray. 2011. *Media, Crime, and Criminal Justice: Images, Realities, and Policies*. 4th ed. Belmont, CA: Wadsworth Cengage Learning.

Surette, Ray. 2015. *Media, Crime, and Criminal Justice*. 5th ed. Cengage Learning.

Townend, Judith, and Cassandra Wiener. 2021. *Justice System Data: A Comparative Study*. Sussex: Legal Education Foundation.

Victor, Daniel. 2023. "Timeline: The Adnan Syed Case." *The New York Times*. Retrieved from www.nytimes.com/article/adnan-syed-serial-timeline-serial.html, accessed 26th May 2023.

Vitis, Laura. 2023. "'My Favourite Genre Is Missing People': Exploring How Listeners Experience True Crime Podcasts in Australia." *International Journal for Crime, Justice and Social Democracy* 12 (2):97–110.

Vogt, Nancy. 2016. "Podcasting: Fact Sheet." *Pew Research Center* 15.

Wästerfors, David, Veronika Burcar Alm, and Erik Hannerz. 2023. "The Bumpy Paths of Online Sleuthing: Exploring the Interactional Accomplishment of Familiarity, Evidence, and Authority in Online Crime Discussions." *New Media & Society*:14614448221149909. https://doi.org/10.1177/14614448221149909.

Wiltenburg, Joy. 2004. "True Crime: The Origins of Modern Sensationalism." *The American Historical Review* 109 (5):1377–1404. https://doi.org/10.1086/530930.

Yardley, Elizabeth, Emma Kelly, and Shona Robinson-Edwards. 2018. "Forever Trapped in the Imaginary of Late Capitalism? The Serialized True Crime Podcast as a Wake-Up Call in Times of Criminological Slumber." *Crime, Media, Culture* 15 (3):503–521. https://doi.org/10.1177/1741659018799375.

Yardley, Elizabeth, David Wilson, and Morag Kennedy. 2017. "'To Me Its [Sic] Real Life': Secondary Victims of Homicide in Newer Media." *Victims & Offenders* 12 (3):467–496.

YouGov. 2022. "True Crime, YouGov Poll: August 29–September 5, 2022." Retrieved from https://today.yougov.com/entertainment/articles/43755-true-crime-yougov-poll-august-29-september-5-2022, accessed 11th January 2024.

6 Spotlight on Sweden

In Sweden, the principle of public access to information ("*Offentlighetsprincipen*"), first introduced in conjunction with the Freedom of the Press Act of 1766, is a key component of the Swedish constitution that promotes transparency and openness in government. Sweden was the first country in the world to grant citizens this right which stipulates that all official documents and records held by public authorities are to be made accessible to the public unless there are specific legal exemptions. Following a reform in 2008 ("*En modernare rättegång*") aimed at modernising the Swedish judicial system to improve efficiency, transparency, and accessibility with digital tools and updated procedures, changes were implemented, designed at streamlining court processes and ensuring that the legal system could better meet contemporary needs and technological advancements. Likewise, in 2016, the UK undertook extensive judicial reforms, particularly through the Her Majesty's Courts and Tribunes Reform Program also aimed at more efficient and user-friendly justice system by digitising court processes and enhancing the use of video hearings. Canada, Australia, US, Singapore, and Estonia are also examples of jurisdictions sharing common goals of increased transparency, accessibility, and accountability through digitalisation.

The digitalisation of the Swedish courts has therefore made it possible for the preliminary investigation report, as well as the audio recordings of examinations and cross-examinations to be requested and received digitally. Upon receiving these files, there are no restrictions regarding their dissemination. It is therefore possible to publish or share them in the media, social media, chat forums, podcasts, documentaries, and so on. Similar drives towards modernising the judiciary through the use of information and communication technologies have been seen across the globe, with increased electronic justice or "e-justice" as it is known a central factor in courts' goals of open justice (Sandoval-Almazan and Gil-Garcia 2018).

All of this means that there is more legal information available than ever before, particularly given the increased drive towards digitalisation during and after the COVID-19 pandemic (cf. Townend and Wiener 2021). However, although the digitalisation of documents and the implementation or increased usage of digital technologies such as video links and live blogging may increase

DOI: 10.4324/9781003344643-6

access to the courts in different ways, digitalisation also brings with it several challenges, many of which result from laws not keeping up to speed with the digital age.

Video links

In February 2022, a trial took place following the largest-ever investigation into the online sale of narcotics, valued at around 10 million Swedish crowns. Nine individuals were charged, and the trial resulted in seven convictions, with three receiving prison sentences of seven and nine years. However, during the trial, one of the legally trained judges participated via video link during significant parts of the examination of defendants and witnesses, and the other legally trained judge also participated via video link during parts of the trial, as both were ill with COVID-19.

According to Swedish law, the general rule is that parties and judges should be physically present in the courtroom, with video link participation allowed only under legitimate circumstances, such as cost, inconvenience, or safety concerns, and only if deemed appropriate for the purpose of the person's appearance in court and other circumstances. The judges' virtual participation in this case appeared to fall into a legal grey area, leading both the prosecutor and the seven defendants to appeal.

The Court of Appeal ultimately disagreed with the district court's interpretation of the law that the judges are also permitted to participate via video link. It ruled that the judges are not permitted to participate via video link and that the remote participation of these judges led to an insufficient examination of the case's details. As a result, the court determined that a procedural error occurred, which likely impacted on the trial's outcome. The Court of Appeal ruled:

> Even if presence via video link means in many respects a better form of communication than telephone and also equates to personal presence for example for parties, video technology cannot fully convey impressions and experiences in all situations in the same way that personal presence can, both between the court and the parties, as well as between the parties (se prop. 2004/05:131 s.90).
>
> (Sverige 2022, my own translation)[1]

Whilst the apparent legal confusion of the district court about how the law should be interpreted is interesting, of more relevance for this book is that the Court of Appeal highlights a key distinction between face-to-face participation

1 Similarly in Finland, the Supreme Court ruled in December 2021 that two criminal appeal court cases where the judge participated via video link constituted a procedural error. This is despite there no legal requisite for the judge to be present in the courtroom under current Finnish law.

and participation via video. The court believes that individuals cannot communicate, experience the trial, or interpret others in the same way through cameras and screens as they can in person. In essence, it argues that the two forms of participation are not equivalent, and this difference is problematic. The Court of Appeal emphasises that seeing a participant in person when they give evidence is crucial for effectively and accurately evaluating their testimony.

However, in 2017, a case heard at the Supreme Court (Case B 279–17) centred on an appeal for a guilty verdict for violent crimes. At the original trial, the defendant was deemed to be a high-risk threat to the plaintiff. The plaintiff was therefore granted the right to participate in the trial without being visible to conceal her current appearance and protect her identity. The defence appealed against this, claiming that not being able to see the plaintiff during the examination and cross-examination constituted a procedural error and that his right to a fair trial was therefore violated.

The Court of Appeal ruled against the defence, finding that the plaintiff participating without being visible "can to some extent have impacted on the possibility of evaluating her account. According to the Court of Appeal it is, foremost the content of her account that is of deciding importance for the evaluation of her credibility." The Supreme Court upheld the Court of Appeals' decision, stating that the presence of additional supporting evidence meant that the defendant could still be considered to have had a procedurally correct trial without being physically present.

In this 2017 ruling, the focus is therefore on the content of testimony, rather than being able to see the plaintiff. In other words, the Court of Appeal ruled that physical presence was not necessary for the defendant to have had a procedurally correct trial as there was corroborating evidence. So, despite the defence arguing that participating via video link is not the same as being in the same courtroom, the Court of Appeal disagreed.

However, in the 2022 ruling, the judges clearly state that participating via video link is not the same as personal presence, and that the defendant did not have a fair trial because the judges participated remotely.

My intention here is not to explore legal arguments and interpretations, rather to argue that the 2017 ruling stating that it is "the content" of the plaintiff's account that is of central importance is a vital point that easily gets lost in discussions, and indeed, research on physical participation in trials. I argue that there is often a tendency for courts to prefer face-to-face interactions, perhaps linked to the traditional assumption that the right to face one's accuser entails physically facing them in a court of law. This is despite there being a general lack of clarity as to what it is about this physical confrontation that is lost when we move this confrontation online.

Live blogs, surveillance, and new practices

The findings in this section are also based on my cross-cultural study between Denmark and Sweden, with primary focus on Sweden.

Despite its relatively recent emergence, live blogging has quickly become a routine aspect of courtroom activities for the legal professionals interviewed in my research in Sweden and Denmark. However, the respondents in my study also exhibit ambivalence towards live blogs, acknowledging their normalisation while also alluding to their potential to change professional practices. Whilst they view live blogs as a routine part of their work, with many suggesting that they have no significant impact on their performance, the presence of live blogging journalists prompts reflection among respondents about their roles in the courtroom. Many of the respondents discuss becoming more self-conscious about their public image, knowing that they are being scrutinised by a larger, virtual audience who are following the trial online stemming from this awareness of the synopticon they now work within. This can lead to small changes in their courtroom strategies, such as explaining a particular legal argument more clearly. This dual perspective is particularly pronounced among the Danish legal professionals compared to their Swedish counterparts. Moreover, live blogs are increasingly utilised as professional tools by Danish legal practitioners, a trend less evident in Sweden. For instance, several of the Danish respondents talked about reading the blogs to gather information regarding what was said in the courtroom, if they themselves are unsure of what was said. This means that the integration of live blogs into legal practices has introduced new time-consuming routines for the Danes, who may feel they have to read the live blog to ensure that they have not missed anything important presented in court. In contrast, the majority of Swedish respondents claimed to not read the blogs, in particular the judges who argued that this would jeopardise their judicial role.

Concerns were raised by the interview respondents about live blogs being used as a marketing tool, which could potentially distort public perceptions of legal processes and professionals. For instance, many of the respondents talked about the risk of lawyers using the extended platform the live blog provides to reach a larger audience and, thus, a larger client base. Using live blogs to convey oneself as a particularly aggressive defence lawyer in order to attract gang members – a growing concern in Sweden – as clients was specifically raised as a potential issue.

Further analysis of the interview material shows that live blogs fulfil a surveillance function and contribute to the construction of surveillance practices, reflecting a broader societal shift towards a surveillance culture and increasing demands for institutional transparency. This also reflects a shift away from the disciplinary function of open justice. This is evident in the absence of talk regarding concerns about guarding against or sanctioning morally undesirable behaviour and conduct. Indeed, only one respondent, a Danish defence lawyer Linus (DK), noted that live blogs can play an important role in monitoring judges who are "offensive," "icy," and racist, thus serving a disciplinary function.

For most respondents, live blogs are seen as a means of enabling "the public to find out immediately what is happening," as judge Mikael (SWE) says, or to "control that we have a functioning legal system," according to defence lawyer Jens (SWE). Other respondents emphasised the role of live blogs in promoting transparency and openness. The mundane way in which live blogs are talked about by all respondents indicates their move towards acceptance as a practice for surveillance (Lyon 2001), in line with the wider trend towards surveillance becoming an integrated part of daily life in all parts and areas of society (Lyon 2007).

This also suggests that the legal professionals interviewed accept being watched by a potentially large audience, the many, though they acknowledge uncertainty regarding whether live blogs are widely read. Nonetheless, they recognise the synoptic role of live blogging in open justice, with Mathiesen's concept remaining relevant in the digital age. Indeed, the digitalised aspect of live blogs extends the timeframe and spatiality of the synopticon – live blogs remain present online long after the trial and can be re-distributed to a wider field beyond the newspaper's readership by downloading or screen-grabbing reports. Thus, whilst distribution of reports is also possible with traditional newspapers, the digital aspect of live blogs enables the ability to "immediatize and immortalize" (Deuze 2012), bringing a new level of institutional transparency (cf. Moore 2018) and surveillance.

This shift indicates that the disciplinary and moral aspect of Bentham's open justice may no longer be as relevant to the legal professionals interviewed in this study. Whilst such understandings may reflect the high level of trust in the legal system and low levels of corruption in Sweden (International 2020; Survey 2020) leading to the perception of a reduced need to monitor the conduct of unruly judges and others, it nonetheless appears that a shift, however subtle, has therefore taken place in the understandings of these judges, lawyers, and prosecutors.

Live blogs are also understood by the respondents in my studies as a tool for legal professionals to observe each other. For instance, several of the Swedish prosecutors and defence lawyers, as well one judge (together with most of the Danish respondents) – talk about reading live blogs to follow colleagues' trials. The respondents talk about reading these blogs partly due to personal interest, but also to give collegial support, as defence lawyer Jenny (SWE) talks about. She recounts how a colleague of hers (who had previously been involved in the case that she was defending but who was unable to attend the trial) approached her directly after the day's proceedings had finished to give feedback on her cross-examination. Jenny says, "it's the only time I've gotten such quick feedback, and it wasn't a negative thing, I was just a bit surprised as I hadn't really understood that it was like that." Although Jenny says that she has read blogs of other trials, her colleague's actions make her aware that she is not only the subject of surveillance, but also the object of other's surveillance (Deuze 2012). It appears that everyone is, indeed, spying on everyone else (Deuze 2012).[2]

2 This state of mutual surveillance has also been described as "omnopticism"(Jensen 2007).

Furthermore, Jenny is saying that she had not realised what a live blog actually is – that her colleague read a blow-by-blow account of her cross-examination – a finding which also suggests that live blogs may not yet be a fully integrated part of legal professionals' surveillance imaginaries (Lyon 2018). This means that whilst for some reading live blogs may be a legitimate surveillance practice, for others it remains less so (Lyon 2018). It also indicates that whilst live blogs have become an accepted part of courtroom work, as prosecutor Noah (SWE) stated – you are "aware that you are being watched the whole time" – live blogs may still be shrouded with uncertainty constituting a form of surveillance that is accepted but which may not be fully understood.

Whilst there appears to be general acceptance that the proceedings and legal professionals are the object of surveillance, there is less tolerance regarding the focused attention on lay participants. For instance, prosecutor Elise (SWE) begins by saying, "for me, personally, it doesn't matter," but that others may find it uncomfortable. She says,

> Others may think it feels unpleasant that what they say and their reactions – above all else – it's not just what they say, but they are perhaps crying or sad or worked up or whatever it may be, I'm talking about the plaintiff and witness and defendant, that they could think that it's unpleasant that it's reported straight out.

For Elise the focus on her in a live blog is unimportant, however she differentiates between how she experiences this and how lay participants might experience the attention. Several of the respondents echoed this response, differentiating between their own acceptance and what they perceive as the more invasive experience of witnesses, plaintiffs, defendants, and family members sitting in the public gallery. Judge Joanna (SWE) also talks about this saying,

> The very presence of journalists can make many defendants and plaintiffs worried; I know they think it's unpleasant, they get a bit scared when they realize that it can come out in the newspaper and whatnot.

Prosecutor Jan has a similar reflection saying that live blogging journalists add a layer of stress on lay participants. He says,

> It's yet another strain to know, it's tough enough as it is sitting there. It's usually empty in the courtroom and it's still really tough for the plaintiff. Every person that comes in the courtroom, it can be a security guard or someone from the public who always turns up who doesn't have anything else to do and will entertain themselves and listen. It can create completely different conditions for talking if there is a journalist live blogging. I can't say that it has ever improved the opportunity for me to conduct a good trial.

For Jan, the added value of the live blog is difficult to discern, rather it constitutes an unwanted distraction and extra level of exposure for lay participants. This is presented as being particularly relevant for vulnerable actors as judge Mikael (SWE) talks about. He says, "perhaps someone who is a little wobbly irrespective, and thinks it's a bit nerve-wracking or scary who perhaps thinks like this."

Here we see that judges, or "powerful agents" as Haggerty (2006) would describe them, who are typically not the target of surveillance, are nevertheless accepting of this focus, but they also attempt to protect those who are traditionally the target of this surveillance gaze (cf. Foucault's 1975/1991 "disciplinary gaze"), namely the vulnerable. Once again we glimpse "surveillance politics" (Haggerty 2006) developing amongst the individuals who are aware they are being scrutinised.

A normal Swedish family

In order to explore which types of crimes are covered in live blogs, I conducted a thematic content analysis of 95 live blogs available on Swedish news websites, published between 2012 and 2020. The results show that half of all criminal trials that are live blogged in Sweden are murder trials (see Chapter 1 footnote 5 for a presentation of the methodology).

Of the 49 murder trials at district court that were live blogged, 27 (55 percent) of these involved male victims, 18 (37 percent) involved female victims, and four (8 percent) centred on child victims under the age of 15 years. A comparison with the number of male and female murder victims in 2012–2020, as shown in the Swedish National Council for Crime Prevention, reveals that, each year on average, around 74 percent of murder victims were male, 26 percent were female (BRÅ 2021), and less than five were children (BRÅ 2024). Of these trials, 13 percent had a female defendant and 87 percent had a male defendant.

To make this more concrete, in 2020, there were 212,580 cases in district courts across the country and of these, 119,921 (56 percent) were criminal cases (Domstolsverket 2021, 9). Of these, 34,403 regarded crimes against the

Table 6.1 Which types of criminal trial are live blogged?

	Total	*Percentage*
Murder and murder-related	49	51.6%
Violence	8	8.4%
Arson	5	5.2%
Sex crime	5	5.2%
Robbery	4	4.2%
Gang crime	3	3.2%
Narcotics	3	3.2%
Other	16	16.8%

person, however exactly how many of these regard murder trials is unclear, but we do know that there were 188 trials that led to a murder conviction, 23 for manslaughter and one for infanticide.

Murder trials thus constitute less than 1 percent of criminal trials held in a district court in Sweden[3] yet half of the live blog coverage. Murder trials, and in particular female murder victim trials, are thus massively over-represented. The choice of trials to live blog appears to follow newsworthy imperatives: covered are trials that are novel, such as the murder of a female victim; that are titillating, such as an axe murder, a newspaper delivery person who was kidnapped, imprisoned, and tortured, and an alleged sex game gone wrong; or that have a female defendant. So, as one of the Swedish prosecutors I interviewed pointed out, "only a fraction of all trials that are held every day in Sweden" are live blogged and, to this should be added, of those, a disproportionate amount of murder trials and certain kinds of murder trials are covered.

A Swedish journalist, Kalle, I interviewed talked about this, saying that certain trials centring on gang members who are victims of crime may not gain as much media attention as those where a "normal Swedish family" is the victim which have a higher "shock value" and "uniqueness" as he goes on to say. Trials which have a degree of novelty also gain more attention, for instance the trial of a so-called moped gang attracted national attention. The suspects were charged with 50 burglaries, classed as grant theft. The novelty here was, as the live blog stated, "it is common for burglars to commit so many crimes, but unusual that they are charged for it" (Nr 74). Here, even a mundane or ordinary crime becomes extraordinary.

This means that there are often trials that are uninteresting from a legal point of view that are live blogged, whilst trials that pivot on unusual legal cases or arguments remain unknown. For instance, Noah, a Swedish prosecutor I interviewed, uses the trial of A$AP Rocky – an American rapper who stood trial in Sweden for an assault he committed in Stockholm – to exemplify this. The trial, regarding a relatively minor crime, gained widespread, international attention including live blogging by several media outlets despite it being a minor, straightforward case. It was the celebrity involved in the trial that boosted it into the international arena. Hence, rather than focusing on "justice-worthy" (Townend and Welsh 2023) trials of notable legal interest, the tendency in live blogs is for newsworthiness to prevail. Lina, a Swedish lawyer I interviewed, talked about this saying,

> I have a lot of cases where there's a lot of legal quirks because I'm mainly in major cases that run over many days where there's a lot of technical stuff and there's often a lot of reasonable points of view that aren't described at all, that are actually, really relevant. Sometimes you have

3 Nine percent of criminal cases are appealed and 36 percent of cases are changed on appeal (Domstolsverket 2021, 23).

> a feeling that it's because it gets too complicated for the journalists to understand it and then they might have to familiarize themselves with it and they don't bother to do that, and then they take a different angle instead.

These findings are in line with previous research from the US which shows that news organisations in the US tend to choose to report on a trial that appeals to readers, "regardless of its importance or implications" (Vinson and Ertter 2002). Trials for violent crime – constituting two thirds of cases covered – followed by those focusing on high-profile events, or novelty cases (such as the case of a parrot who witnessed a murder) were over-represented (Vinson and Ertter 2002, 85). Other subjects that arguably were of more societal relevance and interest, such as civil rights and political corruption, reflected only one fifth of coverage.[4]

Similarly, analyses of news coverage in the UK between 1945 and 1991 reveal a rise in crime-related reporting, with a notable emphasis on violent crime and terrorist offences, a pattern that is echoed in the US (Allen, Livingstone, and Reiner 1998; Livingstone, Allen, and Reiner 2001; Reiner, Livingstone, and Allen 2000; Grosholz and Kubrin 2007).

Additionally, Jewkes (2015, 67) summary of the research on the media and crime stories finds several studies which conclude that the media selectively distorts and manipulates public perceptions thereby creating a false picture of crime which, in turn, promotes stereotyping, bias, prejudice, and gross over-simplification of the facts (see also Mawby 2002). Similarly, a historical study exploring the history of crime news in the UK newspaper press found that the media were regularly involved in constructing moral panics by giving the most attention to crimes that appeared least frequently in official statistics, thereby conveying "a distorted view

4 Vinson and Ertter (2002, 88) also coded court coverage into three broad categories: (1) straight-forward reports on the facts of the case; (2) primarily explanatory stories detailing the law and judicial process involved; (3) entertainment – going beyond the facts of the case to include "graphic details of the crime, descriptions of appearances, dramatic emotional reactions or testimony, and human interest stories about participants in the process." This final category also included commentary discussing strategies, but without linking them to legal or procedural grounds. They found that 75 percent of stories fell into the first category: presentation of the facts of the case, particularly on television. Nearly 20 percent of stories were classed as entertainment, and the remaining 5 percent were more explanatory stories. However, there were differences between the different media types with newspapers including more entertainment (23 percent) and explanation stories (12 percent) than television (15 percent and 3 percent respectively). These findings indicate that the primary form of coverage is informative, with entertainment taking a more secondary role. However, as the authors note, the relative lack of explanation regarding legal processes and procedures which may aide an understanding of the judicial process is worrying. When focusing on the types of explanations given, they found around one fifth explained penalty options, less than a fifth gave procedural explanation such as admission of evidence, and only 10 percent explained relevant laws. Newspapers were more likely than televised reports to give explanations.

of crime" (Wood Carter 2016; see also Jones and Wardle 2008). In the English context, Moran (2014, 152) finds, "news tends to make the extraordinary seem like the everyday," meaning that an unequal amount of reporting focuses on exceptional and extraordinary proceedings and events within, thereby skewing the picture painted of the courts and judicial activity.

The finding that crimes least likely to be committed are most likely to be reported in the media is known as the "backwards law" (Surette 2003) – that such stories stand out, lending themselves to sensationalisation. For instance, female sex offenders gain greater media attention due to their doubly deviant nature (Jewkes 2015), hence the media tends to downplay male violence and overemphasise female violence (Ellis, Sloan, and Wykes 2013). Live blogging thus follows previous trends in constructing certain types of crime as more prevalent than others by reporting on them more frequently.

Which parts of the trial are covered and who are depicted?

My analysis of live blogs also revealed that for some trials, such as for the murder of a teenage girl on her way home from work which consumed Sweden in 2017, the coverage is gavel-to-gavel, covering all day every day. However, if such a large trial continues for an extended number of days, then the amount of coverage may be reduced, with examinations and cross-examinations of key witnesses prioritised. Those aspects of the trial that tended to be covered included the presentation of the facts of the case, the questioning of plaintiff, defendant, and witnesses, and the closing arguments. This contributes towards the construction of a trial as dramatic and exciting, with things happening all the time. The mundane aspects such as complicated legal arguments, technological delays, complicated presentations of evidence, and handling expenses tend not to be depicted.

This finding supports previous research which shows that coverage of trials tends to focus on the start and the end with many aspects of court proceedings and judicial activity in between disappearing in reports, indicating that certain aspects of legal proceedings are missed (Vinson and Ertter 2002; Haltom 1998; Moran 2014). It also ties into Chibnall's (1977) criteria of simplification: for the trial to be newsworthy, certain parts are skipped to retain the reader's interest. This could mean choosing to not cover the trial during complicated presentations of evidence, but it could also entail reporting a summary such as "now the details of radio towers are being explained" rather than reporting verbatim reproductions of what is being said. All of these are subtle ways in which trials are depicted in a slightly misleading manner.

Zooming in on this further, it is also of value to examine which actors are reported on and how as this contributes to constructing understandings and expectations of trials. Of the legal professionals in the courtroom (judge, prosecutor, defence lawyer, counsel for the plaintiff), it is the prosecutor who gains the most coverage in terms of what they do and say in the trial. This can be understood in relation to the legal system in Sweden where the prosecution has the burden of evidence and where the role of the defence lawyer is to find weaknesses in the prosecution's case. This is also explained by journalist Malin, when I asked her who she tends to focus on in live blogs. She says, "I would probably say the prosecutor and suspect perhaps because they are the ones driving, who are most active. The defence lawyer has their own specific times so to speak." Malin is referring not only to the central role of the prosecutor – and indeed the defendant – but also to the order of proceedings which sets out when each party may speak, and which also indicates that objections and interjections by the defence lawyer should be kept to a minimum. This can, at times, lead to the defence lawyer defending their client by remaining passive for large parts of the trial and the defendant only permitted to speak at certain times.[5] Thus, despite, as Malin says, the prosecutor and the defendant "driving" the trial – the defendant's possibility of speech is limited, meaning that her focus switches to the prosecutor.

When the defendant is depicted, it is often in emotional terms, once again fulfilling the criteria of newsworthiness, and with regards to where he or she is looking– a depiction which may serve to capture the only form of action the defendant engages in. For instance, the following excerpts are from a murder trial of a young woman:

> The 22-year-old doesn't express any emotion whatsoever when the medical examiner goes through Tova's injuries. He looks up quickly at the lay judges – a short second – then looks back down at his papers.
>
> (Nr 61)

> When the 22-year-old was previously asked to speak freely, and when he answers his defense attorney's questions, he speaks very quickly. He appears to be very eager to get his story across. However, when the prosecutor has asked questions, the ex-boyfriend has appeared calmer in his responses and tone, although he has responded sharply. The details that seem to provoke strong reactions from the audience and relatives do not appear to affect the 22-year-old much.
>
> (Nr 61)

> The plaintiff's counsel has previously described the 22-year-old as cold and indifferent during the proceedings. Many of the observers likely share the same impression of the man today. Judging by his facial expressions and body language, he hardly reacts to any of the testimonies, or the images shown.
>
> (Nr 61)

5 For instance, the presentation of the facts of the case can take several days, large chunks during which the defence lawyer listens only. This is followed by the defence's position to the charges which may entail a, usually brief, presentation of evidence from the defence. As the prosecution has the burden of evidence, the majority of witnesses tend to be for the prosecution although the defence may also choose to call their own.

Later on, in the same trial:

> It gets emotional for the victim's family during the friend's testimony. There is sniffing from the public. The suspect does not look at the friend. He sits and writes notes or something, and looks down in his papers, just as he has done through large parts of the trial. He shows no feelings.
>
> (Nr 61)

In a double murder trial, the live blog captures:

> The defendant has a beard today. He opens and clothes his mouth, and switches between looking down at the table and towards the prosecutor who is sitting on the other side of the room. He doesn't look at the victim's relatives who are sitting in a row to his left.
>
> (Nr 14)

And in other trials:

> The man's voice shakes when he speaks. He is speaking quite quickly and recounts what happened, and how he experienced it.
>
> (Nr 53)

> The suspect is sitting quietly and is still and his facial expressions do not reveal much of what he feels.
>
> (Nr 31)

In two other murder trials:

> The suspect was crying and looked tense when the guards led him out.
>
> (Nr 12)

> "It's easy to say something about a person who isn't here and can't correct it. She isn't here and can't say anything," he says, and now his voice sounds angry as he becomes upset. The accused is sitting with his arms crossed, leaning forward, and looking at the prosecutor. His hair is parted to the side.
>
> (Nr 11)

Depicting the emotions of the defendant is thus one of the central and most common ways in which the defendant is described in live blogs. Indeed, when the defendant is mentioned, it tends to be in emotional terms. Again, this can be understood in terms of fulfilling the ninth criteria of newsworthiness, namely emotionalisation, and also becomes more understandable if we turn our attention to the comments section which most live blogs have, where readers can post comments or questions to the live blogging journalist. One of the most posed questions is about the defendant's emotional state. For instance, in the double murder trial (Nr 53) mentioned earlier, one of the readers' comments, "Does he look regretful?" to which the reporter replies, "it's hard to say, he shows no feeling, nor does he look at the pictures from the murder site being shown on the big screen." In another murder trial (Nr 16) a reader asks, "How does the 37-year-old seem? Confident and articulate, or hesitant and unsure?" to which the journalist replies, "He speaks calmly and seems confident in his story." In the trial for the murder of a child (Nr 22), the comment section is filled with readers asking how the defendants seem, "what kind of emotional expression do they have now?" "How are they reacting now?" "Does the defendant seem to be troubled by the fact that the victim's father is in the courtroom?" Another asks, "is she composed when she answers each question?" The journalist responds "yes, I think so. Every now and then she draws a breath and sighs heavily."

We can therefore see from the questions posed by readers that emotional expressions are an important part of creating a sense of being-thereness, of being able to understand and picture the events taking place. By describing defendants in emotional terms, either in the live blog itself or in response to readers' questions, journalists are contributing to the construction of defendants as emotionful or emotionless. Indeed, it is the absence of an otherwise expected emotion that is often highlighted, such as when a defendant shows "no emotion" when an autopsy report is read out, or when a witness recounts their experience of a murder attempt.

However, the journalists interviewed in this study take care to present themselves as cognizant of the vulnerable position defendants, together with plaintiffs and witnesses, may find themselves in when participating in a trial. Another journalist, Hilda, talks about this when asked how she depicts what is going on in the courtroom:

Hilda: How we describe them is, perhaps not describing as much, like yeah, feelings and how they look – we should be quite careful with that and think about the fact that it's people sitting there.

Lisa: Is that also the case for judges, prosecutors and lawyers?

Hilda: I think so.

Lisa: There isn't any difference between how you would describe the different participants?

Hilda: No, although on second thought, judges, prosecutors and lawyers have much more power than the defendant or plaintiff or crime victim have. They have a sort of public role in some way, so it wouldn't be a problem to describe if they have an outburst or something, I don't know, or something that sticks out or do something. They have, they are there for a professional purpose I would say.

Here, Hilda is talking about the vulnerable positions participants may be in when witnessing or in other ways taking part in a trial – positions which may entail a power disadvantage. Hilda must therefore take great care to ensure that any depictions do not lead to an increased traumatisation or secondary victimisation which may arise from the ways in which they report the trial and actors within in live blogs. This was an approach echoed by all other respondents in the study, and one that is reflected in the live blogs I analysed with personal depictions of lay participants restricted to emotional and physical displays, but without indulging in descriptions of an intimate or integrity-violating nature.

Women in live blogs

Switching to a gendered lens I also conducted a quantitative content analysis on a narrower sample of live blogs, examining live blogs published on Swedish news websites between January 2018 and December 2020. I found that 38 criminal trials taking place at district courts had been live blogged during this period in the online version of regional, local, and national newspapers, of which 32 were possible to analyse. I then examined how visible female legal professionals are in these live blogs as women are under-represented in certain areas of law but over-represented in others (see Table 6.2). As there are no studies of the Swedish context and, indeed, few studies to my knowledge of how female legal professionals are depicted in court reporting, the presence of female legal professionals in live blogs is an important source of knowledge for understanding courts and the actors within.

The law has traditionally been perceived as a masculine sphere, yet over recent years, more and more women have taken their place in the legal world (Sommerlad et al. 2010; Morello 1986; Menkel-Meadow 1985, 1984). Numerous studies have followed and discussed this progress finding improvement in equal representation in some – but, by no means all – areas of the legal profession, however there is still a long way to go. The further up the career ladder within the lawyering profession one searches, the more pronounced this absence became (Lundetag et al. 2018). Thus whilst Sweden ranks near the top of gender equality (Equality 2021) and gender gap indexes (Forum 2021), equality in the legal profession is lagging behind. Figures show that women are in the majority in law programs across the country, however they constitute the minority in certain key areas of the legal profession (Persson 2018). Criminal law and criminal courts are an outlier as most prosecutors and judges are women, with rising numbers of women working as criminal defence lawyers. I therefore wanted to show whether this equality is reflected in the live blogs.

I conducted a quantitative content analysis in the form of the Bechdel test (also known as the Bechdel-Wallace test). This is a measure of female representation, used primarily in the film and television industry. The test has three criteria: a work must have (1) at least two women in it (2) who talk to each other (3) about something other than a man.[6] I therefore applied the Bechdel

6 The majority of films fail this test, thus revealing the "celluloid ceiling" (Lauzen 2008, 2018) (although this term usually refers to the invisible barriers restraining behind-the-scenes workers, rather than those appearing on screen).

test to live blogs and found that 31 percent (ten trials) passed the test, with interactions between women depicted. However, those interactions that were depicted pertained to interactions between lawyers or prosecutors and witnesses, defendants and plaintiffs, rather than interactions between two female legal professionals. The remaining 69 percent of trials (22) failed the test with no interactions between females depicted. Of the 32 trials analysed, nearly one fifth of the trials (19 percent, six trials) did not mention or depict female legal professionals in any way.

In the following table (Table 6.2) I compare the percentage of men and women working as prosecutors, defence lawyers, and judges, with the percentage of live blogs that depict male and female prosecutors, defence lawyers, and judges. We see that although the majority of prosecutors and judges are women, trials with male prosecutors and judges are more commonly blogged. Female defence lawyers are also disproportionately reported on in live blogs.

Although these analyses by no means provide an in-depth analysis of the depiction of women legal professionals in live blogs, they nevertheless tell us something about who is visible, about who is seen to be working as a judge, prosecutor, or defence lawyer in Sweden today. Judging from this analysis, the answer is: men. This is a highly problematic misrepresentation as it contributes to the social construction of these legal roles as male which, in turn, can lead to a backlash in the number of women aiming to work within these spheres.

How are trials reported?

So far in the analysis, it appears that retaining readers' interest demands making choices as to which parts of the trial to report from, indicating that live blogging may not fully fulfil the educative function of open justice as certain parts of trials and certain actors remain absent in such reports. Live blogging of trials constitutes a particular type of coverage – court reporting in real time whereby journalists should capture the details of events in a factually accurate yet reader-enticing, clickable manner. This means they should attempt to capture and depict a trial which at times may be dry – boring even – in a way that entices readers to keep on scrolling through the report. Although this has always been the case with journalism with stories having to make themselves heard through the noise of competing news events, in

Table 6.2 How many men and women work as prosecutors and how many work on trials that are live blogged

	Prosecutor		*Lawyer*		*Judge*	
	% Working	*Blogged*	*% Working*	*Blogged*	*Working*	*Blogged*
Women	61%	48%	33%	19.5%	53.5%	24%
Men	38%	52%	67%	80.5%	46.5%	76%

Source: (Åklagarmyndighet 2020; Advokatsamfundet 2020; Domstolar 2021)

today's digital age where not only professional news reports contend with informal bloggers and social media posters, but live blogging of trials must also compete against the international overflow of online information washing over the internet.

I begin with an excerpt from my interview with journalist Hilda in which she responds to my question regarding which kinds of trials are live blogged:

> The cases we live report on are often very, very big cases that have garnered a lot of attention, so people become engaged and care deeply about them – they stir emotions and affect people a lot. And I see it as part of my duty when reporting on these cases to inform the public about how things unfold, what happens, and what is said. And of course, in one way, you could say, "Yes, it might be enough just to write a summary afterward," but that's not how the media landscape and climate we have today work. So, I see it as my duty to tell people what happened and depict how the process unfolds. I also think it's important because I believe it can give people a pretty good insight into how the justice system works. I think it's essential to highlight both sides, to show how things work, like with evidence, so people can learn from it. But it's also because people are very engaged and really care about what happens. Reporting is part of my role, you could say.

Hilda tells me that the media landscape of today demands live coverage of events, with continuous updates which she argues is also necessary to educate the public. I will return to the educative function of live blogs later in the chapter, but first I want to highlight that this is a form of court reporting aimed at grabbing readers' attention through the avalanche of other media reporting. Part of this involves setting the scene for readers, many of whom may never have set foot in a courtroom. Journalists talk about that "putting some colour" into the story by describing what is happening in the courtroom, as journalist Kalle describes it, is important to "give the feeling of presence."

My analysis shows that live reporting from trials includes descriptions of the physical characteristics of the courtroom, as this is also an important part of enabling the reader to "see" the courtroom before them, not least in countries where television cameras and regular cameras are not permitted, as is the case in Sweden. Many of the trials that are live blogged are described in terms of who is present in the courtroom, where everyone is sitting, how many people are in the public gallery, whether the relatives of the plaintiff and defendant are present, whether the trial is taking place in a secure courtroom (with reinforced glass separating the public gallery from the courtroom itself), and similar such details. These descriptions tend to be fairly sweeping, with some specific details included to aid the reader in conjuring up the scene unfolding and contribute to a sense of being-thereness. Journalist Sven talks about the importance of setting the scene in this manner as being linked to the level of background knowledge he considers many readers to have:

> You have to try and think that, for most people, even the courtroom is a place where they haven't been that often, so to actually describe what it looks like in there can be relevant for that kind of reader and then I think, yet again, I think that most people perhaps don't know how a trial is formed so you have to explain the whole time: now the prosecutor is presenting the facts of the case and that means this and this, and when you have that information you can start to cover what is being said.

In particularly large trials, as was the case with Akilov, more detailed reports may be written, for instance,

> The trial is being held in the secure courtroom and there is a large security presence. All visitors must have a body search, and everything must be x-rayed. . . . There is reinforced glass between the public gallery and the court and there are lots of police on site, guarding the doors.

In courtrooms where cameras aren't permitted, as is the case in Denmark and Sweden, sketch artists can be used. Whilst courtroom sketches may be included in live blogs of trials with unusually widespread public interest, such as during the terror trial against Akilov or the assault trial against the famous American rapper A$AP Rocky, their use is relatively uncommon. When used, they tend to depict the defendant and/or defence lawyer sitting behind their table in the courtroom. Such descriptions further contribute to painting a picture of the specifics at hand and further add to the sense of being-thereness.

Framing

Trials are also simplified by being framed in particular ways, especially in the portrayal of legal professionals and the emotional dynamics within courtroom proceedings (Flower 2023). Through an extensive frame analysis of 95 live blogs published from criminal trials in Sweden between 2012 and 2020, I found that trials are primarily presented through two primary frames: prosecutorial power and teamwork.[7]

Prosecutorial power is reflected in live blogs' predominant focus on prosecutors, depicting them as central figures driving the trials. In contrast, defence lawyers and judges are portrayed as peripheral characters with their actions often portrayed in subdued terms. The relative absence of defence lawyers and judges in these news reports further contributes to the framing of prosecutorial power, reinforcing the perception of trials being led by prosecutors and

7 For a similar methodology see (Flower 2023).

potentially undermining the significance of defence lawyers and judges. This can be understood in relation to the legal system in Sweden where the prosecution has the burden of evidence and where the role of the defence lawyer is to find weaknesses in the prosecution's case. The prosecutor thus has more court time in the order of proceedings – time where he or she is presenting the case, evidence, questioning, cross-questioning, and summing up.

The defence lawyer, in contrast, may also engage in these parts of the trial, however his or her contribution tends to be more limited. Indeed, it is not uncommon for the defence lawyer to represent their client by remaining seemingly passive for large parts of the trial and the defendant only permitted to speak at certain times (Flower 2019). Thus, as Chibnall (1977, 25) writes, "actions lend themselves far more easily to sensational treatment than do thoughts" – a stone-faced, motionless defence lawyer does not make the news.

This bias towards prosecutors may, however, risk diminishing the perceived importance of the roles of defence lawyers and judges in societal understandings of trials, potentially leading to debates about the nature of their roles. Moreover, when defence lawyers are depicted, it is often in confrontational settings such as cross-examining witnesses and plaintiffs, which may further add to the social construction of defence lawyers as aggressive (Flower 2019).

This contrasts with findings from the US context where it is the defendant who plays the primary role in news reports despite the relatively central role in trials in both jurisdictions.

This disparity could reflect fundamental variations in different forms of reporting: the direct reports in the current study provide blow-by-blow accounts of proceedings, thus accounting for the prosecutor being depicted more often, in contrast to summaries of proceedings, as has been the focus in previous research. This is a key way in which digitalisation has a specific impact on how legal proceedings are reported.

This disparity could also reflect cultural differences, as research shows dissimilarities between how these two countries relate to questions regarding the identity and integrity of defendants. For instance, research indicates that journalists in the US adopt a "watchdog" approach which values full disclosure over the integrity of those depicted, in contrast to Sweden's "protector" line whereby the rights of anonymity weigh more heavily (Smith Fullerton and Jones Patterson 2021). This, in turn can be linked to newsworthy imperatives with the Swedish approach eschewing the personalisation and titillation imperatives to a greater extent. My findings also align with those from a comparative study of the UK, Norway, and Italy, which found subtle differences between how these European neighbours reported on crime (Cere, Jewkes, and Ugelvik 2013).

Further support for this is found in the absence of detailed description of, for instance, a defendant's sex life, or gruesome injuries received by a victim in the live blogs analysed in my study. So, although live blogs are competing for clicks in a highly competitive field, in the Swedish context at least, this has not led to a focus on lurid details, rather the delicate balance between sensationalism and personal integrity is being upheld. This is important as a trial constitutes an arena where one's integrity and private life is outed in a manner perhaps incomparable to any other. Live blogs do not tend to make a spectacle of trials, to the extent of other digital depictions such as podcasts.

My analysis also shows that live blogs construct a frame of teamwork. This is done by portraying interactions between prosecutors and defence lawyers as antagonistic and adversarial, thus creating the impression of opposing teams and by depicting amicable emotions within teams, such as a defence lawyer displaying sympathy and compassion towards their client (the defendant), or prosecutors depicted in this way towards plaintiffs. Emotional depictions are thus used to tie team members together or to distance teams from each other.

For instance, in the live blogs analysed, defence lawyers are most commonly depicted in interaction with the prosecutor, with live blogs reporting such things as "it gets a bit heated, with a fast exchange of words" (Nr 16) between defence lawyer and prosecutor, or the defence lawyer "becomes irritated when the prosecutor doesn't understand his question" (Nr 39). Likewise, depictions of prosecutors showing compassion towards plaintiffs and witnesses, such as "everyone in here understands that it can be tough answering these questions, say if you need a break" (Nr 103) and defence lawyers being described as having "a calmer voice" (Nr 6) when questioning his client in contrast to interjecting to the prosecutor's examination of his client.

Emotionalising interactions in these ways contributes to the depiction of trials as team accomplishments and reinforces conventionalised understandings of legal proceedings as adversarial and antagonistic, despite the Swedish system being a combination of inquisitorial and adversarial. Whilst the role of the judge is not focused upon in blogs – in line with the relatively low-key role a judge has in adversarial trials (in contrast to inquisitorial) and in line with the inquisitorial aspects of the Nordic model of trials, the overarching impression of trials conveyed in live blogs constructs them as adversarial. Moreover, the depiction of prosecutors as confrontational and persistent in their interactions with defendants subtly conveys hostility and aggression, also contributing to the portrayal of trials as adversarial and reinforcing the prosecutorial power frame.

My findings also gather support from Moran (2012), who finds a tendency when reporting about the English judiciary to dramatise events by focusing on the sensational and attention-grabbing and that events are simplified by constructing binary opposites: one side versus the other.

Live blogs can therefore contribute to a nuanced understanding of the emotional dynamics by presenting legal professionals as emotional beings, rather than as emotionless, as is associated with judges and prosecutors (Maroney 2011; Bergman Blix and Wettergren 2018), within criminal trials but they also risk simplifying and potentially distorting public perceptions of legal proceedings. This may have consequences for the continued legitimacy of trials.

Are live blogs entertainment or education?

This brings us to an important balance that must be struck by journalists – educating about trials more broadly and the specifics of the trial at hand versus providing news content that entertains the readers.

A content analysis study of news and editorial stories which mentioned US courts or judges by Vinson and Ertter (2002) explored whether reporters covering trials tend to "entertain by highlighting sensational or dramatic cases and reactions or to educate the public about the judicial system by explaining the process and judicial decisions and why the judges and juries make these decisions" (Vinson and Ertter 2002, 81). They find that entertainment is a key aspect of coverage. As a tool of education, journalistic coverage in the form of reports from trials can constitute an important channel of information regarding legal processes and, incidentally, may also encourage legal professionals to more closely ensure due process; however, the flipside of this is that it may lead to the "dramatization of court reporting" (Vinson and Ertter 2002, 80). Vinson and Ertter (2002) conclude that court reporting does not tend to be entertainment, rather most focus on the facts of the case in a straightforward way. But how does this relate to reporting on trials in the digital age?

In an interview with journalist Susanne, she talks about the challenge of finding the balance between covering trials in a way that will entice readers and adhering to good journalistic practices – a balance which she says has become particularly prevalent and harder to accomplish in today's digital deluge of information:

> Considering how journalism is developing generally we need to be very, very sensitive for the readers' wishes at the same time as we have a journalistic task to do – a journalistic and democratic task, but that the packaging – presentation and packaging of the news – has never been more important in this flow – this digital flow – of news and cute puppies and fake news and real news and because, it's like this, it's never been more important to reach out with good journalism and never been harder, I would say, considering how the flow and demand looks and it really does mean that you need – we find more and more, it is becoming clearer and clearer, is that you have to get close to the people – you have to get close to the people you are reporting about, close to the people you are reporting to, and in that way, live reporting from trials is a good tool, based on what I was talking about with all the nuances, feelings, quotes, this fragment of humanity that comes forth there, in contrast to a judgement on paper.

Susanna describes live blogging as a way of connecting with the reader and of enabling the flesh and blood of legal proceedings to come through. It is a tool for conveying a trial as consisting of interacting, feeling people, rather than merely a written judgement. Thus, the notion of *habeas corpus* – "you must have the body" – plays a central role not only in criminal trials, but also in the reporting of criminal trials (cf. McLaughlin 1998, 74). However, this focus on the body – on the personal – needs to be balanced against ethical guidelines which protect the integrity of individuals depicted in news reports.

The choices made as to what and how to report thus centre on navigating the terrain of newsworthiness and clickability, whilst still ensuring the dignity of those being reported on. As I have already mentioned, this balance also should not be seen in terms of a divide between education and entertainment, rather they should be seen as mutually enriching. Journalist Malin talked about this, arguing that live blogging is a form of education; however, both aspects play a role:

> It's always tricky; you have to be careful when talking about it because almost always when we're live blogging, someone has lost their life. That's why I sometimes struggle with the whole true crime phenomenon, which, you know, is very popular with documentaries and such. On some level, yes, it's "entertainment" in quotation marks – people want to know, they want to consume it, they can't get enough. But it can also be difficult – where's the line between what would be considered consumption? . . . And then you have to be mindful of the tone, but that's the case with everything. Of course, it's more than just dry education. People really want to consume this, and I think many are very engaged. We often notice in these criminal cases that it really touches people – there's a lot of engagement when we live-report. And there are so many who follow it every day, who come down to the courtroom when the trial goes on for several days, you know, those who come back and sit there every day while at work, keeping up with how things are going. And it's like, they might see it as entertainment, but it's also because they're engaged – they really care and can absorb it. I don't know . . . I want to be careful about saying that because it would be wrong, I think, both to the victims and to those who read and engage, because I believe it's about them genuinely caring. That's the thing with crime or legal journalism – very often, it deals with these awful events because they touch on the human condition, and it can be hard to grasp. But that's why so many are engaged – it's sometimes mind-boggling to think about.

Malin raises a very important point here, which is that live blogs are not necessarily an either/or phenomenon – educational or entertaining, rather an understanding of the function of live blogs needs to be more nuanced. If we return to the work of Vinson and Ertter (2002, 81), we see that they work on a binary assumption:

> whether reporters cover the courts to entertain by highlighting sensational or dramatic cases and reactions or to educate the public about the

judicial system by explaining the process and judicial decisions and why the judges and juries make these decisions.

Entertainment, in their frame of reference, is associated with sensationalism and dramatisation, which stands in stark contrast to a more pedagogical approach whereby a trial and the mechanisms within should be clearly explained. When I asked other journalists about how they see balance between education and entertainment, their answers fell firmly in the educational camp. For instance, journalist Susanne answered:

> It's more education than entertainment. I don't know if it is because I'm public service or come from that kind of climate where you are perhaps a little more restrictive, that we shouldn't revel in it, and we shouldn't exaggerate things in that way. And I think that we seldom go towards entertainment in that way, although if there are details that are out of the ordinary then we lift it like a murder weapon that is unusual, or that it was eight shots, but I think that it is more towards education.

Even when dramatic elements are included in Susanna's live blogs, she understands them as a way of helping the public understand the facts of the case, rather than a form of sensationalising entertainment. This is similar to journalist Hilda, who tells me,

> I would never consider live blogging from a trial to be entertainment, really. But the education and information can become very vivid and colourful, so to speak. And sure, sometimes there are things that can lead to a bit of a comical situation, and there can be laughter in the courtroom and so on, and then you might describe it if someone says something a bit humorous or something like that – as long as it stays within those boundaries. But I still see it, just like when we write about verdicts and indictments, primarily as a description of events within the legal system.

For Hilda her role is to pedagogically describe events within the legal system, and that entertainment for her is understood as amusing or light-hearted events that may be reported on.

This brings us to another vital aspect of live blogging: what can and cannot be reported? In another interview I conducted with an experienced Malin – working at a large Swedish newspaper, I ask her if she reflects on the fact that if she writes about something in a very detailed manner, that a witness may be able to read if before they have themselves given evidence (witnesses should not be privy to what is said in court before they have given evidence), she replies,

> The biggest dilemma is when you write about victims and injuries and so on. I can say that the principle we have in Sweden is that we can report

> [in great detail] so therefore I feel that it's not really my job to think, ok, I can't write about a witness who maybe says, "I met Malin at 9pm, then she said he's going to kill me." I feel that I can describe this without having to write something else because a witness is going to come later. Most of it is already in the preliminary investigation so it's obvious that someone can give a completely different version. Sure, a witness can change their mind, but witnesses often give the same picture. So no, I don't actually feel like that, I don't really take that into consideration. . . . I don't usually think about what happens if a witness is sitting and reading this. I don't think it's my job to think that. It should be the judge who decides no, we can't do that. That's what I think.

Malin thus accounts for her actions as not deviant in the sense of law-breaking: she is clearly following the laws which outline access to official documents and proceedings as she says, for instance, "it's the principle that we have in Sweden." For Malin and indeed for the other journalists I interviewed, as long as they follow the ethical guidelines of journalism, they are able to publish incredibly detailed accounts. Again, this is an example of technology moving faster than the law as there are no laws in place which prevent or restrict this. The digitalisation of the preliminary case, which, under Swedish law, is available to the public, is used by Malin as a way of rationalising her intimate reporting as she reasons that the details she is describing can be found online in any case.

It appears that journalists are attempting to navigate the conflict of the media sphere, which attempts to draw in readers, and the legal sphere, which focuses on the presentation of facts. Whilst the journalists interviewed in the current study appear to accomplish this balancing act whilst protecting the integrity of those reported on, increased competition and the drive towards clicks may increase the incentive to move away from this protective approach, to a more clickable tactic. This is important as previous research indicates that coverage may serve to undermine trust in the judicial process, particularly in cases where the verdict does not align with the expectations of readers.

Conclusion

This analysis of the Swedish context shows a number of noteworthy findings which highlight the tension between the rhetoric of open justice and its practice, and between the implementation of digital tools and their legal framework. For instance, whilst live blogs constitute an important way of ensuring the courts remain open to society, their immediacy and level of detail afforded can have more unexpected and damaging consequences which the law, as yet, has not kept abreast of.

It seems likely that this live blogging is a format that will face incursions and perhaps even lead to legal change in the future. Sweden's neighbouring country of Denmark has already banned the direct reproduction of witness testimony in live blogs, and I suggest that Sweden may soon follow suit. It seems apparent that the law has not kept abreast of technological developments and may require revision, for instance, by banning live blogging during certain parts of trials such as witness testimony. More research is needed to the possible risk live blogs pose to the administration of justice, in particular, the threat of witnesses changing testimony. The ways in which live blogs and the legacy of these reports impact witnesses, plaintiffs, and defendants also needs attention. The findings also indicate that the jurisdictional context shapes perceptions of open justice practices, such as live blogs. Future research should focus on how the functions of open justice are understood in countries with lower levels of access to official records, higher levels of corruption, and lower levels of trust in the legal system.

Live blogs balance the line between education and entertainment, with trials reported on in a dramatised and simplified manner. The relative lack of women reported on may serve to highlight awareness that under-representation still exists in the criminal lawyering profession, yet the lack of women judges and prosecutors in live blogs indicates a more worrying trend if we consider that certain types of cases tend to be reported – high-profile and violent crime, perhaps revealing that there is a gendering within the legal profession with regards to which types of cases men and women choose or, perhaps, are allocated. The lack of women may reveal a more concerning lack of women in key positions within the legal profession.

These findings from the Swedish context are particularly interesting as, since 2019, it is not permitted to use electronic equipment such as computers, tablets, and phones in the courtroom without the judge's permission. This is to prevent the trial from being photographed, filmed, or audio recorded, which may be experienced as stressful or anxiety-evoking for the participants within. The aim of this law was therefore to further protect the safety and integrity of those participating in trials. Yet other areas of technology remain unquestioned.

I conclude by underscoring the need for further research to explore the implications of live blogging on the accuracy and transparency of legal proceedings, as well as its potential to shape public understanding of the justice system. Ultimately, addressing these concerns is crucial for maintaining the integrity of the legal system and ensuring public trust in the judiciary. It therefore is apparent that, in contrast to livestreaming, live blogging is perceived by the legal professionals interviewed as being less intrusive. However, this new form of "liveness" from live blogs nevertheless reshapes courtroom dynamics and professional practices in subtle but significant ways.

References

Advokatsamfundet. 2020. *Verksamhet 2019*. Stockholm: Advokatsamfundet.

Åklagarmyndighet. 2020. *Åklagarmyndighetens årsredovisning 2019*. Stockholm: Åklagarmyndigheten.

Allen, Jessica, Sonia Livingstone, and Robert Reiner. 1998. "True Lies: Changing Images of Crime in British Postwar Cinema." *European Journal of Communication* 13 (1):53–75.

Bergman Blix, Stina, and Åsa Wettergren. 2018. *Professional Emotions in Court*. Abingdon: Routledge.

BRÅ. 2021. "Konstaterade fall av dödligt våld: En granskning av anmält dödligt våld 2020." In *Kriminalstatistik*, edited by BRÅ. Brottsförebyggandet Rådet.

BRÅ. 2024. "Dödligt våld i Sverige sedan 1990". Retrieved from https://bra.se/download/18.63eed38e192716a4afccae/1742286318587/2024_6_Doldigt-vald-i-Sverige-sedan-1990.pdf.

Chibnall, Steve. 1977. *Law-and-Order News: An Analysis of Crime Reporting in the British press*. London: Tavistock.

Cere, Rinella, Yvonne Jewkes, and Thomas Ugelvik. 2013. "Media and Crime: A Comparative Analysis of Crime News in the UK, Norway and Italy." In *The Routledge Handbook of European Criminology*. Routledge.

Deuze, Mark. 2012. *Media Life*. Cambridge: Polity.

Domstolar, Sveriges. 2021. "Årsredovisning 2020". Retrieved from https://www.domstol.se/globalassets/filer/gemensamt-innehall/styrning-och-riktlinjer/arsredovisning/arsredovisning_2020_sverigesdomstolar.pdf.

Domstolsverket. 2021. *Domstolsstatistik 2020*. Jönköping: Domstolsverket.

Ellis, Anthony, Jennifer Sloan, and Maggie Wykes. 2013. "'Moatifs' of Masculinity: The Stories Told About 'Men' in British Newspaper Coverage of the Raoul Moat Case." *Crime, Media, Culture* 9 (1):3–21.

Equality, European Institute for Gender. 2021. "Gender Equality Index." Retrieved from https://eige.europa.eu/gender-equality-index/2021/compare-countries/work/bar.

Flower, Lisa. 2019. *Interactional Justice: The Role of Emotions in the Performance of Loyalty*. Abingdon: Routledge.

Flower, Lisa. 2023. "Constructing Clickable Criminal Trials: Framing Trials and Legal Professionals in Digital News Reports." *Emotions and Society* 5 (1):48–66.

Forum, World Economic. 2021. "Global Gender Gap Report 2021." Retrieved from http://www3.weforum.org/docs/WEF_GGGR_2018.pdf.

Foucault, Michel. 1975/1991. *Discipline and Punish: The Birth of the Prison*. Translated by Alan Sheridan. New York: Random House.

Grosholz, Jessica, and Charis E. Kubrin. 2007. "Crime in the News: How Crimes, Offenders and Victims Are Portrayed in the Media." *Journal of Criminal Justice and Popular Culture* 14:59–83.

Haggerty, Kevin. 2006. "Tear Down the Walls: On Demolishing the Panopticon." In *Theorizing Surveillance: The Panopticon and Beyond*, edited by David Lyon, 23–45. Cullompton: Willan.

Haltom, William. 1998. *Reporting on the Courts: How the Mass Media Cover Judicial Actions*. Chicago: Nelson-Hall.

International, Transparency. 2020. "Corruption Perceptions Index 2019". Retrieved from https://www.transparency.org/en/cpi/2019/press-and-downloads.

Jensen, Jakob Linaa. 2007. "The Internet Omnopticon." In *New Publics with/Out Democracy*, edited by Henrik Bang and Anders Esmark, 351–380. Frederiksberg: Samfundslitteratur Press.

Jewkes, Yvonne. 2015. *Media and Crime*. 3rd ed. London: Sage Publications Ltd.

Jones, Phil J., and Claire Wardle. 2008. "'No Emotion, No Sympathy': The Visual Construction of Maxine Carr." *Crime, Media, Culture* 4 (1):53–71. https://doi.org/10.1177/1741659007087271.

Lauzen, Martha M. 2008. *The Celluloid Ceiling: Behind-the-Scenes Employment of Women on the Top 250, Films of 2007*. San Diego: Center for the Study of Women in Television and Film.

Lauzen, Martha M. 2018. *The Celluloid Ceiling: Behind-the-Scenes Employment of Women on the Top 100, 250, and 500 Films of 2017*. San Diego: Center for the Study of Women in Television and Film.
Livingstone, Sonia, Jessica Allen, and Robert Reiner. 2001. "Audiences for Crime Media 1946–91: A Historical Approach to Reception Studies." *The Communication Review* 4 (2):165–192.
Lundetag, Amanda, Claes Hemberg, Maija Inkala, and Omar Ajmal. 2018. *En spricka i glastaket*. Allbright.
Lyon, David. 2001. *Surveillance Society: Monitoring Everyday Life*. Buckingham: Open University Press.
Lyon, David. 2007. *Surveillance Studies: An Overview*. Cambridge: Polity Press. Book.
Lyon, David. 2018. *The Culture of Surveillance: Watching as a Way of Life*. Cambridge: Polity Press.
Maroney, Terry A. 2011. "The Persistent Cultural Script of Judicial Dispassion." *California Law Review* 99:629–681.
Mawby, Rob C. 2002. *Policing Images: Policing, Communication and Legitimacy*. Cullompton: Willan.
McLaughlin, Lisa. 1998. "Gender, Privacy and Publicity in 'Media Event Space'." In *News, Gender and Power*, edited by Cynthia Carter, Gill Branston, and Stuart Allan, 71–90. London: Routledge.
Menkel-Meadow, Carrie. 1984. "Feminization of the Legal Profession: The Comparative Sociology of Women Lawyers." In *Lawyers in Society: Comparative Theories*, edited by Richard L. Abel and Phillip S. C. Lewis, 196–255. Berkeley: University of California Press.
Menkel-Meadow, Carrie. 1985. "Portia in a Different Voice: Speculations on a Women's Lawyering Process." *Berkeley Women's Law Journal* 1 (1):39–63.
Moore, Sarah. 2018. "Towards a Sociology of Institutional Transparency: Openness, Deception and the Problem of Public Trust." *Sociology* 52 (2):416–430.
Moran, Leslie J. 2012. "Every Picture Speaks a Thousand Words: Visualizing Judicial Authority in the Press." In *Intersections of Law and Culture*, edited by Priska Gisler, Sara Steinert Borella and Caroline Wiedmer, 31–49. London: Palgrave Macmillan UK.
Moran, Leslie J. 2014. "Mass-Mediated 'Open Justice': Court and Judicial Reports in the Press in England and Wales." *Legal Studies* 34 (1):143–166. https://doi.org/10.1111/lest.12011.
Morello, Karen Berger. 1986. *The Invisble Bar: The Woman Lawyer in American 1638 to the Present*. New York: Random House.
Persson, Johan. 2018. "Sådan är dagens advokat." *Advokaten* 1 (84):24–26.
Reiner, Robert, Sonia Livingstone, and Jessica Allen. 2000. "No More Happy Endings? The Media and Popular Concern about Crime Since the Second World War." In *Crime, Risk and Insecurity: Law and Order in Everyday Life and Political Discourse*, edited by Tim Hope and Richard Sparks, 107–126. London: Routledge.
Sandoval-Almazan, Rodrigo, and J. Ramon Gil-Garcia. 2018. "Understanding e-Justice and Open Justice Through the Assessment of Judicial Websites: Toward a Conceptual Framework." *Social Science Computer Review* 38 (3):334–353. https://doi.org/10.1177/0894439318785957.
Smith Fullerton, Romayne, and Maggie Jones Patterson. 2021. *Murder in Our Midst: Comparing Crime Coverage Ethics in an Age of Globalized News*. Oxford: Oxford University Press.
Sommerlad, Hilary, Lisa Webley, Lizz Duff, Daniel Muzio, and Jennifer Tomlinson. 2010. *Diversity in the Legal Profession in England and Wales: A Qualitative Study of Barriers and Individual Choices*. London: Univeristy of Westminster.

Surette, Ray. 2003. "The Media, the Public, and Criminal Justice Policy." *Journal of the Institute of Justice and International Studies* 2:39–52.
Survey, World Values. 2020. "World Values Survey Wave 7." Retrieved from https://www.worldvaluessurvey.org/wvs.jsp.
Sverige, Hovrätten för Västra. 2022. "Slutligt beslut." In *B3330–22*, edited by Avdelning 1 Hovrätten för Västra Sverige, Rotel 12. Göteborg: Hovrätten i Västra Sverige.
Townend, Judith, and Lucy Welsh. 2023. *Observing Justice: Digital Transparency, Openness and Accountability in Criminal Courts*. Policy Press.
Townend, Judith, and Cassandra Wiener. 2021. *Justice System Data: A Comparative Study*. Sussex: Legal Education Foundation.
Vinson, C. Danielle, and John S. Ertter. 2002. "Entertainment of Education? How Do Media Cover the Courts?" *Press/Politics* 7 (4):80–97.
Wood Carter, John. 2016. "Crime News and the Press." In *The Oxford Handbook of the History of Crime and Criminal Justice*, edited by Knepper Paul and Johansen Anja. Oxford: Oxford University Press.

7 Conclusion

In this book I have aimed to present a wide-ranging view of the digital courtroom and the ways in which digitalisation shapes how we interact with courts, as well as our perceptions of trials and their participants. By exploring the core themes of participation, attendance, engagement, and consumption, I have illustrated how digitalisation has led to unprecedented openness in courts. However, this increased openness comes with a darker dimension that complicates the transparency central to the idea of open justice. In my analysis I have also demonstrated that many digital technologies originally designed to increase accessibility have been broadly introduced into courts without comprehensive understanding of how these technologies might jeopardise the courts and the legal processes within. In short, although developments of the digital courtroom have been implemented under the banner of improving public access and engagement, many of these tools risk undermining core aspects of judicial integrity, such as the authentic execution of legal proceedings, the portrayal of justice to the public, and the experiential quality of justice for participants. This shift demands a more critical approach to digital integration, one that comprehensively evaluates how these changes might disrupt not only procedural fairness, but also public trust and the perceived legitimacy of the legal system itself.

Several important arguments have been made. Firstly, that a range of digital tools are being used in courts and trials which have numerous benefits, such as using video links to make trials more efficient by reducing the need to postpone hearings due to sickness or enabling victims fearful of their attacker to give evidence from another courtroom. However, with the onset of the COVID-19 pandemic, video links swept across the courts and were implemented in a broader spectrum of trials and for more extensive categories of participants, without robust empirical investigation as to whether this widespread implementation was appropriate. This indicates that our understanding remains incomplete regarding the multitude of ways in which video links impact legal proceedings, alter perceptions of participants, change the practices of legal professionals, or shape the interactions taking place within.

Focused research attention on the digital interaction order and the ways in which rules and roles are constructed and reconstructed through explicit and implicit social processes is vital in order to ensure that legal professionals feel they

DOI: 10.4324/9781003344643-7

are able to perform their roles appropriately; for instance, that a defence lawyer can feel that s/he can defend a client to the best of their ability, or that a judge can maintain order in the courtroom, feelings that are harder to reach when the rules of interaction are unclear. Strategies to replace the well-established physical methods of conveying specific nonverbal, interactional goals in the courtroom, such as a stern look from a judge to a defence lawyer to indicate that a cross-examination is too aggressive or a prosecutor attempting to unsettle a defendant, are currently unclear in virtual justice rituals. This is problematic, as how can a judge indicate that a lawyer is on the cusp of being too aggressive – that an emotional rule is about to be broken – if they can no longer use direct eye contact to convey this? This lack of clarity can lead to feelings of uncertainty in judges, prosecutors, and lawyers as to how to navigate the interactional rules of the courtroom.

Likewise, defendants, witnesses, and plaintiffs might be participating in a trial for the first time and therefore are uninitiated into the interaction order. When the rules of interaction are well established, the judge, prosecutor, or lawyer can explain the rules, roles, and expectations in the courtroom. While these roles will remain unchanged in the virtual setting, the way in which they are performed may change. It is this shift in *how* – the practices involved – that are in transition, making them more difficult to pinpoint and explain to the uninitiated. Importantly, subtle forms of interaction, impression management strategies, and gestures may be more challenging to convey in virtual settings, which can complicate and hinder the possibility of constructing and maintaining a shared understanding. This can result in misunderstandings and a diminished sense of participation which, as a result, may negatively impact participants' sense of justice having been served and ultimately jeopardise trust in the legal system more broadly (Tyler 1988).

Furthermore, there is still much we do not know about virtual justice rituals, leaving us uncertain about their potential for success, particularly if success is defined by individuals feeling fairly treated by the legal system and the perception among legal professionals that they have accomplished their roles appropriately.

In particular, I contend that in order to successfully shift, adapt, or develop traditional justice rituals into virtual settings, we must pay attention to the less tangible and fuzzier aspects of trials: the sensorial experiences of participation which together foster the sense of a certain something going on. These sensorial experiences are crucial for understanding how we can design and construct virtual trials that retain their legitimacy, solemnity, and import.

Within this, increased research attention on atmospheres is vital. Atmospheres are intangible, collectively produced, and emerging from the interactions between people and their settings. They are not simply individual experiences, but social and affective phenomena that involve emotions constructed through senses shaping how people perceive, interpret, and react to each other. The physical environment plays a central role in this: the courthouse, the waiting room, the courtroom, all these spaces pour into the construction of certain kinds of atmospheres. Atmospheres therefore emerge, in part, from the emotional landscapes that shape which emotions can be shown and by whom in different areas of the courthouse. In courtrooms, social norms regulate emotional expressions whilst material arrangements and spatial design construct certain atmospheres. This is an interplay of physical, emotional, and social aspects. Those participating in a trial are thus impacted by everything from the physical layout to the behaviours and emotional expressions of others. Once again, by focusing on the softer aspects of trials, beyond the hard rigidity of the law, it is possible to gain a more complete understanding of the socially intricate tapestry of a trial. In this way we can pinpoint the vital ingredients of successful virtual justice rituals and move forwards in forming the courts of the future.

This is vital as we currently find ourselves on a trajectory toward the de-spatialisation of courts, which could potentially lead to a complete decoupling between the courts and physical presence. The next step involves the dematerialisation of the courts, wherein the physical courthouse is removed. Hearings conducted in virtual reality have already occurred, using basic avatars depicting the different participants in the courtroom. This technology portrays participants more akin to characters in a video game, rather than as living, breathing defendants, judges, lawyers, and so on. However, research is also currently advancing technology that can scan participants' facial features onto their avatars creating a more life-like representation that also reflects the real-time facial expressions of the actual participants. Ongoing research is also focusing on developing hologram technology to be used in trials whereby, for instance, a witness would appear in court as a hologram. Both these forms of participation would remove the necessity of being physically present in the same courtroom during the trial. These developments are steering us closer towards decreased physical participation in trials, even though we are still working to understand their full their implications.

Such developments also take us one step further towards removing the necessity of a physical courthouse. This leads to questions regarding how we can ensure the courts remain a vital institution in society when their physical presence is no longer seen or felt. After all, courts are typically constructed in central areas of cities, symbolising their central role in society, and tend to be designed to reflect the values of justice they stand for, again serving as a visible reminder to all those seeing it. What happens when this symbol of justice disappears? Will the courts retain their sacredness?

Moving to the ways in which trials can now be attended in the digital age, we can keep up to speed with trials in real time, watching livestreams or reading live blogs that give us a sense of being-thereness, as if we were attending the trial on site. And, whilst there are several advantages with these forms of coverage, for instance in fulfilling societal demands of immediacy and enabling people to attend trials of widespread collective interest, perhaps it is time to stop and ask again, how much access is too much? Yes, we live in an age of immediacy, but does this demand that legal proceedings are instantaneously available via YouTube or a news website? What is the added value of being able to see and hear in real time? Transparency continues to be the buzzword of the twenty-first century, but is it necessary for all details of a witness's cross-examination to be directly accessible by those sitting outside the courtroom, waiting to give evidence? These questions are designed to be somewhat provocative, as I wish to kickstart a wider debate regarding an appropriate level of openness.

Turning to engagement, the courts' use of social media to engage with the wider society by informing about decisions, employment openings, and so forth can work towards reducing the gap between this institution and society. However, a balance must be made, once again, between openness and the integrity and rights of all parties involved. This means that all of those participating in a trial are aware of how to use social media appropriately, including judges and juries. The use of social media to engage with wider society can therefore spill over into the misuse of social media with more damaging repercussions. Not only does this relate to the risk of Google mistrials, but also to the risk of going viral, or a trial spiralling into a TikTok trial, the consequences of which can be life changing due to the reach and longevity of the internet.

It is time to stop and reflect on the question that even though open justice may give us the legal right to spread information or legal materials from a trial, does this make it morally right? The journalists I have interviewed in my research draw on their ethical guidelines in the absence of legal restrictions when choosing what to publish, but those outside of the journalism profession – ranging from podcasters to the general public – and perhaps even many of those within journalism, are not bound by such ethical rules or choose not to follow them. Indeed, it can be argued that the widespread dissemination of these materials can be part and parcel of the public shaming process that a trial still, to some extent, constitutes. With a trend towards increasing criminalisation and, hence, an increase in the number of trials to be held, I am calling for a timeout. I am calling for a brief pause to enable detailed empirical examination of the implications that the widespread dissemination and pop culturalisation of trials, brought about by digitalisation, have had on open justice and how this concretely impacts justice and the experience of justice. In the current Swedish context where organised crime is exploding, and where witnesses are already hesitant to give evidence in trials, the risk of going viral or of becoming part of a podcast may constitute the decisive factor for choosing against participating or, indeed, from choosing to perhaps not remember the "truth."

Sweden is currently discussing the introduction of anonymous witnesses, citing Norway as an excellent role model for this system – despite Norway only having used this form a handful of times since implementation. This means, for instance, that judges and defence lawyers will not be able to see witnesses for the prosecution when they are cross-examining them. Again, this takes us one step further away from physical presence in terms of being able to physically see each other, yet again, without fully knowing the implications of this.

The introduction, integration, and use of social media platforms as well as the shifting ways in which trials can be attended from beyond the courthouse, together with podcasts, documentaries, and online forums, have changed the role of the public from passive observer to active observer. Now we can analyse, discuss, and evaluate trials in real time. We can exchange our personal interpretations and judgements in the comments section of live blogs or livestreams, respond to Facebook updates by courts, or use online forums to dissect trials presented in podcasts. This can create a sense of being actively involved in judicial proceedings. We feel we can probe ambiguities, question motives, and query defence strategies. We can ponder the guilt of the accused, the impartiality of the judge, the single-mindedness of the defence lawyer, or the credibility of a witness. We show sympathy for victims, disdain for defendants, admiration for prosecutors. The multitude of ways in which the digitalisation of the courts has enabled this shift from passive to active observer is extensive. However, it remains unclear whether these active observers have any impact on ensuring that legal proceedings remain fair and just. That is, what does the shift from passive to active observer actually entail?

For instance, the possibility of monitoring and discussing a trial in online forums does not automatically mean that the observer also actively reacts when rules and procedures are not followed, for instance, when judicial power is abused or when the rights of those taking part in the trial are not upheld. Yes, widespread media attention drawn to certain podcasted trials indeed has led to cases being re-opened and re-examined and, in some instances, mistrials being called, but the extent to which opening the courts by digital means has led to the accountability function of open justice being fulfilled remains unclear.

Indeed, digitalisation has created a false sense of agency: we feel that we are able to monitor the courts and ensure that the goings on within are conducted correctly, and that within this, we have a sense of power. But how much power do we actually exercise and how much power do we actually have? At the same time, how much power *should* we have over the courts? Scrutiny remains pointless if it does not lead to something. . . . Have we thus developed a false sense of agency: that we have the power to ensure justice is upheld but that we fail to exercise that power? These are questions for future exploration.

Wider trends towards transparency and an increased interest in crime lead to the perfect storm that risks unleashing an avalanche of openness into the private lives of witnesses or the personal experiences that have may have been life-transforming, yet which have been made into content for the latest podcast episode.

Related to this, we see that the functions of open justice have changed, with discipline replaced by surveillance and the truth function no longer fulfilled given the current digital capabilities. The educative function should not be understood as devoid of entertaining undertones, rather entertainment in terms of dramatising and, to some extent, sensationalising trials can lead to their appeal to a wider audience. However, again, this should be a balance that remains even. We currently find ourselves falling into trials being a public spectacle again with podcasts serving as a tool of public shaming.

The quest for open justice is a noble one, yet it must be made with full consideration of the personal integrity and rights of those involved in a trial and it should not, in any way, impact the execution and experience of justice. The law needs to keep abreast of technology developments in order to avoid further mistrials and injustices occurring. My analysis of the Swedish context shows a number of noteworthy findings, in particular that the digitalisation of legal documents and proceedings has led to a worrying distribution and use of audio recordings, case files, and other documents and materials. The absence of regulation here is disquieting.

The goal of this book has been to illuminate and critically examine the multitude of ways in which digitalisation is shaping the courts with a particular focus on the unexpected consequences the intertwining of open justice and digitalisation has had. Digitally enabled open justice has undeniably contributed to the courts being more effective and accessible for many; however, technology often seems to have moved faster than the law, leading to several less valuable consequences such as grey zones regarding the unknown rules of interaction, widespread dissemination of legal materials, and unclear legal regulation.

There are several limitations of this book not least due to the wide range of disciplines I draw on, which includes research in computer studies, media studies, psychology, architecture, geography, philosophy, law, and more. My goal was to tie these various threads together and analyse the digital courtroom through a sociological lens; however, what is needed is an even more thorough interdisciplinary overview to more fully ground a comprehensive sociological approach to understanding the role of digitalisation in courts beyond the scope of this book.

Moving forwards, we need sustained and intricate empirical investigation of each of the central themes discussed in this book for the courts to continue to develop in a digitally and justly sustainable manner. This means studying real-life courts and courtroom interactions on a micro-sociological level to fully access experiences, understandings, and practices.

We also need to critically discuss open justice as it stands today. The concept of open justice is increasingly complex, not only given today's digital context but also given current societal contexts. As already noted, Sweden is facing growing gang-related crime, prompting the government to introduce measures such as anonymous witnesses, which push towards greater secrecy in the justice system. At the same time, there are efforts also aimed at combatting gang crime and preventing youngsters from being recruited into gangs – efforts which centre on more openness, such as proposals to enhance the sharing of information between schools, social services, the police, and the courts to prevent youth involvement in gangs. These contradictory plans – towards both secrecy and openness – reflect the challenge of balancing public transparency with the need for security and privacy and the issues we face ahead.

Digitalisation further complicates the issue. Public access to legal materials, including audio recordings from trials, has resulted in widespread distribution on podcasts and online platforms, raising significant concerns about the privacy and integrity of individuals involved in legal proceedings. In response to these issues, a legal inquiry is currently underway in Sweden which proposes implementing limited access to the preliminary case file until after the final judgement has been published (SOU 2024:51). This restriction would prevent the public, including journalists, from accessing these documents, thereby hindering journalistic investigation that could uncover important details of public interest not presented during the trial.

This issue is further complicated in the Swedish context by the increased durations that suspects spend in custody while awaiting charges (Service 2024; ÅM2023–1418). The proposed restrictions of accessing the preliminary investigation file would hamper journalistic scrutiny of these ongoing cases, including those against minors, and indeed, those trials continuing for a lengthy period of time. This could prevent any irregularities or injustices from being revealed until after the trial concludes and may hinder journalistic efforts to counteract disinformation and misinformation circulating on social media.

I content, therefore, that the tension between open justice and personal privacy requires recalibration. Efforts to classify preliminary case files until a verdict becomes legally binding highlights this issue, as such restrictions limit public access to essential information and undermine transparency and accountability. In a democratic society, access to legal processes is essential for informed debate and institutional oversight. Whilst privacy concerns are valid, restricting access to legal documents erodes the media's ability to scrutinise the justice system, weakens public discourse, and threatens democratic accountability. Ultimately the balance between transparency and privacy must be carefully navigated to preserve both justice and democracy. One potential compromise could involve expanding the scope of confidentiality assessments conducted by courts prior to making preliminary case files accessible to the public. This solution could help reconcile the need for open justice with the protection of personal privacy, allowing journalists to investigate, while mitigating the risk of public shaming on online platforms if personal details remain confidential.

I believe that we find ourselves at a tipping point whereby transparency and openness, on the one side, are balanced against personal integrity and procedural correctness. I have shown that, at times, this balance is disrupted, for instance when audio recordings of trials are used for entertainment purposes, as in podcasts. The digitalisation of court materials and their uninhibited distribution is of particular worry.

In conclusion, I propose a future-oriented perspective with the digital courtroom integrating digital tools without eroding the core value or meaning of the courts. A critical analysis of regulation should be considered to enable an appropriate level of openness. This is a challenging, yet essential, balance as courts will continue to assess the benefits of digital innovations against the need to maintain the solemnity and accountability that physical presence has traditionally entailed.

References

ÅM2023–1418. 2024. *Häktningstider och användning av restriktioner m.m.* Ekobrottsmyndigheten Kriminalvården. Åklagarmyndigheten. https://www.aklagare.se/globalassets/dokument/rapporter/ovriga-rapporter/rapport-regeringsuppdrag-om-alternativ-till-haktning-m-m-ju2023-01342-am2023-1418.pdf.

Service, Swedish Prison and Probation. 2024. "Häktningstider bör kortas." Last Modified 31 May 2023. Retrieved from www.kriminalvarden.se/om-kriminalvarden/nyheter/2023/maj/haktningstiderna-bor-kortas/, accessed 2nd March 2024.

SOU 2024:51. *En mer rättssäker och effektiv domstolsprocess.* Stockholm: Statens Offentliga Utredningar.

Tyler, T. R. 1988. "What Is Procedural Justice?: Criteria Used by Citizens to Assess the Fairness of Legal Procedures." *Law & Society Review* 22 (1):103–136.

Index

Note: Page numbers in *italic* indicate a figure and page numbers in **bold** indicate a table on the corresponding page.

FSC
www.fsc.org
MIX
Papier | Fördert
gute Waldnutzung
FSC® C083411

Kolibri 360 GmbH
Ferdinand-Jühlke-Straße 7
99095 Erfurt, Deutschland
produktsicherheit@kolibri360.de